SECULAR COEXISTENCE IN LEBANON

For Shea,
and to the memory of my parents,
Sami and Hoda Abillama

SECULAR COEXISTENCE IN LEBANON

Christians, Muslims and Subjects of Law

Raja Abillama

EDINBURGH
University Press

Edinburgh University Press is one of the leading university presses in the UK. We publish academic books and journals in our selected subject areas across the humanities and social sciences, combining cutting-edge scholarship with high editorial and production values to produce academic works of lasting importance. For more information visit our website: edinburghuniversitypress.com

Edinburgh University Press Ltd
13 Infirmary Street,
Edinburgh, EH1 1LT

First published in hardback by Edinburgh University Press 2024

Typeset in 11/15 Adobe Garamond by
IDSUK (DataConnection) Ltd

A CIP record for this book is available from the British Library

ISBN 978 1 3995 0754 7 (hardback)
ISBN 978 1 3995 0755 4 (paperback)
ISBN 978 1 3995 0756 1 (webready PDF)
ISBN 978 1 3995 0757 8 (epub)

CONTENTS

Acknowledgements vi

Introduction: An Anthropology of Coexistence 1

PART I MODES OF BELONGING

1 Securing the Religious a/in Place 31

2 *Tabdīl al-Dīn*, Secular Displacement and Religious Conversion 57

PART II FORMS OF LIFE

3 Christian Marriage, Medical Knowledge and the Attributes of the Person 93

4 Conduct and Judgment between the Shariʿa and the Law 121

PART III DISPASSIONATE BODIES

5 Offending the Religious 149

6 The Religious Offended 171

Epilogue 194

References 199

Index 205

ACKNOWLEDGEMENTS

This book would not have been possible without the teachers, colleagues and friends who sustained my efforts to bring it to completion. I want to mention those in Lebanon whose help was essential for my research: Talal Hussaini, Hassan al-Muhib, who at the time was the head of the documentation unit at the Lebanese National Archives, Nizar Saghieh and his Legal Agenda, Nagi Yacoub, Ogarit Younan, and the librarians at the Lebanese University and *Université Saint Joseph* in Beirut for guiding me through Lebanon's legal and judicial sources.

I first read the work of Talal Asad as an anthropology student at the London School of Economics. I came to know him as teacher and advisor at the Graduate Center of the City University of New York (CUNY). His impact on this book is obvious, but it is for his hardly perceptible gestures towards thinking, the subtle power of which I am only now beginning to realise, that I owe him the most. Vincent Crapanzano was always available to listen, and always ready to give, with generosity and broadness of mind. I am grateful also to Mandana Limbert for her patience, as she was among the first to read my hesitant first attempts at writing it up.

Anny Bakalian, the tireless director of the Middle East and Middle Eastern American Center at CUNY, offered a much-needed space for students and scholars of the Middle East to get to know and learn from each other. She was a formidable administrator and remains a friend. Bryan S. Turner and the

Committee for the Study of Religion at CUNY's Graduate Center provided a uniquely challenging multidisciplinary setting in which I was able to present my research when I was still struggling to make sense of it. I thank him and the members of the committee, as well as the fellows of the two Mellon Seminars, *Religion and Violence* and *The Sacred and the Secular*. Also in New York, Louise Lennihan was consistently present in her capacity as department chair to perform the great administrative and logistical feats that were vital for me when I first arrived. The research for this book would have been impossible without her efforts. I thank her, and I thank Ellen DeRiso for her guidance through the bureaucratic mazes of what was then an unfamiliar institutional culture.

This project began to take shape among classmates and colleagues at the Graduate Center. I mention Vivian Berghan, Abu Farman, Saygun Gökariksel, Yizhou Jiang, Banu Karaca, Neri de Kramer, Tina Lee, Abraham Lotha, Adrienne Lotson, Andrea Morrell, Ceren Özgül, Ted Powers, Jeremy Rayner, Ted Sammons, Aseel Sawalha, Katrina Scott, Victoria Stone, Kee Young, and Gabriela Zamorano. Jeffrey Culang, Aleksandra Majstorac-Kobiljski, Shea McManus, Sara Pursley, Noah Salomon, Yunus Doğan Telliel, and Seçil Yılmaz read first drafts, gave comments, and shared their own work. Nada Moumtaz encouraged me to 'pull this project off' and has been involved in it since the beginning.

Osama Abi-Mershed, Rochelle Davis, and Fida Adely welcomed me graciously for a year as a postdoctoral fellow at the Center for Contemporary Arab Studies at Georgetown University. Also at Georgetown, I thank Jeremy Walton for his companionship. At North Carolina State University, I thank Anna Bigelow, Blair Kelley, Seth Murray, Levi McLaughlin, and Matthew Watson. I am particularly indebted to Akram Khater, director of the Khayrallah Center for Lebanese Diaspora Studies, for securing several summer research grants in Lebanon. Rachel Brewster, Ora Gelley, and James Mulholland read early drafts of some parts of the book. I single out Rebecca Walsh for her gift of time to read the introduction with rigour, honesty, and professionalism. She made a real difference in the direction this book has taken.

The staff and faculty at Boğaziçi University's Department of Sociology extended unwavering support at a particularly challenging time. I am grateful to Meltem Ahıska, Ayfer Bartu Candan, Ceylan Engin, Sinan Erensü, Saygun

Gökariksel, Biray Kolluoğlu, Juho Korhonen, Bülent Küçük, Tuna Kuyucu, Güzin Özkan, Ceren Özselçuk, Nükhet Sirman, Kutluğhan Soyubol, Belgin Tekçe and Zafer Yenal. In Istanbul as well, Ayşecan Terzioğlu inviting me to share my work with her and her students at the Cultural Studies Program at Sabancı University.

For their friendship, I thank Samer Frangieh, Alya Karami, Maya Karanouh, Mazen Labban, Stanton McManus, Lena Merhej and Laura Schneider (I apologise to those I might have forgotten to name).

I owe a special kind of gratitude to Shea, who put up with this for so long, to Rania, Fouad, Paul, Tatiana, Nicolaï, and Amina, who have been waiting for it for as long, and . . . to Riley.

All shortcomings are mine.

INTRODUCTION
AN ANTHROPOLOGY OF COEXISTENCE

What might the coexistence of Christians and Muslims look like? How would their coexistence enable and constrain their respective articulations of their distinctiveness and difference? What ways or manners of thinking, doing and feeling might articulate coexistence and enter into the making of the respective sensibility of Christians and Muslims? What is it to say (or be) 'Muslim' and 'Christian' in a secular regime of coexistence? How would the religious figure in it? How, according to what norms or principles, and by what procedures, might the secular, positive law guarantee the coexistence of Christians and Muslims? In what ways might coexistence be connected to such secular liberal values as equality, freedom, tolerance and dialogue? What might the relationship be among coexistence, 'sectarianism' and secularism?

The aim of this book is to answer these questions by way of an anthropological study of the coexistence of Muslims and Christians in Lebanon. I argue that the coexistence of Christians and Muslims in Lebanon is a historically and geographically specific arrangement involving the practical (ethical, political) organisation of a world composed of Christians and Muslims – that is, the making of a world in which they coexist through their distinctiveness and difference.[1] The topography of that world of coexistence takes the shape

[1]In a recently published genealogy of the concept, Meziane argues that secularisation is the process in which the conditions of salvation are created in 'this world' – rather than sought in the 'next' one – through the exploitation of the Earth and its natural and human resources.

of a secular hierarchy of oppositions – between private and public, the intelligible and passional, the legal and religious, reason and faith – in such a way as to ensure that the religious is (are) always encompassed within and, thereby, rearranged by the secular.[2] Implicit in coexistence is the assumption that this world is not a projection of a divine, transcendent, or theologically sanctioned order, but the work of Christians and Muslims in Lebanon and, as such, as much a fabrication of their coexistence as it is for it.[3]

The coexistence of Christians and Muslims in Lebanon is one (and only one) way in which Christians and Muslims might secure their religious equality, religious freedom and religious difference – the equality, freedom and difference of the religious.[4] It is a formation of secular power, one of secular

He takes 'the secular' in the sense of 'this world', identifying the latter with the Earth – a three dimensional geographic and geological entity that sets the horizon for the finality of human aspirations. Mohamad Amer Meziane, *Des empires sous la terre: Histoire écologique et raciale de la sécularisation* (Paris: La Découverte, 2021). I use 'this world' in contrast to speak about an arrangement of concepts, practices and attitudes that are constitutive of the coexistence of Christians and Muslims and touch their bodies in definite ways.

[2] On the concept of 'hierarchy' as a relationship between encompassing and encompassed, see Louis Dumont, 'Vers une théorie de la hiérachie', in *Homo Hierarchicus: le système des castes et ses implications* (Paris: Gallimard (Collections Tel), 1978 [1966]). See also Louis Dumont, *Essais sur l'individualisme: une perspective anthropologique sur l'idéologie modern* (Paris: Éditions du Seuil, 1985 [1983]), p. 301.

[3] Ussama Makdisi has argued that a 'culture of sectarianism' crystallised in the nineteenth century Ottoman empire following the collapse of the centuries-old order that had subsumed and joined together in a hierarchy ruler and ruled, Muslims and Christians. In so far as it could be said that in contrast to that transcendent hierarchical order, what emerged in the aftermath is a modern, immanent formation, then 'sectarianism' and coexistence could be said to be rooted in the same secular realisation, namely, that Christians and Muslims inhabit the same 'world', that they are now left to their own devices to shape it, and that it is up to them to choose the means by which they do so. Ussama Samir Makdisi, *The Culture of Sectarianism: Community, History, and Violence in Nineteenth-Century Ottoman Lebanon* (Berkeley: University of California Press, 2000).

[4] In so far as the religious belong(s) to one of the three monotheisms – Judaism, Christianity and Islam – and in so far as only some 'sects', 'churches', or 'congregations' are admitted as belonging to them. This restriction is contingent. In principle, the category could be more inclusive. There seems to be a consensus prevailing in Lebanon that religion means Judaism, Christianisty, and Islam – the religions of 'the Book' (*ahl al-kitāb*) or, in a modern, Catholic formulation, the 'Abrahamic religions'. For a historically informed critique of the analytic utility of the latter, see Aaron W. Hughes, *Abrahamic Religions: On the Uses and Abuses of History* (Oxford: Oxford University Press, 2012).

power's supports and domains of action: it is the world in which the exercise of secular power over the religious takes place and finds its groundings, its reasons – the world in which as actions in this world the exercise of secular power over the religious may seem sensible.

The coexistence of Christians and Muslims in Lebanon rests on three principles: that Muslims and Christians are secured a place and secured in a place apart within a whole (Lebanon) in which their articulation of their distinctiveness and difference is guaranteed; that they articulate their distinctiveness and difference through marriage and its consequences (the family); and that they keep a check on their religious passions. The three principles are embedded in concepts, practices and attitudes and constitute, by virtue of being so embedded, a sensibility or form of life. That sensibility (or form of life) is coexistence, and it involves an arrangement between Christians and Muslims in Lebanon in and through which the sense of 'Muslim' and 'Christian' (and the sense of 'the religious', generally) answer to the demands of religious difference, equality and freedom.

The positive, secular law provides the means – conceptual and practical, substantive and procedural – by which coexistence is routinised and reinforced, and the common language (or discourse) that enables distinctively Muslim and Christian articulations of religious difference. It is through law that coexistence is given form and, in virtue of that, an intelligibility available to all. The law structures or organises coexistence in terms of its own order of binary oppositions, namely, the personal, transactional and codifiable (recordable, registerable, legible) on the one hand, and what does (or can) not lend itself to be legally (con)figured or represented, but is always present, latent, susceptible to arousal and (potentially) violent – that is, the affective or passional, tied as it is to what it is to say 'Muslim' and 'Christian' – on the other. The passions are to be suppressed so as not to spill out into the open (the public), threatening coexistence and, along with it, the state that depends on it (the public order).

The conceptual and practical oppositions in terms of which coexistence is legally organised find their common point of support in the legal subject: the human person and, specifically, the body with which the human person is taken to be endowed.[5] It is in the legal subject that the two terms are joined

[5] The juridical concept of 'the person' presupposes a necessary connection between a person's rights and her ownership of her body. Marcel Mauss, 'Une Catégorie de L'Esprit Humain: La

(and kept apart), and it is in the body that the coexistence of Muslims and Christians is anchored. The legal subject, which the religious and the individual Muslim and Christian embody, and which constitutes the legal basis of the coexistence of Christians and Muslims in Lebanon, sustains the judicial function as it is performed across civil, criminal, ecclesiastical and shariʿa jurisdictions. The continuum between the secular and religious with which the legal subject provides the judicial function, and the fact that the latter is common to all jurisdictions, informs the method of this study: to examine articulations of the secular and religious across jurisdictions.

A Trans-jurisdictional Investigation: Judicial Events and the Divisions of Lebanese Law

Consider the following: a Lebanese civil judge invalidates a person's religious conversion, considering it legally fraudulent. Her criminal counterpart releases from custody two young Muslim men accused of offending the religious sentiments, claiming to teach them the love that Muslims have for the Virgin Mary. A Sunni shariʿa judge decides to grant a divorcée and a wife an equal share of the deceased man's wealth, invoking the higher purposes of marriage, among which are procreation and preservation of the human kind. An ecclesiastical judge declares a marriage – a Holy Sacrament of the Catholic Church – null and void on the basis of a forensic psychiatrist's assessment of the spouses' 'abnormal' or 'pathological' sexuality.

This is a random selection of judicial events, actions performed by four distinct judiciaries: civil, criminal, Islamic (Sunni), and Christian (Catholic). In so far as they all are judicial events, they have features in common. They consist in an action – invalidating, releasing, granting, declaring – performed

Notion de Personne Celle de "Moi"', *Journal of the Royal Anthropological Institute of Great Britain and Ireland* 68 (1928): 263–81; Simone Goyard-Fabre, 'Sujet de droit et objet de droit: Défense de l'humanisme', *ARSP: Archiv für Rechts- und Sozialphilosophie/Archives for Philosophy of Law and Social Philosophy* 81, 5 (1995): 517–31; Yves Charles Zarka, 'L'invention du sujet de droit', *Archives de Philosophie* 60, 4 (1997): 531–50; Stéphane Mouton, 'Personnalité juridique et sujets de droits', in Xavier Bioy (ed.), *La Personnalité Juridique* (Toulouse: Presses de l'Université Toulouse 1 Capitole, 2013), pp. 47–56; Claire Neirinck, 'La personnalité juridique et le corps', in Xavier Bioy (ed.), *La Personnalité Juridique*, pp. 57–67; Muriel Fabre-Magnan, 'Les sujets de droit', in M. Fabre-Magnon, *Que sais-je?* (Paris: Presses Universitaires de France, 2014), pp. 97–107.

following a decision made on the basis of an argument that gives reasons to it through the assessment of facts. The action is then brought to bear on a Christian's or Muslim's body and its relationship with other bodies. At first glance, it might appear that among the variety of the events cited, those generated by the civil and criminal judiciaries could be classified as 'secular', while those by the ecclesiastical and shariʿa judiciaries, 'religious'. Yet, a closer examination of each would suggest a more complicated picture: all of the events above articulate secular and religious elements; they all display a clear distinction between the two; they all connect the two in one way or another.

Thus, a conversion is invalidated, for it is found to be intended to defraud a relative from her rights to inherit, with the consequence that the latter will now inherit, while the 'convert' return to his initial religion. Two young Muslim men are released, for the judge finds hope for them to be reformed and transformed, having memorised Qurʾanic verses, and learned something about the Virgin Mary and the religion of their Christian compatriots. In the third case, a part of the properties of a deceased man will go to his divorcee, for the judge casts doubt on the moral grounds of his second marriage, adjusting in the same act the definition of marriage handed down by preceding Islamic jurists. Finally, a marriage is declared to be non-existent, for its 'biological' basis is found defective, making it possible for the spouses to be released while remaining in the Church as the Sacrament is safeguarded from the arbitrariness of human volition.

The linkages between the secular and religious elements that structure these judicial events display a sort of asymmetry. They obey a logic that is common to all judicial events of the kind (the kind, that is, that involves the religious), no matter the jurisdiction in which they occur. It cuts across civil and criminal, Islamic and Christian jurisdictions. In the case of the civil and criminal events, the action is carried out in one direction, carrying with it the force of the concepts that support it from the side of the secular authority which enacts it towards the religious (Christian or Muslim/Islamic) who/which receives it, drawing the latter into the domain of law, of legal discourse (and practice), taking it in, constructing it as its object. Whereas it goes without saying that the secular is the basis and agent of the action, the religious, in contrast, is acted upon, singled out, spelled out, encompassed by the demands of (legal) representation or intelligibility.

In the case of the ecclesiastical and shariʿa events, the same asymmetry is on display, but it is, first, more complex than the one that organises the civil and criminal events, and, second, the ecclesiastical and shariʿa events obey a logic that is specific to each of the two religious jurisdictions. They issue an action that proceeds from a religious authority towards the religious, but the action in both cases is accompanied by mediating terms that articulate, differently in each case, the religious and legal. Thus, the civil and criminal judiciaries encompass the religious within the legal, the ecclesiastical judiciaries make the legal available to the religious by way of the medical (medico-legal), while the shariʿa judiciaries do so by way of the ethical (articulations of conduct and judgment).

The four jurisdictions could be grouped into two categories or divisions: the civil and criminal judiciaries could be considered 'secular', while the shariʿa and ecclesiastical could be called, without much controversy, 'religious'. In itself, this classification is trivial. It distracts from the interesting feature of Lebanese law, namely, that each of its two divisions is characterised by a distinctive relationship between religion and law, each performs a specific judicial function, and both take aim at a specific religious object (or element of religion). Whereas the civil and criminal (the secular) judiciaries rule in cases that involve religious conversion and actions that arouse the religious passions – regulating the former, suppressing the latter – the religious judiciaries of the eighteen communities of Muslims, Christians and Jews hold exclusive jurisdiction over marriage and its consequences, such as divorce, annulment, custody, support, inheritance, and other matters that pertain to the family in general.[6]

[6] While it is the case that Muslims, Christians and Jews are officially recognised and have jurisdiction over their marriages and their consequences (the family), this study is restricted to the coexistence of Muslims and Christians. The reason is that fundamental questions about the Lebanese state, such as its political identity, or the form of its legal institutions, which often involve the problem of the status of religion and its relationship with both politics and law, have been (and so far remain) questions about the relationship between Muslims and Christians, and have historically mobilised them as such (and they still do). As I describe it in this book, coexistence is one answer to such questions. The politics of legal reform, which is aimed to 'secularise' Lebanese law (or restore it to its presumed secular essence) almost always ends up touching on fundamental political issues that matter to them (somewhat exclusively), such as the abolishing of 'political sectarianism', the passing

There is a significant difference between the secular and religious jurisdictions regarding the kind of 'religious thing' that is the object of the enactments, or that which counts as religious. What pertains to the 'inner movements' of the subject (that which the subject experiences internally) is placed under the protection of the civil and criminal judiciaries (i.e. the secular), while the subject's 'practical', 'external' relationship with others (a spouse, father, grandmother etc.) is the purview of the religious judiciaries. This division might seem paradoxical to some observers. The securing of the private freedom of belief or conscience (religious conversion) and the sanctioning of what may be expressed in public as or about religion is typical of any secular, liberal democracy. Yet, subjecting citizens to the religious authorities of the religious communities to which they are by law consigned in matters of marriage and the family not only exacerbates a presumably already deeply rooted so-called 'culture of sectarianism', but is a gross violation of the basic principles of secularism. The secular judiciaries are in charge of protecting religious beliefs and sentiments, while their religious counterparts rule over vital swathes of the life of a citizen that ought to be – because they are vital – under the sole jurisdiction of the positive, secular law and secular institutions (marriage and the family).

This division of Lebanese law is an expression of an organisational feature the significance of which for the understanding of secularism in Lebanon has gone unnoticed. It is an aim of this book to show that the understanding of the relationship between the religious and the law, and, therefore, of the sense of 'the secular' in Lebanon, would be more complete if the two parts of the legal arrangement are encompassed within the same analytical project. It focuses on the interlinkages between the two, and between the civil, criminal, ecclesiastical and shariʿa judiciaries through an analysis of their

of a 'civil law of marriage', or the prospects of a fully 'secularised state'. For a history of the relationship between the formation of the Lebanese state and politics of legal reform during the French Mandate over Syria and Lebanon, see Elizabeth Thompson, *Colonial Citizens: Republican Rights, Paternal Privilege, and Gender in French Syria and Lebanon* (New York: Columbia University Press, 2000); Nadine Méouchy, Peter Sluglett, Gérard D. Khoury and Geoffrey Schad (eds), *The British and French Mandates in Comparative Perspectives/Les mandats français et anglais dans une perspective comparative* (Leiden: Brill, 2004); Max Weiss, *In the Shadow of Sectarianism: Law, Shiʿism and the Making of Modern Lebanon* (Cambridge, MA: Harvard University Press, 2010).

enunciations – how, specifically, each articulates in its own ways the secular and religious – drawing the consequences for an understanding of secularism in Lebanon from that analysis.

Secularism and Lebanese Law

Opinions about the legal system in Lebanon are split between two conflicting accounts, each containing a statement about the status of secularism in Lebanon made on the basis of that account: 'partial secularism' and 'managerial (regulatory) secularism'. Each of the two accounts is a version of what has been called 'political secularism', the values, principles or norms that dictate the relationship which the state (as institutions and exercise of power) is to have with the religious (e.g. neutrality, separation, religious freedom), or the practice by which the state determines its relationship with and, thereby, defines, the religious (e.g. the banning of religious symbols in public schools, ruling on the shariʿa concept of *ʿidda*).[7]

In the partial (or incomplete) secularism account, the general scheme of Lebanese positive law leaves out of its purview the personal status of citizens, placing it under religious jurisdictions. The state's sovereignty is, thereby, surrendered to the religious or, conversely, the latter is invited to have a say in what ought to be the former's exclusive and exclusively secular domain. In one variation of the partial secularism account, the interpenetration of law and the religious is objectionable as a matter of principle. 'Secularization – taken as the differentiation of the legislative framework from religious institutions and

[7] Political secularism in this sense is taken to be analytically distinct from secular sensibilities. The former consists in the more or less systematic application (some would say imposition) of secular principles by means of more or less formal practices (policies) with the aims of shaping institutions (and bodies). Examples of political secularism would be legislating for the abolishing of religious jurisdiction over marriage and the family, the banning of ostensibly religious symbols in French *lycées*, or the brandishing of religious freedom as an instrument of foreign policy. In contrast, a secular sensibility would be a more or less widely-shared and diffuse attitude towards religion or the religious, such as tolerance, or the strong preference which an otherwise religious person might have for a civil marriage. Hussein Ali Agrama, *Questioning Secularism: Islam, Sovereignty, and the Rule of Law in Modern Egypt* (Chicago: University of Chicago Press, 2012), and Saba Mahmood, *Religious Difference in a Secular Age: A Minority Report* (Princeton, NJ: Princeton University Press, 2016).

norms', as one author writes, 'remains incomplete in Lebanon'. On one hand, 'the Lebanese state betrays elements of secularism', since 'the Constitution . . . affirm[s] the absolute freedom of belief'.[8]

Yet, on the other hand, according to the same author, the Constitution 'obliges the state to surrender key jurisdictions in the realm of personal status law' to the various 'confessions [communities]' of Christians and Muslims.[9] What the Lebanese Constitution admits, it seems, the law denies. The secular in this variation on partial secularism figures as the absence of the religious, a condition which the Lebanese Constitution meets in regards to the freedom of conscience and belief, but which Lebanese law fails to meet in regards to personal status. A wholesome secularism – what, according to some proponents of this account, ought to be the model aspired to – would require the complete dismissal of the religious from the legal domain in its entirety. The two are, simply, mutually exclusive.

In another variation of the partial secularism account, the objection against the Lebanese legal arrangement places the emphasis on its effects on citizenship. The Lebanese state is characterised by a 'political and legal order that has consistently upheld both the constitutional secularity of citizens' and 'religiously segregated laws to govern marriage, divorce, and inheritance that have actually denied the secularity and equality of citizens'.[10] It upholds 'the principle of religious diversity [and] the equality of all citizens, *and* [the] codification and maintenance of highly gendered and unequal sectarian regimes of "personal status"'.[11] By this account, the Lebanese state's 'surrendering' of personal status to the religious undermines the freedom and equality of its citizens who find themselves bound, by law, to a religious jurisdiction – even if they are not 'really religious' – and subdivided into discrete religious identities with which some do not even identify.

[8] Mark Farha, 'Stumbling Blocks to the Secularization of Personal Status Laws in the Lebanese Republic (1926–2013)', *Arab Law Quarterly* 29, 1 (2015): 31–2. Farha concludes that Lebanon 'combine[s] elements from Ottoman communalism' in its legal arrangement, and 'French Republicanism' in some of its Constitution's 'egalitarian, laic clauses'.

[9] Ibid., pp. 31–2.

[10] Ussama Makdisi, *Age of Coexistence: The Ecumenical Frame and the Making of the Modern Arab World* (Berkeley: University of California Press, 2019), pp. 7–8.

[11] Ibid., p. 10.

The secular in this version of partial secularism consists not in the absence of the religious from the legal, but in the secular principle of citizenship. What is desired is less the exclusion of the religious from the legal as an end in itself (as a matter of principle), but the privatisation of the religious in order to guarantee the equality and freedom of all. This version presupposes a normative idea of 'the private' (and, accordingly, of 'the religious' and 'secular') whereby the religious is (ought to be) a private matter, and 'private' is identified with individual 'belief' and 'conscience'. It is in this respect that secularism in Lebanon is 'partial': what the Lebanese Constitution admits, Lebanese law fails to apply (or extend) in full.[12]

The second, managerial account of secularism, stresses the Lebanese state's prerogative to the management or regulation of the religious. Lebanese law in this account is not (not simply, not just) that which guarantees the equality and freedom of all citizens, but a modality of secular power (i.e the state), and the conduit through which secular power acts on religious bodies.[13] It is not exact, by this account, to say that the religious intrudes upon Lebanese law, or that the state interferes legally in religious affairs. Rather, the state's regulation of the religious confirms its commitment to secularism's principle of neutrality, for, as it carries out its regulatory function, it does not privilege one religion over another.

According to the managerial account, secularism is not lacking from the Lebanese state, but is 'the condition of possibility [of] the nation-state' in general, intrinsic to it as 'the structuring force through which religious and sexual difference is managed'.[14] In this account, 'the secular' consists in the very character of secular power, taken in the dual sense of the state's 'sovereignty' and 'governmentality': the state's claim to, and exercise of, the exclusive right to regulate (and define), and its posture of neutrality towards religion.

Secularism figures in these accounts as a basis of a critique of Lebanese law and, more generally, the state. The latter is singled out as either requiring

[12] See also Morgan Clarke, *Islam and Law in Lebanon: Sharia within and without the State* (Cambridge: Cambridge University Press, 2018), pp. 33, 38.

[13] Maya Mikdashi, *Sextarianism: Sovereignty, Secularism and the State in Lebanon* (Stanford: Stanford University Press, 2022).

[14] Ibid., p. 9.

(legal) reform measures to align it with the standards of a 'properly (liberal) secular' state, or curb the power it wields over bodies. Yet, it is the particular concept of law that each account presupposes that informs the concept of the secular by which it delivers its critique. In the partial secularism account, 'the legal' is the domain of the state's legislation, and a 'properly' secular state would imply a fully secular law. In the liberal variation of the partial account of secularism, 'the legal' is that which guarantees the equality and freedom of all citizens – the constituents of citizenship – while 'the religious' is that which divides and constrains or binds the citizen. In both accounts, 'the legal' and 'the secular' are mirror images of each other, so to speak. What might an alternative account of the relationship between 'law' and secularism, between the legal and the secular in Lebanon look like? Plainly, what *is* the relationship between law and secularism in Lebanon?

The two accounts differ not only in their respective concepts of 'the legal' and 'secular', but also in the part or division of Lebanese law they have their sight on, and on the basis of which they pass their judgments about the status of secularism in Lebanon. The partial secularism account singles out the laws of personal status, while the managerial account points to the state's civil (secular) judiciaries' exclusive right to rule in cases that appear to be 'properly religious', such as religious conversion. What secularism turns out to be in each account, and which part or division of Lebanese law is held in view, are *also* mirror images of each other. The secular judiciaries' taking action that would decide on the status of, say, a religious conversion would appear as 'regulation'; the religious judiciaries' (the very fact that there is such a thing as religious judiciaries) exclusive jurisdiction over marriage and its consequences (including the family) would appear as a violation of the secular, or the 'values' of secularism. What would the secular look like if both divisions of Lebanese law are considered together in a single inquiry that attends to their interconnections?

Apart from the assumptions about the secular and the legal that support them, and the division of the Lebanese legal arrangement which they take as datum, both accounts make their claims about secularism (and about Lebanese law) in terms of its relationship with religion. In the 'partial account', secularism appears to be undermined by religion, which is allowed to encroach upon the law or the state. In the 'regulatory or managerial account' of secularism, the state regulates or manages religion while claiming neutrality towards all religions. In both accounts, 'religion' is presupposed as a category that, in theory, could include any particular religion, but in practice in Lebanon includes *only* Christians and Muslims.[15] So, how is (are) the religious in Lebanon circumscribed to (and by) Christians and Muslims, and how is that to be accounted for? What difference would it make for an account of secularism (and law) in Lebanon if the observation that the Lebanese legal arrangement involves Muslims and Christians were taken into account? What difference would it make if the account proceeded from the observation that it is Christians and Muslims as 'Christians' and 'Muslims' who occupy the legal space in Lebanon?

Interrogating the Lebanese legal arrangement this way, this book seeks an understanding of that arrangement's relationship with secularism and the secular, and, importantly, describes its distinctive rationality. The book proposes an inquiry into the assumptions that support the legal arrangement, the concepts it articulates, the practices through which they are applied, and the attitudes it mobilises. It considers the legal arrangement by looking into the way it works, the kind of work it does, what it puts into play – what it does to and for the religious, how it figures in the determination of such identifications as 'Christians' and 'Muslims', how the religious enter(s) into the reasoning and decisions of the civil and criminal judiciaries.

In this perspective, the sense of the secular suggests not just an ideology, discourse or political doctrine, not to the formal characteristics of the state and its sovereignty, not to the form or functioning of its legal institutions, and not to the explicit exercise of power from which the religious is (ought to be) 'subtracted'.[16] Rather, secularism consists in their organising principle, or the rationality in virtue of which they are made to make sense. The name of that rationality is 'coexistence'.

[15] By law, it also includes the Jewish community; see footnote 6.

[16] There is a considerable body of multidisciplinary scholarship on the inadequacy of the 'subtraction story' of secularism, secularisation, or the secular. The phrase, 'subtraction story', is Charles Taylor's. Charles Taylor, *A Secular Age* (Cambridge, MA: The Belknap Press of Harvard University Press, 2007).

Coexistence as a Secular Arrangement: Difference, Equality, Freedom

In one of its genealogies, coexistence figures as a modern political idea that begins to acquire some discursive appeal around the mid-nineteenth century, at the time when the Ottoman empire was embarking on its comprehensive project of 'modernising' reforms.[17] It delineates the 'imaginative horizon' of political mobilisation and action in a context in which the respective status of and relationship among religious communities was being recast in terms of equality and freedom.[18] The idea is put forth as a viable alternative to 'sectarianism' and a reminder to the members of a diversity (religious or otherwise), that a possibility is available for them to exist together peacefully, equally, and freely within the framework of the same (Ottoman) state.[19]

The Lebanese Constitution states in its Preamble that one of its 'Fundamental Provisions' is that '[t]here shall be no constitutional legitimacy for any authority which contradicts the pact of coexistence (*mithāq al-ʿaysh al-mushtarak*)'.[20] The provision does not specify the identity of the coexisting parties, but subsequent stipulations make explicit that what is implied is the coexistence of Christians and Muslims. Article 24 describes the composition

[17] Makdisi, *Age of Coexistence.*

[18] Vincent Crapanzano, *Imaginative Horizons: An Essay in Literary-Philosophical Anthropology* (Chicago: University of Chicago Press, 2004).

[19] There seems to be an increased scholarly interest in this sense of the word 'coexistence' in Lebanon (or what is now Lebanon) and the Middle East. See, for example, in addition to Makdisi, Theodor Hanf, *Coexistence in Wartime Lebanon: Decline of a State and Rise of a Nation* (London: Centre for Lebanese Studies in association with I. B. Tauris, 1993); Nicholas Doumanis, *Before the Nation: Muslim-Christian Coexistence and Its Destruction in Late Ottoman Anatolia* (Oxford: Oxford University Press, 2013); Roschanack Shaery-Yazdi, 'Rethinking Sectarianism: Violence and Coexistence in Lebanon', *Islam and Christian-Muslim Relations* 31, 3 (2020): 325–40; Christian Lochon, 'Les chrétiens dans l'Orient: l'apport de l'histoire des religions à la coexistence religieuse en Méditerranée', *Cahiers D'Histoire* 145 (2020): 81–99; Carole Hillenbrand (ed.), *Syria in Crusader Times: Conflict and Coexistence* (Edinburgh: Edinburgh University Press, 2020).

[20] Article 10 in Part One: Fundamental Provisions, under the title 'Preamble': Bahige Tabbarah, 'The Lebanese Constitution', *Arab Law Quarterly* 12, 2 (1997): 224–61. 'Mutual existence' is a different category to 'political sectarianism', or '*al-ṭāʾifiyya al-siyāsiyya*', which figures in another stipulation.

of the 'Chamber of Deputies', in which 'the distribution of seats shall be [made] according to [several] principles' the first of which being that of the '[e]qual representation between Christians and Muslims'.

If the Constitution is taken to the letter, coexistence or mutual existence in Lebanon is a political principle: it fixes the state's identity and establishes equality as the rule of representation within it. In so doing, it qualifies the latter as it limits the former, since equality is equality between Christians and Muslims – Muslims and Christians being equally constitutive of the Lebanese state – while the Lebanese state is a state of and for Christians and Muslims (in which the two are equally represented). The difference that is privileged in Lebanon today is that between Muslims and Christians, who happen to be brought together under the sovereignty of the state of Lebanon and encompassed by its laws. Thus, the coexistence of Muslims and Christians is one of the foundations of political authority, serving to (de)legitimise political action and the exercise of power. In this respect, it is a basis of a particular style of politics and, more generally, of the political (as concept and practice).

I make a case in this book for an anthropological account of coexistence. I do not discount the status of coexistence as an 'origin myth', or a Lebanese version of the social contract, and as a historically specific political idea or discourse that derives its force from its opposition to 'sectarianism'. I do stress, however, that coexistence is not just that, but an articulation – an eminently secular one – of a form of life or a sensibility rooted in the contingencies of Christian and Muslim co-occupation of the same juridical or legal space as *Christians and Muslims* (they are encompassed by a common juridical space). It is in virtue of that legal co-occupation that they are bound to law by law, and thereby conjoined through law. I take 'coexistence' in the sense of an organising or structuring principle that transcends Muslims and Christians, their normative, theological categories, and their particularities, while (and thereby) possessing the capacity or power to mediate their relationship and articulate their particularities.

The coexistence of Muslims and Christians in Lebanon, as it takes shape through Lebanese law, brings into play three sorts of relationship: a conjunctive relationship between Christians and Muslims, a hierarchical relationship between them (and the religious, more generally) and the state, and a singular, positional relationship between each of them and the state. In the first place, the 'and' that conjoins the two grammatically articulates their political equality, Christians and Muslims both being in possession of equal rights and enjoying an equal status and representation in the state.[21] The conjunction is twofold, as it is an articulation of equality and (in)difference, through which the distinction and distinctiveness of the two is maintained. The coexistence of Muslims and Christians in this respect consists in a relationship of equality and difference.

Muslims and Christians, equally, freely, and differently, stand in a hierarchical relationship with the state (secular power), which encompasses and incorporates both into its own medium (e.g. political representation, law). In so far as coexistence of Muslims and Christians is their coexistence in Lebanon, it imposes a limit on both – a limit to which they are to accommodate. The state is an abbreviation of secular power in so far as it encompasses – and in virtue of a prerogative of sovereignty to encompass – the religious and mark, thereby, its difference as secular and as power from the religious.

In coexistence, Muslims and Christians enjoy, each separately, a relative freedom (they are enabled and constrained) to determine, to a certain extent and in some respects, their relationship with secular power, and to position themselves differently towards it. What posture they assume enters into the sense of what it is to be (or say) 'Muslim' and 'Christian' in Lebanon.[22] The words 'Christian' and 'Muslim' become two distinct and distinctive articulations of the religious and secular (it does not follow from this remark that they are reducible to their relationship with secular power).

The provision about coexistence in the Lebanese Constitution makes reference to its founding moment, namely, an agreement between Muslims and Christians to commit to it as a matter of principle – the act of agreeing itself being a performance of coexistence (coexistence in action). Clearly, however, the agreement and the promise are not enough to secure it, for otherwise there would be no need to secure it by writing it into the Constitution. This suggests a transactional or contractual sense of coexistence. It is an arrangement

[21] This has not always been the case, and could be otherwise. See note 6, above.

[22] One of the more obvious instances of this difference is the status of the religious judiciaries: the shariʿa judges are state employees, the shariʿa courts are state courts; ecclesiastical judicial institutions are not. See Clarke, *Islam and Law*, p. 35.

between the two parties, their coming to an understanding (e.g. about the pact of mutual existence) that calls for a process of mutual accommodation and compromise that defines their interactions with each other. Implied in this sense of coexistence is that of a laying out of things in a certain order (from which it does not follow that it is protected entirely against contingencies or the threat of disorder).

This order of things might through routine or habituation dictate or, in time require, the cultivation of embodied dispositions and, accordingly, the arranging of concepts, actions and senses to conform to it, at least to a certain extent. Thus, coexistence is an arrangement among parties, that requires a specific arrangement of things, times and spaces, and that calls on the parties to arrange practices, attitudes and perceptions accordingly. It is in this holistic sense that 'the coexistence of Christians and Muslims in Lebanon' figures in this book: as constitutive of a sensibility or form of life, with its distinctive ways of thinking, doing and feeling.

Principles of Coexistence: Belonging, Marriage, Passions

Three principles support the coexistence of Christians and Muslims in Lebanon, or, put differently, the coexistence of Christians and Muslims in Lebanon requires that three conditions (or sets of conditions) be met or satisfied: that a place apart be available to each of them in which they be secured, that marriage (and its consequences, the family) be the articulation of their distinctiveness and difference, and that their religious passions remain in check. These could also be considered the three criteria of coexistence, whereby each is also an articulation of the religious and secular.

The first is that there is a place apart in the greater whole (Lebanon) for Muslims and Christians to exist in their distinctiveness and difference. That there is a place apart in the greater whole for Muslims and Christians to exist does not mean that it is given, but made (made by them, in a sense). It is carved out in a process in which the religious is (are) spatialised, configured through a spatial scheme that transcends them all (i.e. it is secular). Muslims and Christians are secured in a place in which they are enabled (and constrained) to articulate their distinctiveness in ways appropriate to them within the limits which the requirements of their coexistence set, an attachment to a place through which their singular articulations of their respective difference and distinctiveness are guaranteed. Their securing in place consists in arranging their bodies in a prearranged space, in arranging the bodies of Christians and Muslims (the religious), arranging them as (in so far as they are, they possess) bodies in a prearranged space – to a region in a space that is prearranged to contain their bodies (to contain them as bodies).

They are to be secured in their respective place, and to be so by means that mark their place and make known (explicit, recognisable) their attachment to it. It does not always go without saying what those markers are – what counts as a (appropriate) marker, what markers are admitted, where and how they are to be admitted or displayed. They are of concern to secular power, which defines and regulates them, but they are also contested, resisted, manipulated, put to different ends, and so on. This is due in no small part to their ambiguity – whether they are religious or secular, what authority or agency decides and fixes their meaning as one or the other.[23]

There is in Lebanon a complex of formal procedures to accomplish this task of securing Muslim and Christian bodies in place, a complex that is organised around the very words 'Muslim' and 'Christian', the signs that mark the attachment of the Muslim and Christian body to a specific place in the prearranged space. The complex includes: spaces in which the words 'Christian' and 'Muslim' (or words that imply them) are uttered, confirmed, circulated, recorded, deposited, retrieved, copied, and so on (e.g. the office of a notary public); personnel in charge of seeing to their proper utterance and recording (e.g. notaries, registrars); technologies by which they are authorised (e.g. authentication, witnessing, signatures, seals), materialised (e.g. forms, documents, identification cards, records, registries . . .), and, therefore, circumscribed, contained, controlled – and routinised.

[23] See Asad's discussion of 'reading [and fixing] signs' in his analysis of republican *laïcité* and the debates surrounding the headscarf in France. Talal Asad, 'Trying to Understand French Secularism', in Hent de Vries and Lawrence Eugene Sullivan (eds), *Political Theologies: Public Religions in a Post-Secular World* (New York: Fordham University Press, 2006), p. 500. Elsewhere, he writes, '[T]he sign as an object of a knowing mind (a purely cognitive event) is not the same as the sign translated into the sensible body through the cultivation of sensibilities'. Talal Asad, *Secular Translations: Nation-State, Modern Self, and Calculative Reason* (New York: Columbia University Press, 2018), p. 5. It is in the latter, 'embodied' sense, that I mean the word 'marker' here (see also Chapter 1).

Securing Muslims and Christians in place depends on and enacts the secular assumption that, apart from and despite their religious difference as Muslims and Christians, there is a secular substratum common to both of them, which, conversely, constitutes the basis on which the separation between Christians and Muslims could be made, their difference and distinctiveness articulated. In abstract terms, the coexistence of Christians and Muslims in Lebanon presupposes that there is a distinction (the possibility of a distinction) between the religious proper (e.g. religious beliefs, rituals, acts of worship, rites, symbols, doctrines, marriage, and so on) and the secular (the body), and that the religious and the (secular) body (as object), could be severed, or, that the Muslim and Christian is to her body as the religious is to the secular (coexistence presupposes and enacts this conceptual severance).

The enactment of this assumption – coexistence as putting-in-place is, in a sense, the enactment – carries implications. In the first place, to speak of 'Christian' and 'Muslim' in Lebanon is to speak both of the religious and of the arrangement of bodies in a general topography – and to be able to speak about the two separately, as existing in separate ontological and epistemological domains. Yet, what is spoken about exactly is determined in a particular context. Coexistence brings forth or calls for the appeal to 'context' to make sense of the utterance of such words as 'Christian' and 'Muslim'. It brings forth a multiplicity of separate religious and secular (legal, political, moral) domains and introduces, thereby, a multiplicity into (the senses of) 'the religious'.[24] The separation of the religious and the corporeal body opens up a space for a distinctive mode of belonging, as it is up to the individual Christian or Muslim to decide (on) the character of the connection between himself (as possibly religious) and his body (as object in place), and whether it matters that the two be aligned, for example, or not. As much as this is a space of freedom for Muslims and Christians, it is also a space in which doubt may settle, scepticism thrive.[25]

[24] Talal Asad, *Formations of the Secular: Christianity, Islam, Modernity* (Stanford: Stanford University Press, 2003), chapter 7 and, for the differentiation of 'religion' and 'the economy', Nada Moumtaz, *God's Property: Islam, Charity, and the Modern* State (Berkeley: University of California Press, 2021).

[25] On suspicion and the positive law, see Agrama, *Questioning Secularism*, chapter 4. On suspicion as a characteristic of the 'secular autonomous subject', see Asad, Formations of the

The second condition or principle of the coexistence of Christians and Muslims in Lebanon is that difference and distinctiveness be articulated through, or in relation to, the complex of interrelations that is marriage and its consequences (the family). Put differently, the difference between and distinctiveness of Christians and Muslims coexisting in Lebanon resides in the singular ways in which they articulate (join and keep apart) the religious and secular (including secular power or the state) through marriage and its consequences, the ways in which marriage and its consequences enter into their articulations of, or do the work of joining and keeping apart, the religious and secular.

Coexistence – secular coexistence – calls for a rearranging of marriage and its consequences (the family) in such a way as to turn them into the privileged nexus of concepts and practices of religious distinctiveness and difference, that through which Christians and Muslims articulate singularly their difference and distinctiveness. A consequence of this is that 'Christian' and 'Muslim', in so far as marriage and its consequences (including the family) are constitutive of their distinctiveness and difference, and in so far as they are articulations of the religious and the secular, are themselves – the very terms 'Muslim' and 'Christian' – particular articulations of the religious and secular.

The complex or nexus of marriage and the family, is constitutive of a sensibility or form of life specific to Muslims and Christians, respectively, and consists in each case in a specific arrangement of religious and secular concepts, practices and attitudes. Marriage and its consequences (the family) are the legally intelligible relay between Muslims and Christians, their relationship with religious beliefs and rituals, the ecclesiastical or shariʿa jurisdiction to which they belong, the secular positive law to which they are subject, and the moral or ethical norms by which they conduct their life.

A feature of the religious sensibility or form of life is an element of religion or the religious experience that cannot be legally accounted for, namely, the passional. These 'passions', or passional features of the religious sensibility or form of life of Christians and Muslims that are singled out as

Secular, p. 124, and on suspicion's connections with the 'legal concept of the person' and the 'essence of the human . . . circumscribed by *legal* discourse', see ibid., p. 135.

critical for coexistence are the religious sentiments (*al-mashāʿir al-dīniyya*), communitarian impulses (*al-naʿarāt al-tāʾifiyya*), and scholastic or doctrinal ('sectarian') tensions or conflicts (*al-naʿarāt al-madhhabiyya*). It is characteristic of these passions as they are construed or framed by the positive law that they exist beyond or outside of the bounds of secular (public) reason or rationality, cannot be articulated in a common – secular – or worldly discourse, do not enter the constitution of coexistence or the public order that sustains it, and if allowed to be given expression, might pose a threat to coexistence.

Each in its own way, they are of, or are connected to, the order not of secular intelligibility, but religious affectivity, belong not to the domain of secular, worldly action, but of religious expressivity (though they can have worldly extensions, effects). They are dormant and, therefore, could be aroused and externalised. The coexistence of Muslims and Christians in Lebanon requires that the passions remain in check, or, more exactly, the expression in certain ways of certain kinds of passions that might threaten or undermine coexistence and the public (order, sphere, space) remain so.

It is the formation of a 'public', consisting fundamentally in the coexistence of Muslims and Christians, that gives rise to conditions in which the religious passions could be expressed and threaten, therefore, the public. The suppression of the passions from the public (order, sphere, space) is a founding act in the constitution of a public capacious enough to include Muslims and Christians and to sustain their coexistence. This founding yet ambiguous act includes and excludes, admits and suppresses, and thus binds the coexistence and the public it sustains to the religious passions that threaten always to undermine it. In a sense, the public (coexistence) and the private (the passions) are interconnected, interdependent.

Law and Coexistence: Jurisdiction, Codification, Sanction

In the preceding section, I described three principles that I argue are the basis of coexistence in Lebanon. In this section, I consider the relationship between the three principles of coexistence and the positive law. I argue that the three principles involve assumptions about the ways in which groups of Christians and Muslims, who happen to be encompassed by the modern state of Lebanon, are to be identified, differentiated or distinguished, and kept apart.[26] The three principles, which ensure that these desirable ends are met, are embedded in Lebanese law, derivable from it, but are not, strictly speaking, legal. As such, they are free-standing, but internally connected with Lebanese law in virtue of their compatibility with certain features of the positive law.

Put differently, the three principles of coexistence in Lebanon lend themselves to the possibilities of legal articulation, possibilities which the positive law, in virtue of three of its features, makes available. The three features are: jurisdiction, codification and sanction. Jurisdiction is the instrument by which Christians and Muslims are secured a place, and in place. Codification is that by which their difference or distinctiveness is recorded, registered. Sanction is the instrument by which their passions are kept in check.

Jurisdiction secures Christians and Muslims a/in place: (1) it enables them to exercise judicial authority, to perform the judicial function; (2) it circumscribes the scope of that judicial authority within a limited, specific region; (3) it secures them in place as legal subjects, with rights that also limit the exercise of judicial authority. Jurisdiction has a transformative power Muslims and Christians must organise themselves as a jurisdiction – that is, endow themselves with legal institutions, rules of procedure, substantive laws, and insert themselves in the juridical space and its hierarchical organisation – that is, submit to the positive law.

I made the distinction in the preceding section between the features of the Christian and Muslim sensibility through which they articulate their difference and distinctiveness, namely, marriage and the family (the consequences of marriage) on the one hand, and the features of their sensibility that may constitute a threat to coexistence, the religious passions in their three variations. The difference between the two that is pertinent from a legal point of view or for the law is that the former are legible (and intelligible) legally – the law can and does register them, record them, codify them – while the latter are not legible to law, the law cannot and does not register them, record them, codify them, for they are taken to be by nature or in essence opposed to it.

[26] Indeed, the coexistence of Muslims and Christians in Lebanon presupposes that Christians and Muslims are identifiable and separable in definite ways, and that this matters for the existence and identity of the state.

It is in law, in positive, secular law that this opposition between the intelligible and passional matters. It is in law that their separation is a problem at all. Thus, through marriage and its consequence (the family), Muslims and Christian articulate their difference and distinctiveness in a legal medium, in a legal language. They make their differences and distinctiveness legible legally legible and, thus, intelligible. Indeed, the very intelligibility of their articulations of difference and distinctiveness is a function of the law – of their being able to articulate it, make it legible, in law, in legal terms.

The law provides a variety of ways for them to codify, register or record and make legible their articulations of distinctiveness and difference. Formal codification of their religious provisions or norms about marriage and how to deal with its consequences in such a way as to give them legal form (to translate them into codes of law), but also 'registration' in the sense that marriage and the consequences could be captured by, recorded in, official (state) registries, inscribed in documents and archived paperwork. Muslims and Christians 'register' also their difference and distinctiveness through marriage and its consequences through the practice of marriage itself, a mode of registration or recording or articulating that is performative, lived, but made possible, enabled/constrained, confirmed, by and through law, its dependency on law.

The passions are checked by the state-authorised sanctioning force of law. Keeping them in check could be done by suppressing any number of the elements that enter into and determine their stimulation: the actions and words, for example, that might arouse or incite or awaken them, the property of their contents (e.g. love, tolerance), their consequences or effects (i.e. the kind of movements they cause), and the threshold at which they are aroused and their subject provoked into movement (their threshold of stimulability). These could be aroused by words, images, gestures that offend the religion, trigger communitarianism, or exacerbate a doctrinal conflict, drawing them out into the open, into the public.

Another distinction is that between the normal and a pathological threshold of stimulability of the passions, the former being what is accepted or tolerated in the general culture or society. It is the norm of toleration, whereas pathological stimulability tends towards intolerance that render its claims (or the claims of those who suffer from it) questionable or even invalid. In other words, it is both the words, images, acts that might arouse the passions and the threshold of stimulability of the passions that are subject to the state's (law's) sanction, since coexistence depends on both.

Jurisdiction, codification and sanction bring to bear the three pillars of coexistence, and the abstract principle of coexistence, on the subject/body. Their point of convergence and articulation is the subject of the judicial function: the subject of law, who figures as a locus of (personal, civil and human) rights and a human being endowed with a body. The legal subject, common to *all* jurisdictions, is the articulation of the legal and religious – that which is at once their joining and separation. The subject/body is not just the point of physical application of the law (secular power in its enabling and constraining effects) and, therefore, that in which coexistence is anchored. The subject (the body), in so far as it stands at the convergence of the personal and passional (i.e. that which provides the law with what it requires to secure their articulation), is the site, as it were, in which coexistence (and its demands) is intensely 'felt' (for lack of a better word), or acquires the charge of a lived intensity.

Thus, the three principles of coexistence, namely, securing a/in place, marriage (family) as articulation of difference and distinctiveness, and the containment of the religious passions, provide the Lebanese legal arrangement with its organisational logic, its coherence and sense. They also give legal or judicial action in each of these areas of law its basis, grounding, reasons, arguments, and authority. Thus, they are at work through the law, the law puts them into practice, makes them work, makes them real, or, in short, enacts them, bringing them to bear on the bodies of Muslims and Christians. It is through that work, which the law performs routinely, that they are both effective and concealed. Thus, they are the criteria of intelligibility of Lebanese law and its peculiar arrangement, and it is through the analysis of the work they do in their capacity as the structuring principles of legal action that they could be brought out.

What Secular Coexistence Might Look Like

There are implications to coexistence and its three principles. In the first place, the securing of Muslims and Christians a place and in place implies a specific mode of belonging to the two religions. Moreover, the privileging of marriage and its consequences (and the family) as the articulation of the difference between and distinctiveness of Muslims and Christians implies that the two stand on the same, footing as equally valid, interchangeable and comparable forms of life. Finally, the injunction that the religious passions be contained implies that Christians and Muslims be in possession of dispassionate bodies in virtue of which they are to be responsive and responsible to themselves and to each other (at least in whatever counts as a public transaction). Modes of belonging, religion as form of life, and the dispassionate body are the secular requisites of the coexistence of Christians and Muslims in Lebanon; they are constitutive of a secular sensibility which, in so far as coexistence involves an arrangement between Muslims and Christians, is common to both.

The book is accordingly divided into three parts. Each part is composed of a pair of chapters, each chapter proceeding through an analysis of a legal event or a series of legal events that offer insight into one of the three constituents of coexistence. Part I describes the mode of belonging through which Christians and Muslims are secured a place, and secured in place. Part II is focused on the difference between and distinctiveness of the forms of life which are articulated through marriage and the family. Part III traces the profile of the dispassionate body in and through which the religious passions are contained. The analysis draws attention to the variety of ways in which the secular and religious are joined together and kept apart. An argument running throughout the book is that there is a relationship between the three principles of coexistence on the one hand, and the articulations of the secular and the religious on the other. In a sense, each of the principles is a way to constitute the secular – coexistence – by appealing to the religious.

Chapter 1 examines the concepts and procedures by which the legal incorporation of Muslims and Christians is carried out. A twofold translation of the religious into the legal accompanies incorporation: of Muslims and Christians into/as legal subjects and Christians and Muslims into/as legal jurisdictions. As groups (or communities), Christians and Muslims are claimed to possess a distinctive personal status, which translates into formal recognition. If and once granted, recognition – depending, in the last instance, on a political decision – entails the confirmation of personal status and, accordingly, the concomitant jurisdiction. Individual Muslims and

Christians are 'born into' a jurisdiction (they are consigned to their father's jurisdiction), but are free to transfer to another once they attain legal age.

Chapter 2 is an account of the concept and practice of '*tabdīl al-dīn*' ('the changing or switching of religion'). It examines *tabdīl al-dīn* in the context of a legal space organised in terms of religious jurisdictions in which movement across jurisdictions is admissible in principle. *Tabdīl al-dīn* is a complex structure that articulates religious conversion and legal (secular) transference and an entire series of oppositions: the sincere and fraudulent, the authentic and strategic (or tactical, or instrumental), the willed and the coerced, the internal (e.g. beliefs) and external (a performance), and so on. Accordingly, an act of *tabdīl al-dīn*, in so far as it remains questioned, involves both the 'internal' experience of turning away from one 'set' of religious beliefs to another (or none, or vice versa), an 'internal' movement of conscience or the soul, and the exercise or outward manifestation of this change, *and/or* the 'external' switching of religious jurisdictions and consequent change of the regime of personal status under which one falls. Since the relationship between the two movements is not obvious, *tabdīl al-dīn* lends itself to scepticism and, in some cases, suspicion – itself an effect of the secular rationality of coexistence.

Tabdīl al-dīn points towards the suggestion that coexistence presupposes as a constitutive feature the equal validity, interchangeability, and comparability of Islam and Christianity as different and distinct forms of life (or sensibilities). This difference and that distinctiveness reside in their – i.e. Muslims' and Christians' – respective legal availability, or the ways in which Christians and Muslims on one hand, and the secular positive law on another, are rendered mutually available. Their difference and distinction, then – the difference and distinction that matter to their coexistence – consist in: (1) the mode in which a Muslim and Christian figures in the judicial discourse as a subject of that discourse; (2) the mediating function of the shariʿa and ecclesiastic judiciaries between the Muslim and Christian subject of law and the secular positive law; (3) the legal component – or legally authorised component – that ensures the mutual availability of the subject and the law and enables and constrains the two judiciaries as they perform the judicial function. It is in and through marriage, its consequences and the family that legal availability and, through it, coexistence comes alive – enters into the life of the Christian and Muslim.

The secular positive law, while presenting Muslims and Christians with the problem of articulating it and the religious, offers them the possibility of two different solutions, two means to join and keep apart the religious and legal – or ensuring their mutual availability. It is their legal availability that constitutes the common reference that in this respect makes it possible to compare the Christians and Muslims in their coexistence. Chapters 3 and 4 are somewhat of a diptych, the two chapter joined and kept apart by the notion of legal availability. Chapter 3 considers a Christian (Catholic) style of rendering Christians and the secular positive law mutually available. The Christian figures in judicial discourse as a medicalised body and a subject of a (possibly pathological) desire, the ecclesiastical judiciaries exercising the function of extrapolating (translating) the statements of medical experts into an ecclesiastical decision.

The Muslim (Chapter 4), in comparison, is legally available in so far as he conducts himself appropriately (whether in accordance with the shariʿa or 'common sense'), a conduct expected of the judiciaries as well. Harmony (or, at least, lack of conflict) is sought through that conduct between the shariʿa and the secular positive law, in order to protect the shariʿa from the sanctions of the secular positive law. In a sense, the Christian's impulses, as structured through marriage and medical discourse, are the link between the Christian Lebanese subject and the state, while the Muslim's conduct, cultivated in the family with the shariʿa as guide, is the link between the Muslim Lebanese subject and the state.

In opposition to marriage and the family, the religious passions are the sources of difference between and distinctiveness of Muslims and Christians that are not legally codifiable, cannot be registered by the secular positive law, and threaten, therefore, coexistence and the legal order that sustains it. The religious sentiments, the communitarian impulses, and the doctrinal or sectarian tensions are to remain contained and prevented from erupting into the public. On one hand, they could be buffered from provocation (incitement, arousal) by legal measures and judicial action that curb or silence the causes of provocation, such as certain modes of speech, or the projection of certain kinds of image (Chapter 5). On another, their intensity could be reduced by lowering their bearers' threshold of sensitivity to attune it to generally (socially or culturally) accepted or normal standards conducive to mutual tolerance and coexistence (Chapter 6).

In the Epilogue, I revisit the relationship between law and the secular and suggest that the coexistence of Muslims and Christians in Lebanon is a sensibility (form of life) – a secular concept that is embedded in, but neither reducible nor identical to, Lebanese law in its current arrangement. I consider the limitations and paradoxes of the secularising critiques of the Lebanese legal arrangement and the benefits of an anthropological concept of 'coexistence'. Coexistence is not – not just – a passive, peaceful living separately together, nor a cynically instrumental or pragmatic politics, but a problem and, therefore, the grounding of 'the political' – the secular organising principle of a politics of the religious through which 'Christians' and 'Muslims' (in the Lebanese case, but others, in other cases) are (re)composed, conjugated.

PART I

MODES OF BELONGING

1

SECURING THE RELIGIOUS A/IN PLACE

'*Shū al-madhhab*?' – 'what's the *madhhab*?' – asks the woman behind the desk, pen in hand, looking up from the form she is filling out. 'Maronite' (Eastern Catholic), answers the mother of two, standing before her with her children by her side. 'And your husband's?' 'Catholic' (i.e. Melkite Catholic, also Greek Catholic). The *mukhtār*'s office is located on the ground floor of a shopping centre across the street from the large compound that houses the headquarters of the General Security of the Lebanese Republic. The office is also a stationary shop and photocopy centre, providing all the services an applicant for a passport, say, or residency needs for the completion of the required formalities at the GS. The *mukhtār* is an official of the Lebanese state, a local level civil servant whose jurisdiction is limited to a population of fifty to 3,000 souls – a small village or, in a city, a neighborhood or district. One of the *mukhtār*'s main functions is to authenticate a person's identity and status, process paperwork for such transactions as sales contracts and inheritance, or that require attestation of civil (personal) status.[1] The *mukhtār* is a relay between citizens and the Directorate General of Personal Status (DGPS), and through the intermediary of the latter, the Lebanese state. I was in the presence of the *mukhtār*'s wife or sister, I surmise – I know of another *mukhtār*, in another neighbourhood close by, whose twin brother

[1] The office of the *mukhtār* is described in full in the text of a law issued in 1947, available in Arabic at: http://elections.gov.lb/Municipality/2016/Mukhtars/المجالس-الاختيارية/قانون-المختارين-و-المجالس-الاختيارية. aspx (last accessed 29 December 2022).

stands in for him. When the Maronite mother and her two children left, having paid the veiled young woman who had just completed the copies the amount owed, I asked the scribe, 'What kind of document requires that one declare a *madhhab*?' 'An *ikhrāj qayd* , was her reply. 'What evidence do you have that the person is telling the truth? Is the petitioner's word enough?' 'If he lies', she explained, 'and what is written in the form differs from what is in the records, they [at the DGPS] would send the application back.' I found myself in the mother's shoes a year or two later. I was the object of the same question, among strangers (three men, lingerers at the *mukhtār*'s; they were there when I went back again a few times afterwards). I was taking care of a family matter and needed a document issued. 'What's your grandfather's *ṭā'ifa*?', asked the *mukhtār*, instead of *madhhab*, a slippage that made no difference for the kind of information I was expected to and did provide.

Lebanese citizens are routinely called upon to spell out a *madhhab* (or *ṭā'ifa*) before a civil servant, who would prompt them with a question to say, 'Sunni', 'Shiʿa', 'Druze', 'Maronite', 'Orthodox', 'Evangelical (Protestant)', and so on – one among a limited number of designations that signal their attachment to one of the monotheistic religions in the country: Islam and Christianity. They would then spell out this attachment in a public setting, and in the presence of strangers who, in turn, would have likely had opportunities to declare a similar attachment. The declaration of attachment consists in the enunciation of a word – the name of a *madhhab* or *ṭā'ifa* – before an official authorised to translate the verbal sign once she hears it into a graphic inscription on a form, entering it in a blank space next to the name of a category: '*al-madhhab* ______________'. The same solicitation is made to Muslims and Christians, in the same way, and they are expected to answer – and do answer – in the same way. The solicitation does not privilege one over the other, nor single out one or the other.

In discussions about personal status and in the texts that make up the legal corpus of personal status in Lebanon (or marriage and its consequences, the family and the religious jurisdictions), the word '*ṭā'ifa*' is frequently used, along with the word '*madhhab*', as in the phrase, '*al-maḥākim al-madhhabiyya li ṭā'ifat al-muwaḥḥidīn al-durūz* (the *madhhabiyya* courts of the *ṭā'ifa* of the uniate Druze).' The adjective '*al-madhhabiyya*' in the phrase qualifies the courts of the Druze '*ṭā'ifa*', marking grammatically their religious character, in opposition to the civil ('*al-madaniyya*') courts, strictly speaking. The translation into English of the substantive '*ṭā'ifa*' in the preceding phrase varies, as it could be used to say 'group', 'community' or 'sect'. A *ṭā'ifa* is in possession of its own *madhhabiyya* courts, its own *madhhabiyya* jurisdiction.[2]

In some contexts, and among some speakers, as in the example of the *mukhtār* above, the two substantives, *ṭā'ifa* and *madhhab*, are used interchangeably. What is interesting, however, is less what the words refer to, or their formal definition, than their usage and the rules that govern the usage – what their grammar tells about the secular and secularism in Lebanon. Thus, for example, if the *mukhtār* asks about the *madhhab*, I would most likely not ask him if he meant 'religious doctrine', a profession of faith, or, strictly speaking, 'the religious community' or 'group' or 'sect' with which I identify. I would just answer, 'Maronite', 'Sunni', . . .

The attachment declared when one answers 'Sunni' or 'Maronite' has nothing obvious to do with the contents of one's beliefs (religious or otherwise), the truth of one's faith, the force of one's commitment to a religious doctrine, or the authenticity of one's sentiments about a religious group or community. Indeed, it is most likely that any solicitation of information about the preceding, if at all attempted, might in that particular context be taken as an affront, an offence, an intrusion, or a joke. It does not follow from this that hearing someone declare a *madhhab* or *ṭā'ifa* at the *mukhtār*'s should not trigger an impulse for guesswork or inference among eavesdroppers, witnesses or the *mukhtār*. Yet, it is clear from the example that what is on display is a distinctive practice that makes sense in a distinctive context.

The practice would seem to confirm the claim that is often made about the relationship between religion and law, and generally about secularism in Lebanon, that there is an overlap between the two, and that they must be separated. Some would take it as evidence of the 'incompleteness' or 'failure' of secularism, others as evidence to the contrary, for by making a rule applicable to all members of any religion, the practice exemplifies the Lebanese state's 'regulatory' secularism. It is a technology by which the state manages 'religious pluralism' while upholding the principle of neutrality towards all

[2] When speaking about the Christian *ṭā'ifas*, the word '*rūḥiyya* (spiritual)' is used instead in reference to ecclesiastical courts or authorities. It is not used as a category of personal identification in the civil registry (personal status).

religions. It is not the aim of this chapter to make another assertion about the identity of the Lebanese state – whether it is secular or not – but to account for the practice itself as an articulation and enactment of the secular rationality of coexistence.

What is it that is asked for when an attachment to a religious *madhhab* or *ṭāʾifa* is solicited? What is it that one declares when one declares it? How is the religious attachment that one announces or declares to be characterised? In what context would it even make sense to declare one's religious attachment, what context would one be describing in doing so? When Lebanese citizens are called upon to declare a *madhhab* or *ṭāʾifa* before a representative of the state, they are called upon to participate in the execution of a formal procedure by which they would secure their place in a scheme or system of classification. When they specify their *ṭāʾifa* or *madhhab*, declare an attachment to it, and confirm, thereby, what is written, they ascertain that they are in their proper place. What guarantees the propriety of the place – that it is their proper place – is the correspondence between two signs: the verbal sign, said and heard here and now at the *mukhtār*'s, and a written entry made long ago in the civil register elsewhere.

The correspondence between the two is guaranteed by a chain of authorised relays that transmit and authenticate the signs as they mutate from verbal to written, making their passage from a person's mouth, through the *mukhtār*'s ears, from the latter's hand and through the pen she manipulates, onto a form dispatched by the *mukhtār* or an assistant to the civil registry where, on the basis of a census carried out in 1932 (the last official census), the utterance would be confirmed true. It takes that whole chain to constitute the truth of the person's attachment to the *madhhab* or *ṭāʾifa* which he declares before a *mukhtār* when asked, and that truth consists in the proper place which he occupies in a general taxonomy (or scheme). In a sense, to secure the truth of that place is also to ensure that the system or schema remain in place – and that words and persons, and the world they compose, remain in order.

Thus, to spell out one's *madhhab* or *ṭāʾifa* is to articulate the organising principle by which Christians and Muslims in Lebanon distinguish and differentiate themselves from each other, and mark their relationship with the Lebanese state. The scheme within which one places oneself as one utters the word 'Maronite' or 'Druze' (to pick two out of eighteen) is constitutive of a conceptual space that supports a juridical arrangement from which it remains, nevertheless, distinct.[3] It provides the organisational principle by which a conceptual and legal space is subdivided into several distinctive categories and jurisdictions. When citizens declare their *madhhab* or *ṭā'ifa* to a *mukhtār*, they specify their place not only in a category, but in a jurisdiction as well, alongside others of the same kind. They are placing their body (their person) under the purview of a set of criteria and legal rules, and an agency – judicial, religious – that is authorised to interpret and apply them, if need be, in a class of cases that pertain to marriage and its consequences (the family). The difference between one jurisdiction and another is the character of its rules, their sources and provenance, the (religious) tradition they articulate, and their relationship with the Lebanese state.

The legal arrangement and its supportive conceptual scheme are the fabrication of a politics which they sustain. They are the artefacts of the interplay or the play of forces that is constitutive of the relationship between Muslims and Christians in Lebanon, and could, in virtue of that politics, be transformed or modified.[4] It is a system of privileges and rights that gives shape to a kind of politics that takes place around questions regarding the extension of the scheme and its limits, the distribution and granting of the rights to be part of it, the possibility of existence outside it and the form which that existence could take, and the entitlement to decide on such questions. What this politics inevitably must answer as well is what is to count as 'religious' in Lebanon (e.g. a Buddhist community) – indeed, what is to count as 'religion' (e.g. Buddhism) in Lebanon.

[3] This is not restricted to law, as the following example suggests. It defines a sensibility (form of life). I recall listening to a conversation between a mother and daughter in Beirut a few years ago. The mother spoke about a common acquaintance, 'a Shiʿi woman', in her words, who married a 'Christian'. 'Why say "Shiʿi" and "Christian"?', the daughter asked provocatively, with a tone insinuating that she *ought not* to. Visibly irritated, having recognised the tone of the daughter's secularising presumption, the mother replied vigorously, 'Well, the state uses them too!'

[4] The politics of coexistence and of struggle for it is a modern, secular story – it is a history of a secular formation, or a chapter in the history of the formation of 'a secular'. See, for example, Engin Deniz Akarlı, *The Long Peace: Ottoman Lebanon, 1861–1920* (Berkeley: University of California Press, 1993); Makdisi, *The Culture of Sectarianism* and *Age of Coexistence*; Weiss, *In the Shadow of Sectarianism.*

The securing in place, and the securing of place, are accomplished through the mediation of two legal concepts: personal status and recognition, respectively, which the practice (as in the scene above) enacts and articulates. Thus, when individual Christians and Muslims are asked what their *madhhab* or *ṭā'ifa* is, they are being asked to confirm their place, which is secured through their possession of an identifiable, recordable, personal status. That they are secured in place implies that they have a place in which they are to be secured, that they are secured a place, a place carved out in an act of recognition.

Securing in Place: Personal Status

In one sense, the Arabic word *madhhab* is a familiar designation of one of the four schools of *fiqh*, or shariʿa jurisprudence, in Sunni Islam: *ḥanafi, māliki, shāfiʿi* and *ḥanbali,* and the Shi'i *madhhab.* In this scholastic sense, the official *madhhab* that Sunni Muslims go by is the *ḥanafi madhhab*. However, in the secular, legal and administrative contexts in which it is used the word has a wider range, encompassing Christian churches – for example, the Maronite (Catholic), Greek Orthodox, Western Catholic (Latin) or Evangelical – and Jewish congregations (of which three are officially recognised: Aleppo, Beirut and Damascus). When people in Lebanon are asked for their *madhhab* or *ṭā'ifa*, and when they reply Maronite or Sunni, they are asked to declare, and do declare, their personal status.[5]

The Lebanese Constitution stipulates that the Lebanese state 'shall . . . guarantee that the personal status . . . of the population, to whatever [community] they belong, shall be respected'.[6] There are 'records of personal status', and a law that sets the rules by which 'the documents of personal status' are drawn up. There is a 'General Administration of Personal Status', and separate compilations of and treatises on 'the personal status laws' of Muslims and Christians.[7] In ordinary discourse, people speak about Christians and Muslims possessing a distinctive personal status and laws of personal status. The concept of

[5] For a more comprehensive account of the semantics of the two words, see Mikdashi, *Sextarianism*, pp. 100–1.

[6] 'Article 9. The Lebanese Constitution', *Arab Law Quarterly* 12, 2 (1997): 224–61.

[7] A comprehensive compilation of the laws that pertain to the affairs of Muslims and Christians are the two volumes by Aref Zaid al-Zein, *Qawanin wa Nusus wa Ahkam al-Ahwal al-Shakhsiyya wa Tanzim al-Tawa'if al-Islamiyya fi Lubnan* (Beirut: Manshurat al-Halabi al-Huquqiyya, 2003) (Muslims), and *Qawanin wa Nusus wa Ahkam al-Ahwal al-Shakhiyya wa*

personal status is at the root of some misunderstanding about secularism and the secular in Lebanon and the place which religion occupies in the country's legal arrangement. The misunderstanding figures in such assertions as 'personal status laws in Lebanon are religious', 'Lebanese citizens are bound in their personal status to religious authorities', 'the sectarian personal status laws in Lebanon segregate or divide the citizens', and so on. What such phrases do not take into account is the significance of the fact that when Muslims and Christians reply, in certain contexts and situations, 'Maronite' or 'Sunni', they may be articulating a variety of different things, including the legal concept of personal status – a secular concept common to the two of them. What needs to be taken into account is the specific articulation of personal status in Lebanon – that is, the sense and structure of the concept in a context defined by the fact that Christians and Muslims have a place secured for them in and *through* Lebanese law (the Lebanese legal arrangement), an arrangement in which Christians and Muslims coexist in and through Lebanese law and the Lebanese legal arrangement.

The Law of 7 December 1951, 'The Recording of Personal Status Documents', provides the formal description of personal status.[8] In the first part of

Tanzim al-Tawa'if al-Masihiyya fi Lubnan (Beirut: Manshurat al-Halabi al-Huquqiyya, 2003) (Christians). For a compilation and an explanation of the formaltities that are required for citizenship and personal status, with some historical information, see A. Bakkar, *Qadaya al-Ahwal al-Shakhsiyya wa-l-Jinsiyya*, 2nd edn (Beirut: 1987). For examples of treatises on doctrine, including some sample cases, see Wadi Rahhal, *Al-Qawa'id al-'Amma li-l-Ahwal al-Shakhsiyya, al-Jiz' al-Thani: Ahkam al-Zawaj al-Dini wa-l-Madani* (publisher not specified 1997); Nazih Chelala, *Al-Talaq wa Butlan al-Zawaj Lada al- Tawa'if al-Masihiyya: Ijtihadat al-Mahakim al-Ruhiyya wa Dirasa Fiqhiyya Kanasiyya* (Beirut: Manshurat al-Halabi al-Huquqiyya, 2005); Muhammad Kamaleddine Imam and Jaber Abd el-Hadi Salem Al-Shafi'i, *Masa'il al-Ahwal al-Shakhsiyya al-Khassa bi-l-Zawaj wa-l-Furqa wa Huquq al-Awlad fi-l-Fiqh wa-l-Qanun wa-l-Qada'* (Beirut: Manshurat al-Halabi al-Huquqiyya, 2003).

[8] The Law of 1951 has replaced Decree Number 2851 'for the system of civil status and the regulation of its registries', issued by the French Mandate in 1924. The Ottoman 'Law on Civil Status' that was issued on 10 June 1902 stipulates the following: in the first place, 'the civil status enunciates . . . the *millet*, that is, if the individual is Muslim, Christian, or Israelite' (Text XXXIV, Art. 2, 3, 242). Second, 'there will be separate civil statutes for Muslims [and] for every non-Muslim community . . .' (Art. 2, 7, 243). Third, 'The *imāms* and *mukhtārs* of each village or of each neighborhood, and similarly, for the non-Muslim communities, priests and rabbis and the *mukhtārs* of the villages and neighborhoods, are to draw up the acts (*les actes*) of civil status, such as births, deaths, and changes of residence' (Art. 22, 247). George Young, *Corps de Droit Ottoman, Vol. II* (Oxford: Clarendon Press, 1905). I use Young's translation

the law, under 'General Provisions', the first article stipulates that the information that is to be 'recorded in the documents of personal status . . . [is that] related to birth, marriage, divorce, annulment . . ., death, change of place of residence, and switching (*tabdīl*) of *madhhab* or *dīn*'. In charge of drawing up 'the documents of personal status [for] marriage, divorce, and annulment' are 'the husband or wife, and the *madhhabiyya* authority (*al-sulṭa al-madhhabiyya*) that had initiated the contract'.[9] The marriage certificate must include the *madhhab* of each spouse, in addition to his and her name, surname, profession, date and place of birth, and place of residence.[10] The persons concerned alone draw up the documents of personal status in the event of a 'change of the place of residence, and the switching of *madhhab* or *dīn*'.[11]

Among the events that constitute a personal status, marriage – the way marriage is conceived, its relationship with birth and death, and with divorce or annulment, custody, support and inheritance – is singled out as particularly critical to the difference between Muslims and Christians. For, the organisation of the acts and transactions of marriage, its rules and the rights it confers, its ends and the obligations that sustain it, and the procedures by which it is to be completed and dissolved (divorce or annulment), are rooted in specific theologies and religious traditions. It is through marriage that Muslims and Christians, who are otherwise homogeneous in virtue of citizenship, secure at once their heterogeneity and the continued relevance of their theologies or traditions to their lives.

If the civil law draws its general outline by accounting for the series of recordable – that is, memorable – events that constitute an individual's personal life, it is in and through particular religious laws and jurisdictions that the substantive status of the person is defined, his or her personal rights are determined, and his or her body is anchored – secured in place, that is, in so

of Ottoman law with caution. Nevertheless, the text brings out some remarkable differences between the Ottoman and Lebanese laws: a) the suppression of 'millet'; b) the assumption of a single civil status for all Lebanese citizens instead of two, one for Muslims, another for non-Muslims; c) the considerable reduction of the role of the religious or spiritual authorities in the drawing up of official documents.

9 Art. 2, Law of 1951.

10 Art. 23.1., Law of 1951. See Chapters 3 and 4.

11 Art. 2. See Chapter 2.

far as she or he is the subject of the particular law in force in a particular jurisdiction (is a Christian or Muslim legal subject). The 'Law of Personal Status and of Judicial Procedures for the Catholic *Ṭawā'if*', for example, devotes its whole second chapter to 'Of Persons in General'. According to its Article 6, 'Is meant by person (*al-shakhṣ*) – in his legal sense (*bi ma'nāh al-qānūni*) – the site of rights and obligations. In other words, any being qualified to acquire rights and bear obligations.' Article 7 defines personal status as 'the state of living (*ḥālat al-'aysh*) that is distinct from another and fixed in itself (*thābita bi-dhātiha*) with the totality of personal rights and obligations'. Article 8 continues, 'In the Church are natural persons and moral persons and they all enjoy a legal personality'. The 'person' is also explicitly singled out, though not with as much elaboration, in the 'Shari'a Courts Law' of 1962. In its fourth chapter, 'Of Lawsuits (*al-da'āwi*)', in the first section, under the heading, 'The Right to a Litigation (*ḥaqq al-taqaḍi*), Article 25 makes it clear that '[a]ny Lebanese or foreign [not, crucially, Muslim or Sunni] natural or moral person has the right to approach the shari'a judiciary to establish and maintain his rights in matters that enter into its competence'.[12]

In one sense, personal status is a description of features of personhood – the basis of universal citizenship under the law – and of the personal life of a person in which religion and any other substantive source of identity do not figure. 'The personal' is that which pertains to the 'natural person', such as date and place of birth, place of residence, marriage, divorce or annulment of marriage, profession, and death. In another sense, personal status is a marker of a specifically religious difference between Christian and Muslim persons in what pertains to one particular feature of their personal status. In so far as they are citizens, all natural persons have the same personal status; in so far as they are Muslims and Christians, their personal status differs.

The concept of personal status that figures in Lebanese law is the formal (meta-legal, secular) connector that secures the coexistence of Christians and Muslims, and that connects the Christian or Muslim to other Christians and Muslims and to the Lebanese state. It is that in virtue of which the Christian or Muslim identity of the citizen of the Lebanese state is secured, through marriage and its consequences (the family). Thus, it also circumscribes the religious identity within the scope of the personal, retains it only as a personal matter,

[12] Not all religious legal texts make an explicit reference to 'the person' or 'personhood'.

where 'the personal' on the one hand, and marriage and the family on the other, are coextensive. In personal status, neither religious belief or faith, nor ritual or worship, figure (or are at all relevant).

Personal status is an operator of a complex of relations between the individual and the state, between the individual and the religious (other individuals or bodies, community, authority, doctrine, beliefs, etc.), between Muslims and Christians, and between each of them (as a collective or group) and the state. The relationship between the individual and the state consists in what pertains to the 'natural person', namely, its 'body' and its changing 'status': its coming into being (birth), location and movement (residence), union with and separation from another body (marriage, divorce, annulment), and vanishing (death). It is secured by the recording of the coordinates of any single and singular 'body' in (national) time and space, specifying it, thereby, among the multitude of bodies that compose the population. 'Personal status' is a record of the individuating data about a body, that which anchors it in a circumscribed place, for a period of time.

The word '*madhhab*' may designate an entity – person or 'thing out there', a school of thought or doctrine, say. Yet, once it enters into the determination of civil (personal) status it is transformed, becoming part of a constellation of events by which to recognise, differentiate and keep track of bodies (persons) in a legal, juridical arrangement. As it figures in the determination of personal status, its usage marks a relationship between a person and the juridical or legal place to which she belongs (jurisdiction). The concept of *madhhab* articulates a body (person) and a religious jurisdiction. It marks their essential difference and secures their conjoining.[13] This conceptual externality has a consequence in practice. In the first place, to answer, 'Sunni' or 'Maronite', and so on, when one is called upon to specify a *madhhab* is to articulate both one's person and a religious jurisdiction to which one belongs or the regime of personal status under which one falls. Moreover, as the relationship between the person and the religious jurisdiction goes not without saying, it must be constantly solicited, spelled out, and confirmed through practices of registration and an elaborate infrastructure of records and documents.

In spelling out the name of their religion, Muslims and Christians in Lebanon spell out a specific bundle of rights they possess in their capacity

[13] See Mikdashi, *Sextarianism*.

as persons who are subject to the laws of a specific jurisdiction within which they acquire rights, and which the name of their religion articulates as well. The name of the religion, however, articulates the Christian's and Muslim's place as a corporeal body in an arrangement in and through which Muslims and Christians coexist. Their place is secured in the arrangement, and in virtue of the legal arrangement, since 'Muslim', 'Christian', and (in so far as they involve a) personal status, are articulations of particular sets of laws and jurisdictions without which personal status comes to be called into question, its determination turns into a problem.[14]

Securing a Place: Recognition

It is through their laws and in their jurisdictions that Christians and Muslims are, as corporeal bodies, secured in place, securing, thereby, their coexistence in a legal arrangement structured by their coexistence, to answer the demands of coexistence. They are so secured in virtue of their being subjects of law, which confirms their personhood – that is, guarantees their rights *and* secures their bodies (in place). That Muslims and Christians are secured in place presupposes that there is a place secured for them. It is in virtue of the power of recognition that Christians and Muslims are secured a place, recognition being constitutive of religious entities and formations possessing circumscribed jurisdiction over the marriages and families of those persons who belong to them – who are, that is, their legal subjects.

A concept of 'recognition' is given formal articulation in Legislative Decree No. 60 L./R. The decree was issued in 1936 by the High Commissioner of the French Mandate in Syria and Lebanon. It remains today a 'fundamental law' in Lebanon.[15] Its subtitle announces its purpose, namely, the establishing of 'the

[14] See below, the last two sections.

[15] Al-Zein, *Qawanin wa Nusus wa Ahkam* (Christians); Edmond Rabbath, *La formation historique du Liban politique et constitutionnel: essai de synthèse*, 2nd edn. Publications de l'Université Libanaise, 1 (Beyrouth: Libraire Orientale, 1986). A few years after it was promulgated in 1936, Decree No. 60 was followed by another that made it inapplicable to Muslims. What this means today, however, is ambiguous: the ʿAlawis, for example, were recognised in the 1990's, according to an amendment to the annex of Decree No. 60 that lists the names of all of the recognised Christian, Islamic, and Jewish *ṭawāʾif*. Yet, Al-Zein includes it among the legal texts that pertain to the Christians in his two-volume compilation of religious (Christian and Islamic) laws.

system [or order] of religious communities' – '*niẓām al-ṭawāʾif al-dīniyya*'. The decree stipulates the principles of formation of entities – religious *ṭawāʾif* – and their incorporation into a single unified system. The formation and the incorporation, the singular religious *ṭāʾifa* and the plural system or order of religious *ṭawāʾif* are interconnected: for any religious *ṭāʾifa* to claim a place it must be made to 'fit' in place in an arrangement that is supposed to make place for it. For that, it must be recognisable, and it is only so if it conforms to formal criteria common to all.

The decree draws a distinction between two categories of religious *ṭawāʾif*: 'the *ṭawāʾif* that have a personal status', and the ones 'that follow ordinary [i.e. civil] law'.[16] The two are counted as religious, but each acquires a specific organisational character that depends on the way it is legally incorporated. The religious *ṭawāʾif* that are 'legally recognised as possessing a personal status' are 'the historical *ṭawāʾif*'. Those are the *ṭawāʾif* which, at the time the decree was promulgated, had already had their 'organisation, courts, and normative systems (*sharāʾiʿ*, sing. shariʿa) specified in a legislative document (*saqq tashrīʿi*)'.[17] Historical religious *ṭawāʾif* which, not yet meeting that condition 'at the announcement of [the] decree', but have nevertheless 'acquired some privileges, or enjoyed certain immunities' in virtue of prior decrees or ordinances, or 'in virtue of . . . traditions older than a century', are also 'qualified to benefit from legal recognition . . .'[18]

A requirement which any group of people must meet if it were to receive formal recognition as a religious *ṭāʾifa* is that of translating whatever (religious) norms, practices, and attitudes the group might share into a set of codified rules and drawing them up in the form of a legal text (a code). The legality of the text is dependent on, and established by, secular power. The fifth article spells it out: 'A legislative decree authenticates and thereby makes applicable [a *ṭāʾifa*'s] system [of rules], and includes the recognition of the *ṭāʾifa* . . .'[19] Thus, recognition constitutes the religious *ṭāʾifa* as a subject and

[16] See the headings of Parts I and II in Al-Zein, *Qawanin wa Nusus wa Ahkam* (Christians), p. 15 and p. 17, respectively.

[17] Art. 1.

[18] Art. 3.

[19] Art. 5.

agent of secular power (in a sense, it entails the conversion of the religious *ṭāʾifa* into a modality of secular power). According to Article 2, recognition converts a religious *ṭāʾifa* into a 'moral personality',[20] and gives 'the text in which its system is specified . . . the force of law'.[21] The rules which the legal code of an officially recognised *ṭāʾifa* stipulates are applicable to the individuals who compose the *ṭāʾifa*, which, in virtue of recognition, has jurisdiction over them who are, in virtue of that same law, legal subjects – that is, natural persons, endowed with a body, and enjoying personal rights.

Decree No. 60 L./R. draws formally the outlines of the internal organisation of the religious *ṭāʾifa* in such a way as to define the scope of its jurisdiction. Its legal text must include a detailed listing of the religious *ṭāʾifa*'s hierarchy or 'the ranks of spiritual leaders and religious employees, the procedure of their appointment, and the [scope of their respective] authority', 'the rules by which its internal organs are established (e.g., courts, councils)', 'the scope of the authority of its religious courts and their laws of procedure, and legislation (*tashrīʿ*) concerning personal status in all what is related to [its] normative systems'.[22] Apart from this 'internal' limit to a religious *ṭāʾifa*'s jurisdiction, the act of recognition imposes an 'external' limit, namely, the hierarchical order of Lebanese law with the fundamental principles of which they are bound to conform. Article 5 continues, pointing out that recognition is granted a *ṭāʾifa* 'on condition that [its code] do not include a text that violates the general security or morals, or the constitutions of states [and] of [other] *ṭawāʾif*, or the stipulations of this decree [Decree No. 60 L./R.]'.[23]

The implications of recognition to the coexistence of Muslims and Christians in Lebanon, and its relationship with the secular and secularism, extend beyond what is stipulated in Decree No. 60 L./R. In the first place, recognition is a matter of law. Recognition is the spawning of an entity or formation that is both religious and legal, but the religious component of which is translated and transposed into 'the juridical (or legal)', as law. Moreover, recognition grants the entity or formation a jurisdiction – it

[20] Art. 7.
[21] Art. 2.
[22] Art. 4.
[23] Art. 5.

authorises a circumscribed exercise of legal power over its members through the performance of a judicial function – that is as enabling as it is constraining to it, for it is to be performed and exercised in conformity with the fundamental norms and principles of the Lebanese state, under the permanent threat of the positive law's sanctioning power.

It constrains it to submit to the positive law (substantive and procedural) and the rules of that law's secular reasoning, it puts it in the spotlight of the state's surveillance and control, and in as much as it binds its members to it by law, it enables them to release themselves from it, also by law. The act of recognition takes place in (brings into play, puts to work) a single formal system of rules and procedures which all groups must submit to if they wanted to receive the state's recognition. The recognition granted entails the group's inclusion into a system or an order (of religious *ṭawāʾif*, of religious jurisdictions). It is incorporated as a part is into a whole, alongside other 'parts' (a single religious *ṭāʾifa*), having the same relationship with the whole, and with which it has features in common. Once a 'religious community' or 'group' presents itself for recognition, it makes a concession, agreeing to submit to the play of identity and difference whereby no single religious *ṭāʾifa* is privileged over the rest.

Existing, non-recognised 'religious communities' are faced with the permanent secular horizon of recognition, and the privileges and constraints it provides. Moreover, since any group of people could be formed and has the right to claim the status of an officially recognised religious *ṭāʾifa*, a politics of recognition takes shape in which it is incumbent on the state – and on the officially recognised religious *ṭawāʾif* which it embodies – to decide whether to extend official recognition or not, and for what reasons. The granting of recognition involves two kinds of transaction. One transaction takes place between the state and an existing religious community or newly formed group, whereby recognition is granted in accordance with the stipulations of Decree No. 60 L./R. Another transaction is not explicit in the decree, but is internal to the religious community or group, whose members face the permanent possibility of 'self-juridification' – that is, of fashioning themselves (their group, their community) into the entity or formation prescribed by the decree in order to receive official recognition.

Thus, it would seem that the transformation wrought by the possibility of recognition begins prior to its actual granting. It begins with the positing of recognition as a possibility and, therefore, as choice. It entails the positing of a 'religious community' or 'group' before a possible future the pursuit of which is decided exclusively by its own members (or some of them). Put plainly, members of a group or a religious community must come to a decision to seek official recognition and transform themselves in doing so into a religious *ṭā'ifa* as outlined in Decree No. 60. They are faced with the task (the problem) of organising themselves in terms of criteria that meet conditions stipulated by law (legal criteria). The mere prospect of receiving recognition sets the future of any religious community or group, altering its temporality, reorienting its members, and restructures, thereby, its (internal) politics (it gives rise to a politics).

Politics of Coexistence

Decree No. 60 L./R. stipulates the rules by which a religious *ṭā'ifa* is to take a form appropriate for recognition. Recognition secures a place for a religious community or group in the general arrangement that is coexistence – it is through (and in) recognition that coexistence is defined: the coexistence of Muslims and Christians in Lebanon is the coexistence of Muslims and Christians in so far as they are officially recognised by the Lebanese state. The decision to grant recognition and secure a place for a religious community or group – to rearrange coexistence – is a matter of politics, of political contingencies and reasons of state.[24]

The decision to recognise a religious *ṭā'ifa* falls under the 'discretionary authority (or power, *al-sulṭa al-istinsābiyya*)' of government and is made 'in light of the general interest'. Among the considerations which the government takes in its assessments of the general interest is 'the Lebanese public order', which, in a sense, constitutes the limits of politics (of 'the political'). An opinion issued by the Lebanese state's legal adviser offers insight into the ways recognition works.[25] In 1956, the Commission of Legislation and Consultations (*Hay'at*

[24] The French Mandate in Syria and Lebanon granted the Shiʿa and Protestants official recognition by decree prior to the promulgation of Decree No. 60 L./R. in 1938. In the decades that followed independence from the Mandate, official recognition was granted Armenians and Assyrians in the 1950s, and more recently, Copts and ʿAlawis.

[25] The opinion is from the 1950s, but is illuminating. Such cases seem rare. I came across this series of opinions while scouring legal texts that touch upon religion in compilations of rulings from the civil jurisdictions. The opinions of the 'legal adviser' are distinct from judicial

al-Tashrīʿ wa-l-Istishārāt, CLC) of the Ministry of Justice was asked to give its 'opinion about the splitting of the Gregorian Armenian Orthodox *ṭāʾifa*' subsequent to 'the election of [its] Catholicos . . . on February 20, 1956'.

The transcript of the CLC's opinion details the case as follows: after 'a group of members (*farīq min abnāʾ*) of the Gregorian Orthodox *ṭāʾifa*' called into question 'the validity of the election, . . . a bishop (*muṭrān*) . . . advanced several claims (*istidʿāʾāt*) to the Office of the Presidency of the Republic, the Prime Ministry, and the Ministries of Interior and of Justice'. He 'declar[ed] his dissociation from the new[ly elected] Catholicos, his and his followers' splintering from the . . . Gregorian Armenian *ṭāʾifa*, and their joining the Independent . . . Gregorian Armenian *ṭāʾifa*'. The petition was aimed to compel 'the Census and Personal Status Directorates [to] register the statements of all persons seeking to join the new *ṭāʾifa*, which [would] amount to around two thousand and three hundred statements'.[26]

The CLC points out one last fact before proceeding to argue the case: 'most of the requests had already been transferred to the Ministry of Justice, which stated . . . that the recognition of new splinter *ṭawāʾif* . . . is a discretionary matter incumbent on the council [of ministers] to assess in light of the public interest'. It then breaks down the problem into two separate 'legal points': first, 'the Census and Personal Status Directorates' refusal to register the requests' of the defecting members; second, 'the [official] recognition of the defection and of the founding of a new *ṭāʾifa* called "the Gregorian Orthodox Independent Catholicossate"'.[27]

Regarding the first point, the CLC first spells out the two fundamental principles of 'the freedom of belief' and the 'right to switch religions'. 'It is known', it stresses, 'that the Constitution enshrined the freedom of belief, and it is also known that it is the right of every Lebanese to change his *madhhab*'. However, the freedom and the right – or, rather, their exercise – takes place

decisions, strictly speaking, compiled in separate volumes and have their own title. The opinions are an answer to questions raised by the government or a state organ to the 'jurisconsult' at the Ministry of Justice. They are not binding.

[26] One final request by the bishop: 'that the new independent *ṭāʾifa* be given what belongs to it of the monies mobile and immobile'.

[27] CLC 1956, p. 9274.

in a specific context and are enabled and constrained by that specific context. The context which the CLC has in mind is one constituted by 'the number of legally recognized *ṭawā'if*', which is 'limited' by law to the ones listed in 'the Annex to Decree No. 60'.

The CLC then points out that 'the person may leave his *madhhab* and join a recognized *ṭā'ifa* among the *ṭawā'if* specified in the law', concluding that 'the Census and Personal Status Directorate cannot register a person's declaration of belonging to a *ṭā'ifa* that is not recognized and does not have legal being (*kayān qānūnī*)'. Therefore, 'the change of *madhhab*' of the bishop and his followers 'cannot take place', since it could only take place 'within the constraints defined by law'. In other words, the transfer to the Gregorian Orthodox Independent Catholicossate cannot take place because there is no such being as the 'Gregorian Orthodox Independent Catholicossate' (at least not in a legal sense) to which they wish to transfer.

Regarding the second point – the bishop's and his followers' defection – the CLC reasons on the basis of its understanding of their intention to defect, specifically, what they intend to accomplish by defecting. The CLC seeks the intention – and, therefore, the formulation of its opinion in the case – in what the defection might result in. If the defection is 'not aimed to found a new *ṭā'ifa* with its own personal system (*niẓām*, order), courts, and private (*khāṣṣa*) normative system, and 'if it is due to an internal disagreement about the validity of the election', then 'no change of *madhhab* would have taken place', and it is the dispute about the election that is to be dealt with. This can be done by 'appeal[ing] to the competent authorities', namely, the judiciary, and 'there is no need to register the defectors' declarations'. (The CLC is addressing the Census and Personal Status Directorates, which solicited its opinion about the appropriate response to the bishop and his followers.)

If, however, 'the defection is aimed to establish a new *ṭā'ifa* under a new name to which the defectors would join – as it appears to be the case . . . – then for this *ṭā'ifa* to acquire legal being (*kayān*), . . . it must be recognized in accordance to the procedures specified in Decree No. 60/L.R'. Only then will the defectors be able to 'change their identity cards and their *madhhab* inscription on it'. The CLC then outlines the procedures of official recognition: first of all, it 'must take place through a legal text', but 'it is up to the council of ministers to agree on that recognition'. Once there is agreement, the council 'would submit a proposal for a law to parliament', which would then discuss it and vote accordingly for or against it. If the council of ministers 'refuses' to grant the new *ṭāʾifa* recognition – 'a discretionary matter which it has the right to consider in light of the public interest' – its decision could not be appealed for it is connected to the relationship between the executive and legislative powers.[28]

Twelve years later, it was the State's Advisory Council's turn (*Majlis Shūra al-Dawla,* henceforth, SAC) to give an opinion in a dispute among the members of a religious *ṭāʾifa*. On 21 February 1968, the SAC was approached with a petition to pronounce on the validity of an ordinance issued by the Ministry of Interior confirming the appointment of 'Mr J. as bishop and representative of the Antiochian Catholic Apostolic Primary Orthodox Church and *ṭāʾifa*, and of the Byzantine Syrian Rites (*ṭuqūs*)'. According to the plaintiffs, Mr J. had petitioned the Ministry of Interior to recognise him as bishop of the church and (spiritual) representative of the *ṭāʾifa*. The Ministry of Interior forwarded his request instead to the Ministry of Justice, which gave an opinion to the effect that the *ṭāʾifa* in question is not officially recognised. Nevertheless, the Ministry of Interior proceeded to issue the ordinance, claiming that Mr J. is the *ṭāʾifa*'s bishop and representative in Lebanon. The plaintiffs asked the SAC to determine whether the Ministry was authorised to issue such an ordinance, arguing that the *ṭāʾifa* in question was not recognised, since its name was not included among the *ṭawāʾif* listed in Annex No. 1 to Decree No. 60 L./R. of 1936.

The SAC begins its argument by stating that 'the state has left the issue of deciding the matter in accordance with the principles of justice and equity (*al-ʿadl wa-l-inṣāf*)', in other words, according to the Civil Law.[29] Referring back to 'Legislative Decree No. 60 of 12 March 1936', the SAC reasons that for a *ṭāʾifa* 'to adopt a spiritual leader', it must 'be recognized in Lebanon', as stipulated in the Decree. The annex to the latter 'does not include the *ṭāʾifa* mentioned in the Ministry of Interior's ordinance, which considered Mr J. its spiritual leader'. The recognition of a *ṭāʾifa* 'falls within

[28] CLC 1956, pp. 9247–8.

[29] For the history of the identification of the *Droit Civil* with 'justice and equity', see Krynen Jacques. *Le Théâtre Juridique : Une Histoire De La Construction Du Droit.* Gallimard (2018), p. 19.

the scope of legislation', the ordinance constituting 'a contravention to that legislation' and is, therefore, 'legally not valid'.

In so far as it is granted through legislation, the official recognition of a religious *ṭā'ifa* consists in a decision of political (civil, secular) representatives – the legislature and executive – of all of the officially recognised religious *ṭawā'if*. Religious or spiritual representatives have, ostensibly, not only no say – the granting of official recognition being an eminently secular matter – but, in so far as their 'representativeness' presupposes the 'being of an officially recognised religious *ṭā'ifa*', they are, in an important sense, indirectly dependent on the secular power in whose power it is to bring into being a religious *ṭā'ifa* which, then – and only then – the 'spiritual' leader could lead. The very office or status of 'religious or spiritual representative' of a religious *ṭā'ifa* depends on a decision made by the secular representatives of all the religious *ṭawā'if* that had already received official recognition.

This internal 'splitting' of a religious *ṭā'ifa* is marked by the distinction made in the preceding opinion between 'a bishop of a church' and a 'representative of a *ṭā'ifa*', and the distinction between a 'religious or spiritual leader' of a *ṭā'ifa* who, as Decree No. 60 L./R. spells it out, represents it before civil authorities, and the political representatives of a *ṭā'ifa* at parliament or the council of ministers – that is, who are supposed to represent it in the state. Thus, for an individual to belong to a religious *ṭā'ifa* is to be subject to the 'general will' of all the others in so far as it is exercised through the state's legislative procedures and political processes. It is as if the state in which all officially recognised religious *ṭawā'if* participate through their secular representatives, and in which their separate 'wills' merge, were also the passage through which – the medium in which – they are able to carry themselves beyond their identities, transcend their particularities.

The formal concept that articulates the consensus of all the religious *ṭawā'if* is that of 'public order'. The relationship between public order and the system of religious *ṭawā'if* is constituted and guaranteed by law. In a ruling issued in 1972, the Court of Cassation points out that 'the positive rules [of each *ṭā'ifa*] in the . . . system do not violate the Lebanese public order'. It argues that, 'if a foreign law contravenes the [legal or normative] system of one or several *ṭawā'if*, and 'if its stipulations are in agreement with . . . the stipulations of other[s]', then the foreign law 'would not constitute a violation of the Lebanese public order'. However, if there is among the *ṭawā'if* in Lebanon 'a consensus (*ijmāʿ*) on a matter of importance and submit it to a single stipulation which the foreign law violates, then this consensus is considered to be similar to a Lebanese public order'. The consensus of the religious *ṭawāʾif* in Lebanon is constitutive of a public order that 'would prevent the application of the foreign law'.

Limits (and Limitations) of Coexistence

The coexistence of Muslims and Christians, the securing of a place for them and securing them in a place, in the safety of the assumption that all in Lebanon are Christians or Muslims, is not an entirely stable construct. In the first place, it must answer to the claim that there are people in Lebanon who think that what matters is not their religion or 'religious identity', and who want to be recognised as individuals, as human beings. What place is (to be) secured for them (if at all)? How are they to be secured in place? By what law are mere human individuals governed in matters that pertain to their personal status – by what law is their personal status to be defined? Is it necessary to grant them first official recognition as a non-religious, civil, *ṭāʾifa*? Do 'civil *ṭawāʾif*' exist, or would it make sense, and what sense would it make, to speak of a 'civil' or 'secular *ṭāʾifa*'? How would an answer to any or all of these questions bear on the coexistence of Christians and Muslims? How would the coexistence of Christians and Muslims, as a principle of public order, determine the answers to these questions? In short, what are the limits (and limitations) of coexistence?[30]

In 2010, the CLC, on the request of the Ministry of Interior, gave an opinion in a case in which two plaintiffs against the Lebanese state claimed that they did not belong to any religious *ṭāʾifa*. In the CLC's words, the case requires that it give an opinion on the determination of the 'status of Lebanese [citizens] who seek not to belong to any *ṭāʾifa*'.[31] The CLC proceeded on the assumption that not belonging to any *ṭāʾifa* implied not belonging to any of the officially recognised religious *ṭawāʾif*, and this implied belonging to a 'non-religious' or secular *ṭāʾifa*. It argued that a 'civil *ṭāʾifa* (*ṭāʾifa madaniyya*)

[30] The part that follows is a slightly revised version of a section in Raja Abillama, 'Contesting Secularism: Civil Marriage and Those Who Do Not Belong to a Religious Community in Lebanon', *PoLAR: Political and Legal Anthropology Review 41*, S1 (2018): 148–62.

[31] CLC 2012, p. 4.

to which the Lebanese can ask to belong does not exist in the law', from which it follows that an individual 'cannot . . . switch to a different position (*waḍʿ*)', before a law is passed through which a 'civil *ṭāʾifa*' would be officially recognised (and brought into existence).[32] 'It is necessary to enact a single law' first, the CLC concluded, in order to make it possible for 'a Lebanese [citizen] to belong to other than the religious *ṭawāʾif*'.[33]

The CLC's argument rests on (and articulates) an anthropology and ontology that, prioritises the '*ṭāʾifa*' ('group', 'community', 'collectivity', 'society', and, ultimately, 'the state') and an opposition between 'religious' and 'secular' – the two names of two different and distinct kinds or categories of '*ṭāʾifa*' ('groups', 'communities'). This conceptual scheme supports the CLC's interpretation of the plaintiffs' claim that they do not belong to any religious *ṭāʾifa* – as implying that they belong to a 'non-religious' or 'civil' *ṭāʾifa* (which does not exist), rather than non-belonging *tout court*. It also leads the CLC to assert in its conclusion the decisiveness of the principle of sovereignty and, hence, of the principle of coexistence (between Muslims and Christians) over questions of personal status and 'recognition' – over who is to be secured a place, how to be secured in place, and, indeed, of what 'securing' and 'place' consist in.

The scheme that supports the CLC's opinion is contradicted by another opinion, issued by another legal advisory organ of the state's, which prioritises not 'the group', but the individual, not the *ṭāʾifa*, but 'the human being'. The effect of this legal antithesis is that 'the individual' and 'the human' on one hand, and 'the community' and religious *ṭāʾifa* on another, now appear mutually exclusive. Moreover, once the bare, mere, 'private individual' is set as the premise, then, and in accordance with equally secular principles (a secular, that is, as in the preceding logic) what to do with the religious and secular is not (no longer) a 'public' matter (for the CLC, or any other state organ to pronounce on), but one within the individual's exclusive purview. This was the argument made in the same case around the same time by the Higher Advisory Committee at the same Ministry of Justice in which the CLC is housed. The HAC argued that 'the Lebanese [citizen] who does not

[32] CLC 2012, p. 9.

[33] CLC 2012, p. 10.

belong to a *ṭā'ifa'* (*not* a religious *ṭā'ifa*) has, nevertheless, a determinate personal status in Lebanon.[34]

This divergence between the two opinions, which is rooted in the binary opposition between 'individuality' and 'community', 'humanity' and 'sociality', and so on, enters into the different ways in which the ordering of sources of legal norms and rights is viewed – into the very ordering of the sources of norms and rights. The stakes of this divergence is the character of the Lebanese state, but it is an articulation of a more general problem, namely, what takes precedence, Lebanese law or the Universal Declaration of Human Rights – sovereignty or human rights? The CLC upholds the former, the HAC, the latter. At stake in the divergence of opinion between the two advisory committees is the status of Decree No. 60 L./R. and of the limits (and limitations) of the coexistence of Muslims and Christians as an organising principle.

Some lawyers, jurists and activists in Lebanon attribute to the Decree what they consider to be the prominence of the religious in Lebanon, especially in matters of state. They would like to see it abrogated, in the conviction that abrogating it would reduce the power of the religious *ṭawā'if*, if not eliminating it altogether. For others, with a more moderate attitude towards it, Decree No. 60 has the virtue of placing under the rule of law the relationship among three features of the Lebanese state that would otherwise be in conflict: 'the state and its sovereignty, . . . the [religious] *ṭawā'if* and their laws, and the existence of the individual and his [or her] human rights'. The Decree's success, however, depends on the condition that it be applied correctly, which, they argue, has not been the case so far. While as a law (a text), the Decree is balanced, in practice, the religious *ṭawā'if* have been privileged over and against both the state and the individual.[35]

[34] Higher Advisory Committee, Consultation of 11 February 2013, 'The Extent to Which the Civil Marriage Could Be Contracted in Lebanon', pp. 4–5. For an account of the circumstances in which the two opinions were elaborated see Abillama, 'Contesting Secularism'.

[35] This account is based on a conversation in Beirut in 2014 with Talal Hussaini, lawyer and legal researcher. He, along with his brother – a former MP and head of parliament – and a group of lawyers, politicians and activists from the Civil Center for the National Initiative (CCNI) were (at the time) working to establish the foundations of a new state, *al-dawla al-madaniyya* (the civil state). Abillama, 'Contesting Secularism'.

The reason, according to that argument, why religious *ṭawā'if* are so prominent in Lebanon resides not in Lebanese law, but in the twofold assumption that all in Lebanon are religious and belong to a religious *ṭā'ifa*', and that the latter is the basis of life and history (that which the CLC's opinion presupposes). What some of these lawyers and jurists (and activists) argue is that people who do not belong to a religious *ṭā'ifa* do in fact exist in Lebanon, and that the essentially free individual is the basis of collective life, and the subject of history (premises implicit in the HAC's opinion).[36] The disagreement between the two attitudes is a disagreement over what could be claimed to 'exist', and, as will be clear below, over what could be claimed to constitute 'reality'. What could be claimed to be the case – what exists, what is real – enters into the structuring of attitudes and thus determine the interpretation of the law and the scope of its application. (of Decree No. 60 L./R.).

Several decades ago, a prominent Lebanese jurist and constitutional historian wrote that the claim that there are people (in Lebanon) who do not belong to a religious *ṭā'ifa* is a description of 'a mere illusion that has no connection or possibility of a connection with tangible reality'.[37] Some dispute the validity of this assertion, insisting instead that those who do not belong to a *ṭā'ifa* are 'real beings as [is known] from [their] stories . . . and . . . their actions'. According to the proponents of this opinion, the existence of those who do not belong has for long been denied in Lebanon, despite the fact, as they see it, that it is acknowledged in Article 10 of Decree No. 60, which stipulates that 'those who do not belong to a *ṭā'ifa* are subject to the civil law in matters of personal status'.[38] They argue that the only 'tangible reality' that is relevant in identifying the ones who do not belong to a religious *ṭā'ifa* is 'administrative reality', of which the 'records of personal status' are the only admissible evidence.[39]

'Administrative reality' is, however, itself the terrain of contestation between two claims: on the one hand, individuals (of legal age) have the right, and may exercise the right, to decide to have the *madhhab* recorded

[36] The argument is developed in full detail in a book he published in 2013. Talal Hussaini, *Al-Zawaj al-Madani: Al-Haqq wa-l-ʿAqd ʿAla al-Aradi al-Lubnaniyya* (Beirut: Dar al-Saqi, 2013).
[37] Ibid., p. 98; Rabbath, *La formation historique*, p. 104.
[38] Hussaini, *Al-Zawaj al-Madani*, p. 98.
[39] Ibid., p. 99.

in their identification documents; on the other hand, Lebanese law requires that the General Administration of Personal Status specify the religious *ṭāʾifa* of Lebanese citizens by inscribing it in their personal status documents, the consent of the individuals concerned hardly sought. This contestation over the control of the administrative practice of registering a *madhhab* (or religious *ṭāʾifa*) – and its undecidability – is the administrative, practical articulation of an ambiguity residing in the way 'the religious' figures in the Lebanese Constitution and Lebanese law. The Lebanese Constitution admits the 'absolute freedom of conscience and belief', while Lebanese law (Law of 1951) makes it a requirement that individuals declare a *madhhab* or religious *ṭāʾifa*, which would amount to a requirement to belong administratively to a religious *ṭāʾifa*, and identified, thereby, as 'Christian' or 'Muslim'.

In 2009, the Ministry of Interior ordered the General Administration of Personal Status (GAPS) to desist from registering the *madhhab*, and to leave the decision to do so to those concerned (e.g. parents of a newborn). Since then, people have been able to choose to register their children or not, and adults to strike out the reference to *madhhab* in their personal status documents. In the autumn of 2013, the President of the Republic of Lebanon issued a statement 'congratulat[ing] the Lebanese people on . . . the first newborn to be registered without a *ṭāʾifa*'.[40] A form of grassroots activism has

[40] 'First child of civil marriage couple born last month without sect', http://www.dailystar.com.lb/ArticlePrint.aspx?id=235973&mode=print; 'Lebanese couple announces country's first "sect-less" baby', http://america.aljazeera.com/articles/2013/11/1/lebanon-s-first-sectlessbaby.html; 'Meet Ghadi, the first "sect-less" baby in deeply divided Lebanon', http://www.cnn.com/2013/11/28/world/meast/lebanon-sectless-baby-jamjoom/; 'Baby Ghadi's religion isn't on his birth certificate, a first for sectarian Lebanon', http://www.huffingtonpost.com/2013/10/30/baby-ghadi-religion_n_4178489.html; 'Trending: The baby making history in Lebanon', http://www.bbc.com/news/magazine-24725799; 'Ghadi, premier bébé libanais "libéré de toutes les contraintes religieuses"', http://www.lorientlejour.com/article/839551/ghadi-premier-bebe-libanais-libere-de-toutes-les-contraintes-religieuses.html; 'Confessions – Ghadi, le premier bébé libanais sans religion', http://bigbrowser.blog.lemonde.fr/2013/10/29/confession-ghadi-le-premier-bebe-libanais-sans-religion/; 'Ghadi, un bébé laïque pour le rêve d'un Liban déconfessionnalisé', http://www.liberation.fr/monde/2013/12/10/ghadi-un-bebe-laique-pour-le-reve-d-un-liban-deconfessionnalise_965572; 'Né sans religion. Ghadi, le bébé de l'espoir au Liban', http://www.parismatch.com/Actu/International/Ne-sans-religion-Ghadi-le-bebe-de-l-espoir-au-Liban-535189.

gathered round it, with individuals approaching the GAPS with a request that the *madhhab* or religious *ṭā'ifa* be struck out of their personal status records and documents.[41] This contestation is waged in terms of rights: whether the individual has a 'human right' – whether, that is, it is a human right – to decide what (religion) to declare in and through the records of personal status, or whether it is the law (and, therefore, the state) that determines the right to do so or not. It is also a contestation over 'the religious' (e.g. freedom of religion), from which questions about rights are inseparable – or, rather, over the very separability of 'rights' (the secular) and the religious – and the boundaries and relationship between the religious and the (secular, civil) state. It is, thus, a contestation of the coexistence of Christians and Muslims in Lebanon – in so far as coexistence implies the securing of Muslims and Christians in place (bodies in jurisdictions), of securing a place (a jurisdiction) for Christians and Muslims (as corporeal bodies).

It is in contestation that the limits (and limitations) of coexistence are made explicit and called, thereby, into question. For, the contestation is over bodies (Christian, Muslim, or otherwise), over the securing of bodies (in order to secure bodies) in place, and over bodies that might be out of place. In a sense, it is a contestation over the very concept of body which the coexistence of Muslims and Christians in Lebanon presupposes and articulates, and, in a

[41] The activism came to my attention when someone in Beirut whom I had just met and who, after I informed her of the research I was carrying out at the time, announced that she had recently had her documents modified. I had the opportunity to have the contents of that conversation confirmed twice. The first time was by a friend, whose sister had also sought to have her religious community struck out of her *ikhrāj qayd*, and who, when I asked, generously provided me with a copy of the document. A digitised copy of the document in my possession shows a diagonal stroke marked by hand over and against the horizontal line on which the name of the religious community to which she belongs (is presumed to belong) would be written. It would seem that even that refusal to declare one's belonging to a religious community, or one's refusal of belonging altogether to a religious community which that inscription is supposed to signify, would still leave its trace – would still be declared. The second confirmation – with variation on the first account – came to me at the end of spring 2021, when, again, someone I had just met who also asked me about the work I do, claimed that there are hundreds of similar cases, and that he is in possession of numerous samples of *ikhrāj qayd* to show it. He announced also that he himself had successfully had his religious community – 'Armenian Orthodox' – not exactly struck out, but entered instead as 'Buddhist'.

more general sense, what concept of 'body' is to support what (whose) 'coexistence'. While 'administrative reality' delineates the terrain on which the contestation is waged, it is the datum itself that is contested – what 'reality' one speaks about when speaking about the reality of Christians and Muslims and about in Lebanon; what makes them available to identification and gives force, thereby, to such assertions as, 'there are Muslims and Christians in Lebanon'.

Conclusion

It is clear that if it is the case that the coexistence of Christians and Muslims in Lebanon is rooted in their historically and geographically specific coincidence in a common juridical-political space, coexistence is, nevertheless, a normative construct. It is one and only one way of interpreting and doing something with that contingency. Thus, coexistence is neither an ideology nor a mere political idea, but, as a norm (or a complex of norms), is embedded in an open set of interconnected practices that are constitutive of a form of life (or, if one takes into account the body, a sensibility). One constellation of practices is that through which Muslims and Christians are secured in place, and secured a place. Other ways of imagining of coexistence are possible or, put differently, coexistence could be otherwise. Moreover, it does not follow from the fact that Muslims and Christians are secured in/a place that they are permanently bound to it. As the next chapter shows, Lebanese law provides rules and procedures that enable (and constrain) the movement of individual Christians and Muslims across religious jurisdictions.

2

TABDĪL AL-DĪN, SECULAR DISPLACEMENT AND RELIGIOUS CONVERSION

In February 1951, Olga and Caesar petition the Lebanese Court of Cassation to decide if, according to an Orthodox ecclesiastical court, they are divorced, or, as the Catholic judiciaries maintain, they are still married. The Court decides in favour of the Catholic marriage.[1]

In 1967, Tania approaches the Cassation claiming full rights over her father's inheritance. The Cassation rules in favour of Tania, against the Administration of Public Islamic Endowments.[2]

Salah, Tony, and Hanan appear before the same court in 1970 with a petition to rule that Salah's claim to place a hold (*ḥajr*) on his granddaughter's – Hanan's daughter – person and properties is invalid. The Cassation Court issues a decision in Hanan's favour, against the maternal grandfather.[3]

On 27 April 1984, Shafiqa petitions the Maronite (Catholic) First Instance Court to appeal a decision to dissolve her marriage issued by the Orthodox

[1] Cassation Court (henceforth, CC), Decision No. 110, 18 September 1951. *Al-Nashra al-Qada'iyya* (Beirut: Ministry of Justice, 1952), pp. 253–8.
[2] CC, Decision No. 8, 23 June 1967. *Al-ʿAdl: Majallat Naqabat al-Muhamin* (Beirut: Bar Association, June 1967): 171–2.
[3] CC, Decision No. 271, 26 March 1970. *Al-ʿAdl* (March 1970): 429–30.

Ecclesiastical Court. The court issues a ruling declaring instead that the case falls beyond its purview.[4]

In 1994, a woman whose name is not given in the case transcript appears before the Higher Sunni Shariʿa Court with a request to be separated from her husband, with whom she is bound by a Catholic marriage. The court issues a ruling declaring instead its lack of competency in the case.[5]

In 2002, Vivian files a complaint against her husband Ibrahim and his lawyer before the First Instance Civil Court in Mount Lebanon, petitioning the latter to annul an agreement made by the spouses to end their marriage. The court issues a decision to accept her claim and abrogate the agreement, ending thereby her Catholic marriage.[6]

All of these cases involve disputes between previously or, in some of them, still married spouses or members of a family. All have as their final point of appeal the Cassation Court, the highest instance in the Lebanese judicial hierarchy with the competence to arbitrate between parties in such cases. The shariʿa and ecclesiastical courts receive their share occasionally, but whereas the secular court makes a decision that settles the dispute, the religious judiciaries proclaim their lack of competence. Despite the fact that the religious judiciaries in Lebanon have exclusive jurisdiction over conjugal and domestic disputes, they seem to surrender it in such cases to the civil courts, which, under ordinary circumstances, do not.

What explains this jurisdictional displacement? Why are these cases and the Christians and Muslims caught in them transferred from the religious jurisdictions to which they belong, to the secular jurisdiction of the Lebanese state, to which they do not? If it is the case that marriage and its consequences fall under their jurisdiction, then why do the religious judiciaries reject them? A

[4] Maronite Unified First Instance Court (henceforth, MUFIC), Decision No. 17/84, 26 February 1985. *Al-Sharq al-Adna: Dirasat fi-l-Qanun* (Beirut: Faculté de droit et des sciences politiques, Université Saint Joseph, 1985): 198–200.

[5] Prosecutor General at the Higher Sunni Shariʿa Court (henceforth, PG), Decision No. 483/94, 19 December 1994. Elias Abou Eid (ed.), *Al-Qararat al-Kubra fi-l-Ijtihad al-Lubnani wa-l-Muqaran/Les grands arrêts de la jurisprudence libanaise et comparée*, 36 (Beirut): 9–19.

[6] First Instance Civil Court (henceforth, FICC), Decision No. 54, 17 May 2022. *Al-ʿAdl* 4 (May 2022): 750–4.

theme runs through them all, marks them as a particular class of personal status cases, and appears to justify the exceptional civil legal treatment they receive. Caesar and Olga, both Maronite Catholics, switched their *madhhab* to Greek Orthodoxy Orthodoxy; Tania's father, Greek Orthodox, had allegedly changed his religion to Sunni Islam; Hanan, once a Muslim, switched to the Christian faith; the Maronite Catholic Vivian and Ibrahim switched to Syriac Orthodoxy. In the first case, the Cassation ruled on the basis of its assessment of the spouses' switching their *madhhab*, and it ruled in favour of Tania in the second case, after concluding that her father's change of religion was incomplete. In the case of Salah, Tony and Hanan, it ruled against the maternal grandfather, singling out the mother's changing of her religion, and abrogated the agreement between Vivian and Ibrahim because it involved a change of *madhhab*.

Why is the changing of religion (or *madhhab*) in cases of marriage and its consequences a reason to uphold the rights of one person against another, or to quash the decision of one religious jurisdiction while confirming that of another? What sense and what force does a change of religion possess? When secular jurisdictions hear cases that involve a change of religion, and when religious jurisdictions turn away from them, are they confronted with the same thing – do they have the same idea of what is a change of religion? Do the shariʿa and ecclesiastical jurisdictions? Why, in the first place, is a person's change of religion worth the attention of the highest judicial instance in the country?

The Problem of *Tabdīl al-Dīn*

The judicial cases that prompt the questions articulate a complex of three relations: between two or more (natural) persons; between (natural) persons and a secular and/or religious jurisdiction; between two secular and/or religious jurisdictions. The relations are between persons (human, conjugal, familial), between persons and things (relations of property), and between jurisdictions (relations of authority). The claims that are advanced to the court are, accordingly, claims over persons, claims over things, and claims of competence.

> Olga and Caesar, for example, approach the Cassation having in hand two decisions from two religious courts that entail two opposite outcomes. Olga is granted an Orthodox divorce, while the Catholic Rota, before which Caesar had ended up, upholds their marriage.

Tania, a Greek Orthodox, wishes the Cassation Court to overturn a decision issued by the Beirut Islamic Shariʿa Court in favour of the Public Administration of Islamic Endowments (*al-awqāf*) in Beirut that excludes her from her father's inheritance.

In Hanan's case against her father Salah, the Cassation is asked to decide which one of two decisions is valid: the one that is issued by the Sunni Shariʿa courts granting Salah his request for a hold over his granddaughter's person and properties, or that by the Orthodox Ecclesiastical Court refusing his request and contradicting the Sunni ruling?

The decision to dissolve Shafiqa's marriage is issued by the Orthodox Ecclesiastical Court, and she herself had to seek an annulment of her Catholic marriage to a once-Maronite man who had decided to contract an Islamic marriage to another woman while they – i.e. he and Shafiqa – were still bound by their Maronite (Catholic) marriage. The Maronite court considers that the case falls beyond its purview, as does the Sunni court when the unnamed woman approached it for a ruling, since her husband had converted to Islam in the Kingdom of Saudi Arabia while both were still bound by their Catholic marriage.

In so far as persons, things, and jurisdictions are all either Christian or Muslim, disputes are averted, but once their separation is not (or no longer) a matter of course, then disputes arise, and the Cassation Court is called upon to arbitrate. That which the Cassation (or any court, for that matter) singles out as the root of the dispute and the apparent confounding of identities is a change of religion (or *madhhab*) that had taken place either in the past (i.e. prior to the initiation of the case), or in the present, while a case is still being heard by one court or another.

The change of religion, which acquires its sense and force in so far as it is situated in a judicially construed context, is suspected of being the cause of the dispute or conflict – is disruptive, that is, of the complex of relationships that make up the judicial situation. Accordingly, the court proceeds by investigating the change of religion, identifying it in the context of a sequence of legal facts.[7]

[7] The same applies to the religious courts, with the difference that they abstain from investigating the change, declaring instead their incompetence in the case. I discuss this in the last two sections.

There is a fourth, 'internal' relationship to be added to the three 'external' ones mentioned above, one that is not explicit or immediately obvious in the case, namely, that which *tabdīl al-dīn* (or *madhhab*) brings into play between the subject and herself in the act itself. This relationship constitutes a more serious problem for the judiciaries to investigate because they run the risk of impinging on the beliefs or the conscience of the Christian or Muslim who decides to change his religion (i.e., of violating the secular principles of neutrality and separation).[8]

In addition to the claims of right of the various disputants, be they persons or jurisdictions, what is at stake in any act of *tabdīl al-dīn* – what any act of *tabdīl al-dīn* brings into play – is those 'internal' and 'external' relations. Thus, implicit in such cases is the pervasive problem that in each and every case of change of religion there is a chance that the change be motivated by an authentic religious conversion; implicit in each and every case of change of religion is the possibility that a secular, legal displacement be the outward expression of an authentic religious conversion.

The problem is rooted in the Lebanese version of the idea of religious freedom. The Lebanese Constitution stipulates, first, that 'there shall be absolute freedom of conscience', and, second, that 'the personal status . . . of the population, to whatever religious sect they belong, shall be respected'.[9] While it is not spelled out in it, the text suggests that religious freedom in Lebanon is to be taken in the sense of the two clauses, which describe the shape it takes in the context of the coexistence of Muslims and Christians. In the first clause, the freedom of religion is encompassed by the more general category of 'freedom of conscience' (the latter could include atheism, for example) which, in so far as it is absolute, entails the absolute freedom to change one's religion. The second clause presupposes the difference between and distinctiveness of

[8] Clearly, this does not apply to cases in which the subject of the change is no longer in existence. Yet, in a sense, in so far as beliefs and 'conscience' are legally or judicially inscrutable, they have something in common.

[9] 'Article 9. There shall be absolute freedom of conscience. The state, in rendering homage to the God Almighty[,] shall respect all religions and creeds, and shall guarantee under its protection the free exercise of all religious rites provided that public order is not disturbed. It shall also guarantee that the personal status and religious interests of the population, to whatever religious sect they belong, shall be respected': 'The Lebanese Constitution', *Arab Law Quarterly* 12, 2 (1997): 224–61.

Christians and Muslims (a 'pillar' of coexistence) and of the legal arrangement that mediates and guarantees it. As it was described in the preceding chapter, the coexistence of Muslims and Christians is a matter of law and order (legal, public), the two being mutually dependent. The problem of *tabdīl al-dīn aw al-madhhab* is that it carries the potential to subvert that order and unsettle coexistence. *Tabdīl al-dīn*, to put it in slightly different terms, is a calling into question of the arrangement through which Muslims and Christians in Lebanon are held together and kept apart – that is, a calling into question of their coexistence.

The idea of 'religious freedom' which the two clauses articulate presupposes a sort of dualistic metaphysic of mind and body that is consistent with the anthropological assumption that supports the positive law, namely, the idea of a legal subject, the single and singular rational human person in possession of her body. Accordingly, this dualism implies that it is possible to separate the 'internal' forum of conscience and the 'external' domain of action. When it comes to *tabdīl al-dīn*, specifically, it implies that it is possible to separate religious conversion and legal displacement, and gives rise to the concomitant problem of determining their relationship.

Tabdīl al-dīn is an articulation of both/either the movements of the soul (conscience) and/or the movements of the body (an action) in (juridical) space, across boundaries (jurisdictions), relative to other bodies (legal subjects). A change of religion (or *madhhab*) matters legally. As an external movement, it carries with it the possibility of disputes over (personal) rights and jurisdictional conflicts and constitutes, thereby, a threat to the legal and public orders on which coexistence depends. Yet, to prohibit *tabdīl al-dīn* or *madhhab* entirely as a way to preempt its potential for disorder is to undermine the freedom of religion and, more generally, the freedom of conscience.[10]

Thus, a space is carved out for a discourse concerning the truth of *tabdīl al-dīn* and a set of practices through which to tell apart its two terms – to tell whether an act of switching religion (or *madhhab*) is an instance or expression

[10] The freedom or right to religious conversion was the privileged vehicle and measure of the freedom of religion in the late Ottoman Empire. Selim Deringil, '"There is No Compulsion in Religion": On Conversion and Apostasy in the Late Ottoman Empire: 1839–1856', *Comparative Studies in Society and History* (2000): 547–75, and Mahmood, *Religious Difference*.

of a religious conversion or a mere matter of legal displacement, if it is internal or external, a matter of conscience or law, private or public, sincere or fraudulent, and so forth.[11]

The problem of *tabdīl al-dīn* in Lebanon is one in which the status and limits of religious (judicial) authority and the reasons (of the Lebanese) state are called into question. *Tabdīl al-dīn* holds the prospect of calling into question the (legal) arrangement through which Muslims and Christians coexist in Lebanon, calling into question their very coexistence.

What *Tabdīl al-Dīn* Looks Like

A sentiment of suspicion accompanies *tabdīl al-dīn aw al-madhhab*, within or without the law. However, judicial suspicion in particular, and the questioning to which it leads, has to do with the setting in which an act of switching a religion or *madhhab* takes place, or the circumstances that surround it. What matters legally about the change of religion is the legal context in which it is executed, questioned, and judged. The context consists in all of the other legal or legally relevant actions that pertain to a case of personal status: the actions of spouses and family members, the procedures of administrative organs of the Lebanese state, and the decisions of civil, ecclesiastical and *shar'i* judiciaries.

A judicial examination of a change of religion or *madhhab* proceeds typically on the basis of a narrative composed of a sequence of legal events that culminate in a person's (or persons') appearance before the court. The narrative is a judicial construction of the person's actions in the context in which

[11] The legal problem of changing religion is not unique to Lebanon. In the United States, for example, it assumes the form of 'the problem of religious conversion fraud' in the context of asylum policy. Asylum is granted to claimants on grounds of 'persecution or a well-founded fear of persecution on account of . . . religion' in their home country (8 USC § 1101(a)(42)(A)(1994). Tuan N. Samahon, 'The Religion Clauses and Political Asylum: Religious Persecution Claims and the Religious Membership-Conversion Imposter Problem', *The Georgetown Law Journal* 88, 7 (2000): 2211). However, the US Immigration and Naturalization Service (INS) suspects cases of 'eleventh hour' conversions, requiring the administration to determine 'whether a religious convert is an imposter or a legitimate member of a religious group . . .' This is 'complicated' by the First Amendment, which imposes on the INS the delicate assignment of determining the sincerity of conversion while avoiding the 'impairment of free exercise' and the 'imposition of a religious orthodoxy'. Ibid. 2211–38.

they are carried out, and in which the force and sense of a change of religion could be assessed.

> Olga and Caesar 'belong to the Maronite *ṭāʾifa*' and were married as such in the Maronite Church on 6 May 1926. Thirteen years later, on 10 June 1939, 'the wife petitioned the Maronite Archbishopric's registrar in Beirut' with a request for 'separation (*hajr*) and support (*nafaqa*)'. The Archbishopric seems to have succeeded to 'reconcile' the spouses, but on 27 April 1940, 'each filed a [separate] complaint against the other at the same Office'. When the Office 'ordered [them to return] to marital cohabitation . . . [t]hey appealed [the] decision before the Maronite Patriarchal registrar', which issued a decision 'on 4 December 1941 to overturn the first instance ruling . . . and grant Olga separation from her husband Caesar for a year and a half'. In 1942, 'the husband filed a new complaint at . . . the Maronite Diocese in Beirut', which 'dismissed [two years later] the claim of annulment due to fear . . . consider[ing] instead the marriage void' due to the incestuous proximity of the spouses. However, the 'Defender of the Matrimonial Bond' appealed the decision before 'the Maronite Patriarchal Administrative Office', the latter 'overturn[ing] the first instance decision and dismiss[ing] the case'. The husband, Caesar, 'objected', but his objection was rejected by the aforementioned authority, which 'decided on 24 August 1945 to leave the matter to the Holy Council of the Eastern Churches'. Five months later, 'upon a Papal summons, the Council transferred the case to the Roman Rota'. So far, the spouses have remained within the Catholic hierarchy, but as their case lingered at the Rota, they step outside the boundaries of the jurisdiction to which their marriage and its consequences belongs – to which they legally belong – to petition 'the Orthodox Bishop of Mount Lebanon' with a request that they be 'accept[ed] . . . into the Orthodox *ṭāʾifa*'. On 15 October 1947, Olga 'petitioned the Orthodox Court in Mount Lebanon for divorce with compensation'. This would have raised no suspiction, as their marriage and its consequences would have been transferred to the Orthodox jurisdiction following their *madhhab*, in accordance with Lebanese law, which stipulates that the transfer of jurisdiction *follows only once the* religion or *madhhab was officially registered.*[12] Yet, the couple filed for an Orthodox divorce before completing

[12] Legislative Decree No. 60 L./R., 1936, Article 23: 'If one of the spouses left his *ṭāʾifa*, the marriage and the documents that pertain to the system of personal status remain subject to the

> the formalities required for 'their switching to the Orthodox *madhhab* to take effect'. Nevertheless, and despite the fact that they formalised their *madhhab* 26 January 1948, several months after they had filed for divorce, the Orthodox court issued a divorce ruling three days later. The Cassation Court pursues the investigation further. Olga 'went back to her Maronite *madhhab*' on 23 March 1948 'claim[ing] that she was coerced to sign the divorce decision', and appealed 'the first instance Orthodox decision before the [Orthodox] Patriarchal Court in Damascus'. On 26 May 1949, the latter 'decided to repeal the [Orthodox] first instance ruling . . . and to consider the two parties married'. Caesar appealed before 'the Orthodox Court of Appeals', which 'overturned the last decision and dismissed [Olga's] appeal on 11 January 1951'. Meanwhile, elsewhere, the Rotal Court 'was interrogating Caesar, who swore an oath before it that he was still a Catholic, and that he adopted the Orthodox *madhhab* without applying for it'. When the Rota 'ruled on 12 April 1949 that the annulment does not hold, Caesar . . . appealed . . . to another circuit, which rejected his appeal on 1 April 1950'.[13]

Some of the salient features of *tabdīl al-madhhab* (this applies as well to *tabdīl al-dīn*) are on display in Olga's and Caesar's narrative. *Tabdīl al-madhhab* is an action, it presupposes a subject and carries effects in 'this world'. It is a single and singular positive fact, localisable, therefore, in time and space, and recordable – its localisability and recordability being mutually dependent (that it is to be recorded officially is required for the change of religion or *madhhab* to be recognised as such). It is ambiguous, for it may or may not be deliberate, intentional, or purposeful, and it may be motivated by secular and/or religious motives, or be based on secular and/or religious reasons.

While it is not, strictly speaking, a legal action, its effects – those that matter judicially at any rate – are the legal effects which it brings upon 'this world' in so far as 'this world' is legal, or legally constituted (or that part of this world over which the secular positive law has claim). A change of religion

law according to which the marriage was celebrated or the documents drafted or contracted. However, if both spouses left their *ṭā'ifa*, then their marriage and the documents and obligations that pertain to personal status will follow the law of the [new *ṭā'ifa*'s] system starting from the date on which their leaving [conversion] of their *ṭā'ifa* was recorded in the records of personal status.' Al-Zein, (Christians).

[13] CC, Decision No. 110, 18 September 1951.

or *madhhab* consists in an intervention in the legally constituted relationship between persons (marriage, custody, support . . .), between persons and things (inheritance), and between religious authorities (judiciaries and jurisdictions). Its force and sense are tied to 'this world' in which it is performed – a world composed of a series of chronologically arranged facts in which the change of religion or *madhhab* is inserted in an orderly fashion (or ought to fit).

In Olga's and Caesar's case (and others of the same kind), a feature of this legal world is the judicial process, or, more exactly, a complex of three separate judicial proceedings which the couple's *tabdīl al-madhhab* brings into contact. Theirs is a representative of a kind of case and sets an early precedent for subsequent cases of the same kind, involving a Catholic couple seeking another way out of their marriage than annulment by switching to an Orthodox jurisdiction (or any other jurisdiction) in which divorce is admitted.[14]

> Four years later, in another case, the Cassation Court is called upon again to uphold one of two ecclesiastical rulings. The Orthodox decision would dissolve Zahiyya's and Toufic's marriage; there is no mention of the contents of the Maronite ruling in the published case transcript, but the Cassation explains that the two rulings are mutually 'contradictory (*mutanāqidayn*)'. The Cassation reports that for the duration of their marriage, the spouses 'were . . . Maronites' and 'had remained' so, living together 'in continuous cohabitation for fourteen years'. On 29 July 1954, however, they proceeded to convert ('*'amadā ila taghyīr madhhabihima*') to Orthodoxy 'at the civil registry', signing two days later 'a statement before the notary public (*kātib al-'adl*) in Tripoli' in which they claimed that 'one divorced the other, considering that they are of the Orthodox *ṭā'ifa*'. They 'filed for divorce on 3 August 1954', that is, as the Cassation goes on to emphasise, 'five days after' they had changed their *madhhab*. A day later – six after they made the change – 'on 9 August . . . the Orthodox Ecclesiastical Court issued a divorce ruling'.

In the two preceding cases, the spouses were Maronite (Catholics) and their marriage was subject to the rules of Catholic Canon Law, which admits only the possibility to annul, under stringent conditions, what it considers to

[14] It is early relative to the history of the Lebanese Republic, which was proclaimed so in 1943 – the case is from 1951, and the marriage itself was contracted in 1926 under French Mandate over Syria and Lebanon.

be essentially a Holy Sacrament of the Church.[15] In both cases, the Cassation's narrative suggests a connection between the spouses' intention to 'divorce' and their decision to switch their *madhhab*. In both cases, finally, the change involves two Christian churches, displacing the spouses (back and forth a few times in the first case) between two ecclesiastical jurisdictions. In the next two cases, the conflicts are between shariʿa and civil jurisdictions – that is, between Muslims and Christians (the latter fall under the civil 'Law of Inheritance for non-Mohammedans' of 1959).

> The facts of Tania's case against the Administration of Islamic Public Endowments (henceforth, AIPE) in Beirut begin when, upon the death of her 'father Jean (John) . . . in Beirut on 22 January 1967', a civil court decides to allocate his property to her and his mother Souraya. However, two months later 'Beirut's Shariʿa Court' decides to designate the AIPE as his rightful heir, 'considering [that] Jean [is] Muslim'. On 6 April 1967, Tania 'petitioned the Cassation Court' with the claim that the Shariʿa court had no authority over the case because he 'was legally Christian' – *legally* Christian, and remains so, even if he had changed his religion, since the change did not occur according to Article 41 [of the Law of 7 December 1951, 'The Recording of Personal Status Documents'].[16] The article describes the formality required for a change of religion or *madhhab* to be considered accomplished – that is, for it to have legal effects (for a full description of the formality, see below). As defendant, the AIPE countered Tania's claims, its lawyers presenting the court with 'a certificate announcing his Islam (*shahādat ishhār al-islām*, also, make public) registered [in Egypt] at the Documentation Office in Cairo (*maktab al-tawthīq*) on 12 June 1966'. The AIPE advanced two claims: first, that the certificate is evidence that Jean's change of religion did in fact occur; second, that 'the formality cited in Article 41 . . . is not an essential (*muʿāmala jawhariyya*), but a bureaucratic formality (*muʿāmala qalamiyya*)'.[17]

> In *Nader* v. *Labban*, Abla and George were married on 11 January 1958 at Beirut's Capuchin church as Roman Catholics (*latīn*, officially a *madhhab/ṭāʾifa*).

[15] The two cases occurred in the 1950s, a decade or so after the proclamation of Lebanese independence from the French, and a decade or so before the Second Vatican Council of 1965, which 'modernised' the annulment of marriage. They precede by three decades the promulgation of the new Code of Canon Law of 1983 and the Canon for the Eastern Churches. See Chapter 3.
[16] I discuss the text of this law in Chapter 1.
[17] CC, Decision No. 8, 23 June 1967.

He later 'embraced the Islamic religion into the Sunni *madhhab* (*iʿtanaqa al-diyāna al-islāmiyya ʿala madhhab ahl al-sunna*)' and had his religion 'registered on 15 Decembre 1967 at the Administration of Personal Status according to procedure and the law'. George died soon afterwards, his wife Abla receiving promptly from the single civil judge a confirmation of his death. The civil court designated her as 'sole heir' since George died a 'Christian'. Some time in 1968, the late George's 'paternal cousins' manage to 'acquire from the shariʿa court' a 'notification' in which it was claimed that they were 'sole heirs because the deceased died a Muslim and the Islamic religion does not grant a non-Muslim [a right to inherit] (*lā yūrith*)'. George's cousins appealed also the civil court's decision, which 'revoked [its] earlier decision' on grounds of 'incompetence . . . after it was proven that the deceased . . . died a Muslim'. Abla petitioned Beirut's Civil Court of Appeals to overrule both the civil (appeal) and the shariʿa rulings. She claimed that her husband's *madhhab* after the two married had 'no effect . . . since [their] marriage remains subject' to the jurisdiction within which 'it was contracted[,] according to Article 23 of Decree No. 60 L./R.'. It follows that the distribution of the deceased husband's inheritance is to be carried out in accordance with the 'Inheritance Law for Non-Mohammedans'. She also claimed that inheritance in this case falls within the jurisdiction of 'the civil court[,] considering that [George's] switching from Christian to Muslim constituted an evasion of the law (*iḥtiyāl ʿala al-qānūn*)' that was 'intended to dispossess his wife from her legitimate (*sharʿi*) [share in the] inheritance'.[18]

The dispute in the two cases is rooted (and is traced back by the courts to) the husband's/father's change of his religion at some point in the near or distant past. In both cases the change leads to a dispute over his inheritance the settling of which depends on answering the question of who is the rightful heir, and by what law. In Tania's case, the answer depends on determining the identity of the deceased – whether, that is, he died Muslim or Christian – which, in turn rests on the validity of whatever attests or authenticates it. A distinction is made between a legally effective and, therefore, judicially relevant change of religion, and a change that is ineffective, the decisive fact being the bureaucratic formality required by Lebanese law, the only

[18] CC, Decision No. 9, 20 October 1983. *Al-ʿAdl* 1 (October 1983): 235–40.

official and judicially admissible evidence that the change of religion had taken place.

In Abla's case, the answer depends on determining the identity of the marriage – whether, that is, the marriage is Christian or Islamic, which is a matter not of the religious authority before which it was celebrated, but on the location in which it was registered after the change of religion (or *madhhab*) – whether, that is, it was transferred via a transfer of documents to the same jurisdiction to which the switch of religion was carried out. If it did not, then the determination of the identity of the rightful heirs would follow the identity of the marriage, which is decided on the basis of the marriage certificate, not the religion or *madhhab* of the deceased.

Abla's husband's switching from the Christian religion to Islam has no effect on her rights to inherit since he did the switch on his own. The two were neither divorced nor was their marriage annulled before George took a second wife, and they never transferred their marriage to the shariʿa jurisdiction (i.e. from the Roman Catholic to the Sunni), George having contracted a second marriage as a Muslim. Similarly, in the case below, the husband exercises his right to change his religion on his own, despite being bound to a marriage and a family that belonged to a different religion. He displaces himself across jurisdictions with the result that he dies leaving two marriages, two families, and two religious jurisdictions in dispute over his inheritance.

> Ibrahim and Isabel married in the Maronite Church in 1936, and when trouble stirred between them he left for 'Kuwait [where he] switched to Islam in 1953'. He then contracted a 'second Islamic marriage in 1960', 'registered [it] in Beirut at the shariʿa court in 1962', and a few years later switched back to 'Christianity[, choosing] the Orthodox *madhhab*'. He 'died in 1973' leaving behind two wives and six children, four from his first marriage, two from the second. When the second wife, Giselle, petitions a civil judge, he makes a decision to distribute Ibrahim's fortune over all of them, including the first wife and her four children. The latter manage to get the decision quashed by a higher court, which designated them as sole heirs. Giselle appeals that decision a first time and is defeated, petitioning for a second attempt on 9 May 1978.[19]

[19] CC, Decision No. 11/1981, 18 December 1981. *Al-Sharq al-Adna*: 352–64.

A *taghyīr al-dīn* in such cases could also be a pretext to lititgate, as in Georgette's case against her second husband's son from a previous marriage, who calls their marriage into question by claiming that her and his father's *taghyīr al-dīn*, which took place before their marriage, was intended only as a means to free themselves of their previous marriages.

> Georgette, Greek Orthodox, and Antoine, Maronite Catholic, are bound by a Maronite marriage. They sign a notarised agreement on 24 July 1971, proclaiming their 'embracing of (*iʿtināq*) the Orthodox *madhhab*', enabling themselves thereby to petition the Orthodox ecclesiastical court for a separation (*faskh*). Georgette, authorised by an Orthodox bishop (*muṭrān*), then married Shafiq in August 1971, the two remaining childless when he died eight years later. On 15 December 1980, Shafiq's son François, from a previous marriage, managed to acquire a ruling from a Maronite archbishopric 'confirm[ing] Georgette['s]' first marriage and considering them both 'unqualified to contract a subsequent correct (*ṣaḥīḥ*) legitimate (*sharʿī*) marriage'. Georgette challenged the Maronite archbishop's ruling, claiming the Orthodox archbishopric as the only competent authority.[20]

Sincerity, Public Order, Personal Rights

François makes the additional claim that the change of religion of his step-mother and her ex-husband is an attempt at 'legal evasion (*iḥtiyāl ʿala al-qānūn*)' that is intended 'only' as a means to 'acquire a ruling of dissolution' from the Orthodox Church. Doing do, François is arguing that, even if the court finds that the marriage of his step-mother and father were regular (legally valid), her intention to divorce her first husband is nevertheless based on an insincere change of religion – insincere since they utilise it as a pretext to accomplish legal ends – and, therefore, carries no legal effect.

Whether the assertion is true or not does not matter in this case, for the change of religion is executed in conformity with the law. Nevertheless, it helps bring to view the criteria according to which a change of religion (or *madhhab*) is judged: (a) whether it is carried out in conformity with the legal rules of marriage and its consequences (i.e. it does not impinge on the personal rights of others) and the order of jurisdictions (i.e. it does not undermine the

[20] CC, Decision No. 7, 1 November 1983. *Al-ʿAdl* (November 1983): 197–200.

legal order); (b) whether it is legally sincere (i.e. it is not intended as a means to evade the law or commit legal fraud); (c) whether it is accompanied by a bureaucratic formality (also in accordance with the requirements of Lebanese law) and is, therefore, complete and demonstrable.

François's assertion that his mother and her first husband had committed legal fraud remains difficult to substantiate; not so in the case of Olga and Caesar. Eleven years after their first petition to separate, they succeeded in obtaining two decisions: Olga from the Orthodox court ruling for divorce, Caesar from the Catholic court confirming the marriage. They were at once married and not married, and the Catholic and Orthodox jurisdictions (and, by extrapolation, the two *madhhabs* and churches) in conflict, as a result of the couple's choice to change their *madhhab* and initiate a parallel judicial inquiry to the one that was still in process within the Catholic jurisdiction.

It was Caesar who made the appeal, requesting the Court to confirm his and Olga's divorce, in accordance with the Orthodox decision. The Cassation defines its task to be to decide which of the two decisions is valid: the latter, or the Catholic Church's decision to confirm Caesar's and Olga's marriage? The first step in its reasoning is to consider if it falls within the scope of its jurisdiction to question the decisions of the religious judiciaries, which would be the case only if the latter: (a) violated fundamental legal norms or, (b) overstepped the limits of their jurisdiction into that of another.

Moreover, legal evasion (*iḥtiyāl ʿala al-qānūn*) might lead to a violation of the legal 'principle [that] it is not in anyone's capacity . . . to prevent [a person] from being judged by his natural judges (*al-quḍāt al-ṭabīʿiyyīn*)'.[21] In Olga's and

[21] The notion is of French derivation, one of its earlier official appearances being in the Laws of 16 and 24 August, 1790, aimed at organising the judiciary after the Revolution and ratified by Louis XVI. Emmanuel Jeuland, 'Le droit au juge naturel et l'organisation judiciaire', *Revue française d'administration publique* 125, 1 (2008): 33–42. In the New Lebanese Law of Procedure (NLP) of 1983, the expression is mentioned once in a section stipulating the rules specifying judicial competence. 'Locational competence (*al-ikhtiṣāṣ al-makānī*)' corresponds to the jurisdiction to which a person belongs by virtue of residence. 'In cases relating to the bond of marriage', Article 104 of the same law assigns ordinary competence to the court in 'the defendant's last residence in Lebanon' (NLP 1983: Bk. I, Pt. 2, Ch. 5, Sec. 1; Art. 104) Moreover, Article 97 states that his complaint would be dismissed 'if the plaintiff's intention in choosing a defendant's court is merely the removal of competence from the natural judiciary in order to cause the opponent harm'.

Caesar's case, evasion would threaten to 'corrupt the legal norms' and cause a conflict between the Catholic and Orthodox jurisdictions, the prevention of which gives the Court of Cassation 'the right to examine' the case in hand 'to solve the issue of competence'. More specifically, the Cassation considers it its 'duty to examine if the purpose (*al-ghāya*) of . . . [Caesar's] complaint is to turn the defendant [Olga] away from her natural judges'.

In what way could Caesar's complaint turn Olga away from her natural judges? How is the Cassation to know what other purpose Caesar might have to file the complaint – other, that is, than the apparent aim of having the court settle the conflict between the two religious jurisdictions? In other words, how is the Cassation to know what Caesar's 'real' intentions are, and – more to the point – why would it suspect that he had other intentions? The Cassation's suspicions are aroused by the change of *madhhab* or, rather, the frequency, manner and circumstances in which it is carried out in the context in which marriage, its consequences and the family, fall under the jurisdiction of a multiplicity of Christian and Islamic jurisdictions. It is by changing one's *madhhab* that one has the power to displace someone else – a spouse, children – from his or her natural judges; it is by examining the change of religion or *madhhab* that the court gains insight into the purpose of a change of religion and, therefore, the intention in a claim or complaint.

The court cites Article 23 of Decree No. 60 L./R. of 1936, which stipulates that if 'both spouses leave their *ṭā'ifa*, [then] their marriage and the documents and obligations related to [it]' become subject to the 'laws of their new system (*niẓām*), starting on the date [the change] was recorded in the civil registry'. The court then qualifies the rule, adding the condition that it applies only in so far as 'the purpose of [the change of religion or *madhhab*] be not the corruption of rules of public order and competence, and legal evasion'. There is 'evidence' that Olga's and Caesar's *madhhab* 'was a result of complicity for the purpose of breaking the rules of public order and the transfer of . . . [judicial] competencies'. They appear to have 'intended (*'amadā*) the *madhhab* with the purpose (*qaṣd*) of ridding themselves of their natural judges'.[22] How does the Cassation figure out the spouses' intention?

[22] CC, Decision No. 110, 18 September 1951.

Olga had petitioned the Orthodox Court in Mount Lebanon 'before registering the change at the civil registry' – that is, when the marriage was not yet under its jurisdiction. This fact 'shows clearly that the parties intended . . . to break the rules of public order that determine the competent court, namely, the Maronite'. The Cassation found further evidence that they were 'not sincere (*ghayr ṣādiqīn,* also, dishonest),' and the change of *madhhab* 'fraudulent', in the fact of Olga's 'return to her Maronite *madhhab*', and in Caesar's 'declar[ing] under oath before the Rota that he was still upon his Catholic faith'. On the basis of all of this, the Cassation ruled in favour of the decision of the Catholic jurisdiction, concluding that the 'Maronite court and, therefore, the Rotal Court, which is its final instance, [are] competent . . . and repealed the ruling issued by the Orthodox ecclesiastical court'.[23]

A few years later, in a similar case, the same Court of Cassation ruled that the spouses' change of religion was legally 'irrelevant (*lā ʿibra li taghyīr al-dīn*)', since the 'purpose' of the change must not be 'the corruption of the foundations of public order or legal evasion'.[24] It argued that the 'spouses' [of religion] . . . did not follow . . . from conviction (*iqtināʿ*), but was an act of legal fraud by which they intended to' evade 'the authority of the Maronite court' – their 'natural judge' – 'obstruct[ing]', thereby, 'the application of all legal rules'.

A formally similar argument is put forward in 1983, by one of three judges in the case of *Nader* v. *Labban*. The court refrains from investigating the possibility of legal fraud considering it to require an examination of the subject's intention, which is a matter that concerns the subject and his conscience. The court nevertheless finds fault in the change of religion on the basis of the fact that it violates the legal order of competencies and jurisdictions. In a dissenting opinion, one of the three judges on the case points out that among 'the facts' which the ruling seems to have overlooked is that 'the late George . . . had a disagreement with his wife, the appellant, and left her [for] another woman to whom he willed his properties (*awṣa laha bi amlākih*)'. In addition, George 'had already switched' a third time (he did so first from Islam to Catholicism) from 'his Latin *madhhab* to Orthodoxy'

[23] Ibid.

[24] CC, Decision No. 36, 3 April 1956.

before switching back to Islam. Moreover, the dissenting judge pointed out, George 'was not satisfied by the announcement of [his return to Islam] to his relatives and . . . the shariʿa judge, but made sure to complete the formalities in the registry of the General Administration of Personal Status in order to secure secular consequences (*mafāʿīl zamaniyya*)'. These 'facts', argued the judge, are 'sufficient to prove that the hidden purpose' of George's change of religion was to 'dispossess his wife' and constitutes, therefore, 'legal evasion'. George's change of religion is legally irrelevant and does not, therefore, 'alter the system of inheritance' to which he was subject 'prior to that act'.[25]

The disagreement between the court and the dissenting judge is an articulation of a tension among the three criteria of a proper change of religion or *madhhab* that I mention at the beginning of this section. It highlights specifically a tension between the first two criteria – that a change of religion conform to the rules of law and the order of jurisdictions and be enacted through a bureaucratic formality – and the third – that a change of religion not be intended as an act of fraud and legal evasion.

The disagreement reveals another feature of the three criteria, namely, that whereas the first two are positive criteria, the third is a negative criterion. The ruling and the dissenting opinion are two different answers to the same question: if it were shown that a change of religion (or *madhhab*) violated the rules of marriage and the family, was not carried out in accordance with bureaucratic formalities, and was intended to evade the law, which of them would be decisive for the judge: the first two, or the third? In other words, if the first two were confirmed, would the third not fall out of the ruling as superfluous?

The answer seems to depend on the sort of theory of law that frames it: the court, which takes into account in its ruling only the positive criteria, seems to construe the legal order as a positive hierarchy of rules in the maintenance of which intentions do not figure; in contrast, the dissenting judge seems to hold the view that the law and the legal order rest on intentions, from which it follows that the truth of intentions must by the basis of judgment, or at least figure in a judicial decision. An implication of this is that for the dissenting judge, the change of religion (or *madhhab*) is *not* in iteself (rather than its effects) beyond the purview of the secular, civil judiciary and its authority to rule. This dialectic

[25] CC, Decision No. 9, 20 October 1983.

seems to be rooted in (and a surfacing of) the conceptual indeterminacy of 'intention': is it external, written into bodies and discernible in actions, or does it reside in the internal obscurities of the soul (mind, etc. . . .)? If both, what is the relationship between the two – is there continuity or discontinuity between them? If so, is it possible to infer one from the other, and how is the inference to be done? These questions have a bearing on the distinction between 'religious conversion' proper, and 'secular legal displacement' – on the way, that is, they are articulated through *tabdīl al-dīn aw al-madhhab.*

The Question(ability) of Intentions

In several of the cases analysed in this chapter, at least the ones prior to the 1980s, the civil court's concept of intention does not describe 'internal' or 'mental' states, but is embedded in the actions through which it is articulated. Thus, in the earliest of the cases in the series, that of Olga and Caesar, evidence of the spouses' intention to change their *madhhab* is sought in the legal effects of the change, evident in the action and its consequences and requires no further investigation. Their intention to change their *madhhab*, as it surfaces through the Cassation's narration of the facts of the case, is to evade the law and is, therefore, a threat to the foundations of the legal order. The threat of disorder or, more exactly in Olga's and Caesar's case, the disorder they caused in fact by obtaining two contradictory rulings from the Catholic and Orthodox jurisdictions, is sufficient evidence in itself of their intention to evade the law and commit legal fraud, and provides the court the reasons it requires to make a decision.

They are guilty of disrupting the public order because they acted in a way that caused the disruption of the public order, whether they were aware or knew that they were doing so or, if they did so deliberately or not. 'Evidence was available', the court points out, 'that the spouses' leaving their Maronite *ṭā'ifa* was . . . a result of complicity that is intended to disrupt the principles of public order' and evade 'the authority of the ecclesiastical courts'. The evidence 'was inferred from the case and its circumstances' as they emerge from the description of the facts or the sequence of actions and counteractions.

The court presents the evidence: the 'spouses are initially of the Maronite *ṭā'ifa* and subject to the Maronite ecclesiastical courts'; the Maronite court had rejected their claim and transferred the case to the Roman Rota; while the case lingered there, the spouses proceeded to 'switch their *madhhab*' – and this revealed their 'intention to rid themselves of their natural judges'; they filed their complaint before the Orthodox ecclesiastical court while not yet registered as Orthodox – this 'show[ing] clearly' that 'the parties intended to disrupt the rules of the public order'; Olga returned to the Maronite *ṭā'ifa* in the meantime, while Caesar swore before the Roman Rota that he was still a Catholic.

What the court does not say, however, is that the case and its circumstances presuppose a scheme that makes it possible for certain actions and facts to be singled out *as such* and organised in a way that makes legal sense. Implicit in the enumeration of the evidence is that scheme. The narrative that is woven from the sequence of legally relevant facts depends on a hierarchy of norms and procedures that presupposes a definitive configuration of secular – legal and, crucially, moral – categories and concepts, such as public order, intention, evasion, conversion, *and* religion. It is that scheme that makes it possible to single out the facts as legally relevant, to arrange them in a narrative (itself presupposing a normative construal of the temporality of individual action), to construct, thereby, a case, and conclude that Olga and Caesar were 'dishonest', their change of *madhhab* a means to evade the law. It is in virtue of that scheme that the judiciaries (and even the actors of the change of religion) to know that a change is (could be) intended as a means to evade the law – to know, that is, what a legally fraudulent change of religion looks like.

Caesar and Olga were able to do what they did in virtue of the distinction between the two domains of religion and law. This includes the distinction between religious and secular (legal) intent, which makes it possible for the court to pronounce on the change of religion (or *madhhab*) while claiming tacitly neutrality towards religion, in so far as it is pronouncing on the legal intention of the *tabdīl*.

It is in the constitution of an autonomous, secular, legal order, through which the religious, in what pertains to the changing of religion, is consigned to the internal forum of the individual subject's 'mind', and action follows the subject's awareness of the conditions in which he is to act, that reside the enabling conditions of this peculiar sort of action which is *tabdīl al-dīn aw al-madhhab*. It is in virtue of that order that contains it that the latter acquires its uncanny power to cause disorder and undermine the distinction between the religious and secular on which that order depends.

What guarantees the interdependent soundness and safety of switching religions, and what ensures the stability of the order over which it casts its pervasive threat is the eminent subject of law: the subject who, whether Christian or Muslim, is capable of knowing the distinction between the religious and secular (legal), and who, on the basis of that knowledge, proceeds willingly to change his religion (or *madhhab*) and who, therefore, is responsible of the change. (I discuss the relationship between the will and *tabdīl al-dīn* in the following section.) Conversely, in so far as he is a subject of law, and in so far as the change of religion (or *madhhab*) is intentional, it is possible for the judges to hold the subject of the change accountable, and assign *guilt*. Would it not be a violation of the principle of neutrality and the freedom of conscience to scrutinise the subject's beliefs? Is it necessary to do so at all?

The First Instance Civil Court in Mount Lebanon explained the difficulty clearly in a decision issued on 17 May 2002. The 'freedom of belief' is a 'pillar of individual freedom', the court argues, pointing out that it was 'consecrated by (*karrasa*) the Declaration of Human Rights and the Lebanese Constitution'. It then admitted its own lack of competence to 'interfere in the doctrines of persons and examine the depths of their hearts to prove whether their faith is correct (*ṣaḥīḥ*)'. However, it argued, if 'the official appearance' of legal evasion is available to it, it may 'intervene', on condition that the 'aforementioned appearance indicates (*yadull*) clearly that . . . a change of religion was enacted fraudulently[,] which is a violation of the public order'.[26]

The critical distinction in this case is that between 'the depths of hearts' – the forum internum – and the 'external appearance' (in so far as it is official, that is, in accordance with the law). The implication is that, while a direct examination of the former remains beyond the purview of the court, the latter (the appearance) is nevertheless a sign of fraudulent intent. While a sign is sufficient in itself to warrant suspicion and subsequent examination of fraudulent intent, it falls short of constituting evidence – so far, at any rate, and the question urges itself how the court would proceed to demonstrate the presumption of a connection between conscience and appearance.

[26] FICC, Decision No. 54, 17 May 2022.

(A question may be asked here: Is it not conceivable that an 'innocent' intent or a sincere change of religion lead to a legal violation or constitute a threat to the public order?).

In the case of *Francois* v. *Georgette*, one of the claims against the defendant was that her and her ex-husband's change of *madhhab* from Maronite Catholicism to Orthodoxy was fraudulent because they had intended it as a means to acquire a divorce. The court begins its argument by stating the general principle that 'limiting personal freedom and coercion in [matters of] religious doctrine is absolutely not the legislator's intention'. Such a constraint would be contrary to 'what is customary' on the one hand, and against 'the essence of all religions' – that is, religious freedom – on the other. The court's aim is to justify its inability to subject the couple's change of *madhhab* to examination. It would, however, call into question its validity if 'the nullifying means of evasion with the purpose of violating public order and intentionally damaging the interest of others are evident and certain'. The distinction the court is drawing here is between the examination of a *religious conversion* proper and a *secular, legal displacement.* It is the latter that may be carried out with an intention to harm the interests of others and violate the public order. Accordingly, it is the latter that may be scrutinised and judged, on the basis of the available evidence. 'This case', the court maintains, 'lacks such evidence'. Since the court's examination of the defendant's conscience is out of the question, 'legal evasion remains unproven, because the change of *madhhab* is a matter of religion and religious beliefs', and these are 'difficult for the civil courts to delve into in order to say whether faith exists or not'. A change of religion (or *madhhab*) is 'limited to the relationship between the human being and his conscience' (not, notably, between the Christian or Muslim and 'God', 'faith', 'religious authority', 'the religious community' or any other possible 'factor') – that is, a private affair in which the court cannot interfere.[27]

Regarding George's switching to the 'Christian *madhhab*' and the accusation of 'evasion', the court recognises that '*taghyīr al-madhhab* . . . is a personal act related to the individual "self" (*nafs*), thoughts, and beliefs[,] and is a basic human right the legislator guaranteed the citizen'. It then draws

[27] CC, Decision No. 7, 1 November 1983.

a distinction between 'motivations (*dawāfiʿ*)', namely, 'mere belief (*iʿtiqād mujarrad*) and the appeasing of conscience (*rāḥat al-ḍamīr*)', on the one hand, and his equally possible 'intent[ion] to harm (*ilḥāq ḍarar*) his wife the appellant's right' to inherit on the other.[28]

Proceeding without the need to question the former, the court indicates that 'assuming' the latter – 'this harmful and unrighteous act (*hādha al-ʿamal-al-ḍārr wa ghayr al-muḥiqq*)' on the part of her ex-husband – was indeed the case, then 'all she could ask for . . . before the competent civil court . . . is compensation from his legitimate heirs'. This solution ensures the separation between the religious jurisdictions in matters of inheritance, secures 'the public order established in Lebanon', without impinging on the 'personal freedom [of] belief.[29]

The Will to *Tabdīl al-Dīn*, its Freedoms and their Limits

The reference to the freedom of belief and conscience brings out the relevance of the second criterion of *tabdīl al-dīn aw al-madhhab* mentioned above, namely, that a change of religion (or *madhhab*) be carried out according to proper bureaucratic form. It also brings out the reason why 'the outward formal appearance' of a *tabdīl* is considered to be a 'legitimate' basis of judgment for the civil courts. An answer is given in the case of Abla and George, in which the court cites Article 11 of Decree No. 60 L./R., which 'stipulate[s] that every mentally sound adult has the right to leave or embrace a *ṭāʾifa*'. A change of religion, moreover, is legally effective only in so far as it is registered in 'the records of personal status'. Citing the Lebanese Constitution and the Universal Declaration of Human Rights, the court adds that the requirement to register a change of religion or *madhhab* is 'nothing but a confirmation of the freedom of belief, one of the fundamental personal freedoms'.

Article 41 of the Law of 7 December 1951 describes in detail the formality required for any change of religion or *mahdhab* to be considered accomplished. First, 'any petition concerning *taghyīr dīn aw madhhab* is to be sent to the Registry of Personal Status to amend the record'. The petition 'must be supported by a statement from the leader of the *madhhab* or religion to be

[28] CC, Decision No. 9, 20 October 1983.

[29] Ibid.

embraced (*iʿtināq*)' and be 'accompanied by the signature of the postulant'. Then, 'the personal status clerk will . . . summon [the postulant] and ask him, in the presence of two witnesses, if he remains on his decision. If the postulant answers in the affirmative, 'a report (*maḥḍar*) to that effect is drawn up on the petition and the [postulant's civil or personal status] record amended' to reflect the change.

This description of the formality articulates the change of religion or *madhhab* as a process the starting point of which is not determined, but which must end by a demonstration of the petitioner's will that is expressed in writing in an official document. The inscription and the document in which it is inscribed secure for the court the authenticity of the postulant's free will for it presupposes that the formality of *tabdīl*, which involves a performative and discursive operation which consists in his insisting on the finality of his decision to change his religion (or *madhhab*) in the presence of two witnesses and a state official had taken place.

What is supposed to be a matter of conscience and belief is secured as such by means of an act that is carried out in the presence of witnesses and public officials – i.e. *tabdīl al-dīn* turns out to be a matter of personal freedom *and* a public performance through which the latter is put on display and ascertained. The contents of the postulant's beliefs and conscience, or the reasons for his decision to change his religion or *madhhab* are not solicited, concealed within a domain the connection of which with action remaining a matter of inference and suspicion. It is easy to see that the function of the formality is to enact the separation of the private and public, the religious and secular – precisely the same problem to which the judiciaries seem to be responding when they are called upon to settle a dispute that involves a change of religion or *madhhab*.

The stipulations of Article 41 are in some cases the only reference the court requires as a basis to settle a dispute. In the case of Salah, Tony and Hanan, the court rules that the shariʿa decision to grant Salah a hold (*ḥajr*) over his granddaughter is invalid because changing religion 'according to procedure . . . extracts the [one who changes] from the authority of the court of his previous religion (*yukhriju al-muʿtaniq al-jadīd ʿan sulṭān maḥkamat dīnihi al-sābiq*) and subjects him to [that] of his new religion'.[30]

[30] CC, Decision No. 271, 26 March 1970.

In *Tania* v. *The Administration of Islamic Public Endowments in Beirut*, the Court's inquiry begins by 'noting that the deceased Jean, the plaintiff's father, is Greek Orthodox and was registered as such in the census of 1932'. Tania, his daughter, is also Greek Orthodox, because she falls 'under his name' at Beirut's Personal Status Registry. Yet, the shariʿa court claims to 'derive its authority . . . from Jean's certificate of his change of religion to Islam', which it uses to justify its decision to exclude Tania from receiving her share of her father's inheritance. Was that enough?

The court considers 'the point of the inquiry' to be whether 'Lebanese law considers a change of religion accomplished' when it occurs 'before the religious authority of the adopted religion', or only after 'other procedures' are performed 'before Lebanese civil authorities'.[31] It cites Article 41 and 'conclud[es]' from its 'text' and 'expressions' that 'the certificate of the change of religion to Islam' by itself 'is insufficient'. The *tabdīl* must be complete, and for it to be so – in other words, for it to be officially recognised – it must be registered.

'In Lebanese law', the Court explains, 'to correct the record of *taghyīr madhhab aw dīn* . . . the postulant must himself demonstrate his will plainly'. Given the absence of documentary evidence that Jean 'performed the formality . . . before the Administration of Personal Status', his will to change his religion remains undemonstrated and, therefore, the change 'incomplete in the view of Lebanese law', for which he 'remains . . . Christian Orthodox'.

The rationality of the procedure is ambiguous, however. It is considered to be designed to make sure that the postulant is not coerced, but it could also be taken to have a protective function. Thus, it makes it possible to circumvent the 'effects' which *tabdīl al-dīn aw al madhhab* might have on 'Lebanese society[,] which consists of multiple [religious] *ṭawāʾif*' and the *tabdīl's* 'important legal consequences' on that society, 'especially in matters related to inheritance and personal status'.[32]

The transfer of authority across religious jurisdictions is a 'matter related to the social and procedural public order (*al-niẓām al-ʿām al-ijtimāʿī wa al-uṣūlī*)', and the 'legislator's intention in imposing' a formality to execute

[31] The terms with which the Cassation defines the problem are almost identical to those which the Sunni Court used to rule that the case falls outside its jurisdiction.

[32] CC, Decision No. 8, 23 June 1967.

a change of religion is to maintain it 'under civil surveillance (*al-raqāba al-madaniyya*)'. This is another way of saying that there is a limitation to the 'freedom of belief', for it 'does not render permissible the evasion of established rights acquired by' a person as a result of 'an act of marriage in a binding legal institution' that falls outside 'the scope of the freedom of contract'.[33]

In *Giselle* v. *Isabel*, the Cassation Court decides to dismiss the former's case and grant the first wife Isabel and her children full rights of inheritance, 'because', among other reasons, 'the Constitution, if it did guarantee the freedom' to change one's religion 'did not guarantee the freedom to escape from the consequences of marriage' by contracting another. Although the second marriage 'was possible due to that change', marriage in general 'is . . . not a requirement that may not be detached from religion'. The Cassation finds support for this proposition *in* religion itself. Thus, 'if even the Muslim's freedom' may be 'limited' by his wife's condition (in the marriage contract) [that he commit to] monogamy, then 'a Christian attached to another indivisible marriage . . . whose system of personal status does absolutely not accept plural marriages' is even more so; 'neither he, even if he change his religion, nor his second family may limit the rights of a family resulting from a first marriage'.[34]

If the protection of secular order falls under the jurisdiction of the civil (secular) judiciaries, and if *tabdīl al-dīn aw al-madhhab* is essentially a matter that concerns the Christian and Muslim (individual) subject and her conscience and beliefs (within the bounds of that order), then what do the religious judiciaries, whose jurisdiction it is to deal with conjugal and familial disputes, have to say about *tabdīl al-dīn* when they discover it in a dispute of the sort? The problem they face could be described as follows: the religious judiciaries, in so far as they are religious and, therefore, their authority is at stake when a Muslim or Christian changes her religion or *madhhab*, must justify their incompetence to hear a case that involves an act which is (ought to be) relevant to them *religiously* and beyond their purview *legally*. One way to respond – and they have the responsibility to be responsive – to the problem is to spell out, qua religious jurisdictions, a distinctively religious (normative) attitude

[33] Ibid.

[34] CC, Decision No. 11/1981, 18 December 1981.

towards *tabdīl al-dīn*, while providing secular (legal) reasons to justify their lack of competence to decide (i.e. to act legally on the change of religion). The next two sections discuss, respectively, a shariʿa and an ecclesiastical approach to the problem of *tabdīl al-dīn aw al madhhab*.

The Civil Muslim

On 19 December 1994, the prosecutor general at the Higher Sunni Shariʿa Court elaborates an opinion regarding an appeal against the first instance court involving a change of religion. The appellant objects to the lower court's decision 'for it was based on the reasoning (*al-ijtihād*) of the Cassation Court's General Assembly . . .' These precedents 'establish that the formalities (*uṣūl*) for changing religion . . . are obligatory and related to public order'. Moreover, that same reasoning considers 'the certificate of declaration of Islam issued by the Islamic religious authority (*al-marja al-dīni al-islāmi*) . . . insufficient by itself to consider . . . Muslim' the person who performs the change.' Finally, pointing out the distinction between 'positive law' and 'God's shariʿa', the appellant concludes by asserting that 'it is impermissible (*la yajūz*) to ignore the rules of the shariʿa'.[35]

The prosecutor general, however, sees things differently. Having restated the plaintiff's demands as reasons for his intervention, he proceeds to enumerate the steps required, by law *and* shariʿa, to convert to Islam. He begins with the 'benevolent Islamic shariʿa, which considers the embracing of the righteous religion (*iʿtināq al-dīn al-ḥanīf*) to have taken place after the postulant's (*al-rāghib bi tabdīl dīnih*, lit. the one who desires to change his religion) uttering of the *shahādatayn* [that there is no god but God, and that Muhammad is His Prophet], and by releasing (*tabriʿatihi*) him from any other religion [than] the religion of Islam'.

The prosecutor cites two clauses from the law of procedure for the shariʿa judiciary, one specifying the judges' sources of authority in a descending order of priority (the first being the 'most probable sayings of Abu Hanifa', followed by the Ottoman 'Law of Family Rights'), another defining the Sunni judiciary's competence. He closes his argument with a reason he derives from Lebanese Sunni legal memory. '[T]he Sunni shariʿa courts,' he reminds the

[35] PG, Decision No. 483/94, 19 December 1994.

appellant (and the court), 'used in the past to go by the shariʿa rule that *ishhār al-islām* alone was enough to grant it civil consequences (*mafāʿīl madaniyya*)'. However, he continues, they 'used to be confronted, when their decisions were blocked', by the claim that they had 'contraven[ed] essential formulations related to public order'. A consequence of this was that 'the Cassation Court consider[ed] [the Sunni decisions] non-executable and void'. The prosecutor then gives detailed summaries of five Cassation Court rulings on the changing of religion (to Islam) – one from 1967, two from 1970, and two from 1972 – and proceeds to elaborate an interpretation of what they mean for Islam and Muslims. The five decisions have in common Article 41, Law of 7 December 1951, the object of the appeal in the present case. How does the prosecutor general at the Higher Sunni Shariʿa Court justify the obligation that it obey the rule of secular, positive law?

With the backing of 'Article 1 of the Law Organizing the Shariʿa Judiciary' he states 'that the [latter] is part of the state's judicial organs (*tanẓimāt*)'. This implies that, according to 'the Law of Civil Procedure', the Cassation Court possesses 'the right to examine' a shariʿa court's decisions 'for incompetence . . . or contravention of essential formulations (*ṣiyagh*, singular *ṣīgha*) relating to public order (*al-niẓām al-ʿām*)'. This means that the Cassation Court has 'the right to regulate (*al-raqāba*)' the court's decisions 'if it transgresses the limits of its competence, or if it contravenes essential formulations'.

This is the case for two related reasons: first, to ensure the proper organisation and functioning of the legal process 'among the shariʿa, *madhhabiyya*, and ecclesiastical (*rūḥiyya*) courts', and second, to 'prevent transgressions among them[,] for the sake of securing accord (*al-wifāq*) among the *tawāʾif* of which Lebanon is composed'. What justifies the Cassation Court's role of overseer is the aim of realising 'judicial safety among all "religious" courts'.[36]

Does this mean that judicial safety overrides religious considerations or, more seriously, constitutes an affront to Islam? Answering this question in the negative, the prosecutor explains that 'it must be acknowledged that *al-dīn al-ḥanīf* (the Righteous Religion) is neither a state religion, nor the religion of the majority of Lebanon's population'. Moreover, 'it is not permissible to deny that in Lebanon positive or *taʾifiyya* laws exist that must be applied to the

[36] Ibid.

citizens of the country'. For these reasons, it is no 'embarrassment (*iḥrāj*) to Islam if it was in agreement with the other religious systems (*al-anẓima al-dīniyya*)', for 'Islam is inside every Muslim and has nothing to do with its civil dimensions (*abʿād madaniyya*). Therefore, 'the Muslim remains a Muslim or becomes a Muslim if he was not one originally regardless of personal status records'.

The issue is not one of 'doctrine [since] the Muslim [can] practice his religion's norms (*sharāʾiʿ*) . . . without the mediation of his record in the civil state's registries . . .'; he does not require 'an identification card to indicate that he is a Muslim (*min al-muslimīn*)' for him to 'pray at the mosque and fast'.[37] In regards to the Sunni judiciary, 'there is no embarrassment [either]', the prosecutor asserts, 'if it applied the rules of Lebanese positive law since it must respect that law, as does the ordinary [civil] judiciary'.[38]

A change of religion to Islam entails another kind of problem, which the prosecutor describes as follows: 'the Lebanese Christian citizen who truly wishes to change his record to Muslim, can do so easily, and there is no legal obstacle that prevents him from doing so'. It is for this reason that 'his announcing his Islam by merely uttering the two testimonies' is 'not enough to consider him a Muslim', at least not 'in the light of the Lebanese positive codes'. The announcement 'must necessarily be followed by an amendment to his civil status record (*al-nufūs*)'.[39]

While it is unclear what it could mean to truly wish to change one's record to Muslim, what the prosecutor highlights are the legal and political stakes involved in a change of religion or *madhhab* – the freedom to carry it out, and the ease, specifically, with which it may be carried out in virtue of that freedom. He continues, 'legal protection, judicial competence, and the exercise of worldly and political rights are connected[,] in the Lebanese system[,] to those records'. Where exactly is the problem? While the prosecutor has so far been emphasising the separation of the civil and the religious, he now points out that they are not so easily severed, the link between the two consisting in that indivisible legal subject, the 'individual person (*al-shakhṣ al-waḥīd*)'.

[37] Ibid.

[38] Ibid.

[39] Ibid.

The prosecutor articulates this problem when he insists that a person 'cannot be considered a Muslim according to the document of declaration of Islam' on the one hand, 'and a Christian according to his record at the personal status registry' on the other. '[I]s he Muslim here', he asks, rhetorically, 'and non-Muslim there?' In a legal regime that is set up in such a way as to guarantee religious distinctiveness and difference, and in which official documentation, rather than specifically religious practice (as prescribed by the shariʿa in this case) is the instrument by which to secure religious identity, is it so easily separable from that instrument? Accordingly, how is the person's identity as Muslim (or Christian, for that matter) to be determined? How is that presumed identity kept from splitting apart? The prosecutor finds the answer in 'Lebanese law', which 'proscribed' – and, he could have added, enabled – 'this duality of belonging (*al-izdiwājiyya fi-l-intimā'*) to more than one *ṭā'ifa*'.

So how would the shariʿa courts handle a case of 'a Muslim not registered as a Muslim'? They have the 'right . . . to consider [that he is not] a civil Muslim', for legal and political reasons.[40] Considering him so (*musliman madaniyyan*) does not mean that the court 'doubts' his faith, but is rather a way to protect the Islamic judiciary. The prosecutor general is concerned that the shariʿa court's decision be defeated by a civil court. Thus, the reason the shariʿa judiciary is not authorised to hear an unregistered Muslim's case is not that it cast his Islam in doubt, but that 'all of the Cassation Court's rulings were annulling its [own] decisions', and because of the 'requirements of coexistence' between the different religions in Lebanon.

Given these considerations, completing the 'civil appearance (*al-maẓhar al-madani*)' of the change of religion or *madhhab*, which, according to the prosecutor, is a mere formality after all, is a minor affair. 'If he neglects' to do so, the prosecutor points out, 'he has only himself to blame, not the shariʿa judiciary'.[41] The prosecutor's function is to safeguard the authority of the shariʿa courts, Islamic public order and the Islamic interest by making sure that the secular positive law and the shariʿa are 'not opposed', but 'complement[ary to] each other for the good of the Islamic *umma* (*fi sabīl khayr al-umma al-islāmiyya*)'.[42]

[40] Ibid.

[41] Ibid.

[42] Ibid.

The Permanent Mark of Baptism

How do ecclesiastical courts explain their lack of competence to settle cases of personal status that involve a change of religion or *madhhab*? Shafiqa's story begins with her marriage to Pedro 'according to the Maronite Catholic *madhhab* (*'ala al-madhhab al-mārūni al-kāthulīki*)' in Accra on 29 July 1939. Thirty-two years later, Pedro 'became a Muslim (*aslama*)', married Slovakia, and had three children who remained illegitimate because 'he could not register them under his name'. According to the plaintiff, one of the 'proposed solutions' is that she and Pedro change their *madhhab* to Greek (*rūm*) Orthodoxy 'in order to divorce' and clear the way for Pedro to have his marriage with Slovakia validated and their children registered.

Shafiqa 'accepted the offer . . . [for the sake of] the innocent children and', the court adds, out of greediness for the ten million Lebanese Liras paid her from her husband's immense wealth'. Forty-one years after his first marriage and nine after his change of religion to Islam, Pedro finally managed to acquire a divorce ruling from the Orthodox ecclesiastical court and get his (Islamic) marriage to Slovakia validated, as it had until then remained non-existent from a civil legal standpoint.

In her petition to the Maronite ecclesiastical court Shafiqa asked the court to overturn the Orthodox ruling, to 'therefore nullify the subsequent marriage', and to 'consider the three children . . . *awlād zina* (illegitimate)'. Slovakia's response was straightforward: the Maronite court is 'not competent' to hear the case 'according to Article 23' of Decree No. 60 L./R., which stipulates that 'if the spouses changed their religion or *madhhab*, then their marriage and the documents and obligations related' to it 'would be transferred to the corresponding jurisdiction'.

The court's response begins with a formulation, enunciated recurrently by civil judges in similar cases, of a distinction between 'freedom of belief (*ḥurriyyat al-mu'taqad*)', which is guaranteed by 'the Constitution', on the one hand, and the act of 'ridding [oneself] of the religious judiciary' under whose jurisdiction one falls on the other. Article 23 is an articulation of both, freedom and public order, conversion and marriage – that is, the logical distinction between them and the contingency of their connection. In other words, it admits the possibility of either and of both, but the court argues that it was stipulated in order 'to protect the freedom of conscience', rather than 'encourage legal evasion'. This sense of the article must be the correct one, because 'it ought not to be (*lā yajūz*) that such a fraudulent intent be attributed to the legislator'.

Invoking good faith and judicial sincerity as the fundamental principles of legal order (and, therefore, of its own authority), the ecclesiastical court declares that 'the Catholic Church, with what it feels about the obligation to proselytise and spread Christ's teachings, upholds' the freedom of belief. Accordingly, the 'Maronite *ṭāʾifa*' (*not*, notably, 'the Church', which suggests that the court speaks: (a) in the name of the Maronite *ṭāʾifa* in its secular and religious constituents; (b) as a Maronite institution specifically, rather than an institution of the Catholic Church) considers the Maronite who converts with 'a firm belief in Islam or Orthodoxy' a 'miscreant and dissenter (*jāḥidan wa māriqan*) and, therefore, excluded from, and stripped of his rights, in it'. However, due to 'the permanent mark of baptism', he remains 'tied to [the *ṭāʾifa*'s] past, present, and future laws', by which he will be 'judged' and 'redeeming punishment be imposed on him if he repents and returns to it'.

The court emphasises that belief is the true basis of conversion, ruling out secular or temporal motives or intentions, such as converting to acquire a divorce (a distinction which the civil, shariʿa, and ecclesiastical court all have in common). Whatever might be 'the Maronite['s]' motives to convert – 'conviction', 'deceit', 'legal evasion[,] or love of money or status' – and even if he legally divorces and remarries, the Maronite Church (note that the subject here is the Church, not the *ṭāʾifa*) still considers 'null' both 'his divorce and his new marriage' and, therefore, 'his children from [the latter] illegitimate . . . despite what Article 23 stipulates'.

The Church, the court continues, is concerned with the 'spiritual aspect' of the change of religion – i.e. religious conversion, not legal displacement – and is 'uninterested' in its 'strictly civil consequences', such as 'support', 'inheritance', or 'dowry', the settling of which 'it leaves up to the civil courts'. The court's religious – Christian, Catholic – attitude towards the conversion of one of its own and the secular reasons it gives to explain its lack of competence to hear the case are mutually reinforcing. Thus, it argues that the current case is not 'presented according to proper [procedural] form', which, since its 'object' is 'inheritance', ought to consist in asking the following question this way, 'In the view of the Maronite Church, is the marriage of Shafiqa . . . and Pedro . . . still valid when he died?' This would have enabled the

Maronite court to 'decide upon its authority to at least present the Church's correct teaching on this issue'.

The Maronite court interprets the distribution and separation of religious jurisdictions in a way that construes these jurisdictions as a representation of the various *madhāhib*. In a subtle statement, it draws a distinction between the 'legal actions of another [religious] *ṭāʾifa*', which the ecclesiastical court is 'not to judge . . . and declare null' on the one hand, and the decision of another religious court as a legal action that is performed regardless of whether it 'represents' the people that fall under its jurisdiction or not. The court considers the latter the formal legal expression of the 'system of religious *ṭawāʾif*' described in Decree No. 60 L./R. and, therefore, a strictly legal matter.

The Maronite ecclesiastical court explains that, contrary to what Slovakia claims, it is not the case that it lacks the competence to hear the case – which is a civil procedural reason – but rather, in moral-religious terms, that it is 'not concerned (*ghayr maʿniyya*)' about 'declaring null and void' a ruling of 'divorce' issued or 'a marriage' contracted in a 'non-Catholic *ṭāʾifa*'. 'In other matters', it concludes, 'the decision is left to the civil authority the laws of which we must respect and act upon, unless it contravenes the essence of religion.'

Conclusion

Tabdīl al-dīn aw al-madhhab, or the changing of religion or *madhhab* is ambiguous. It is not always obvious or explicit whether it involves a religious conversion, whether what is being intended by it when it is executed is a legal displacement, or whether it is both. A person may 'experience' a religious conversion while stopping short from pursuing a legal displacement. Conversely, another may execute a legal displacement while not going through any religious conversion (prior to or accompanying the act). Some opt for a legal displacement with exclusively secular intentions in mind, whether in good or bad faith, while a religious convert might make the choice to transfer her marriage and the legal affairs of her family in order to be consistent with her new faith. For their part, the civil judiciaries pronounce on *tabdīl al-dīn aw al-madhhab* insofar as it entails a secular displacement – in so far, that is, as it includes an action and carries, in the Lebanese legal arrangement, legal effects. The religious judiciaries pronounce on it as well, but only in so far as it involves religious conversion, and they do so in their religious (shariʿa, spiritual, moral) capacity (keeping in mind that the shariʿa and ecclesiastical pronouncements on it differ).

Whatever the case may be, *tabdīl al-dīn aw al-madhhab* in both of its components is a matter that concerns the (individual) subject (the Muslim and Christian person) and her relationship with her conscience and beliefs, be they religious or secular. This assumption, on which the preceding possibilities all depend, is cross-jurisdictional, as it supports the reasoning and decisions of the secular (civil) and religious (shariʿa and ecclesiastical) judiciaries. This is plain enough in the preceding analysis, but what is not so plain is that implicit in *tabdīl al-dīn aw al-madhhab* is the secular idea that 'Islam' and 'Christianity' (and religions in general) designate equally valid, comparable, and interchangeable forms of life in and out of which an individual may enter and exit at will.

PART II

FORMS OF LIFE

3

CHRISTIAN MARRIAGE, MEDICAL KNOWLEDGE AND THE ATTRIBUTES OF THE PERSON

'. . . I don't believe in the institutional and clerical baggage of religion, . . . it is too complicated and burdensome to marry in Lebanon . . . suffocating with its ritual and paraphernalia, its conspicuous celebrations and dress codes.'[1]

'Examination *(al-faḥṣ)* . . . must . . . [show] that there is nothing that impedes the valid contracting or permitting of the marriage. . . . The priest [is called upon to] examine with earnestness what might constitute an impediment to the contracting of the marriage. [He is to] ask the engaged couple, carefully and each separately, if need be, if they are constrained by any impediment and if they – especially the fiancée – are free in giving their consent, and if they know enough Christian catechism . . . It is up to the local Church leader to stipulate specific rules regarding this examination that is incumbent upon the priest.'[2]

'It is incumbent on any petitioner [male or female] for marriage to acquire prior to the processing of the marriage contract before any religious or civil authority a medical certificate . . .', which 'includes the results of clinical, microscopic, and radiological tests for diseases that are defined by a decision issued from the minister of public health . . .'[3]

[1] Informant, Melkite ('Greek') Catholic, about her choice to contract a civil marriage.

[2] 'What Must Precede the Marriage Covenant', Title 1, Law of Marriage for Eastern Catholic Churches, Canon 9.

[3] Articles 1 and 2 of Legislative Decree No. 78, 9 September 1983. 'The Requirement for a Medical Certificate Before Marriage'. Al-Zein, *Qawanin wa Nusus wa Ahkam* (Christians).

'Announcements (*al-munādāt*) [take place] at the church, three Sundays or other holidays, consecutive, during the Holy Mass attended by a large number of people . . . hang the names of the petitioners to the marriage in public on the door of the parish church or other churches, for the duration of eight days, such that in that period coincide two major holidays . . . [The faithful are to] reveal to the priest or the local Church leader what impediment [to the prospective marriage] they might have noted.'[4]

'There is no divorce here, go see the Orthodox.'[5]

'These [the ecclesiastical court's archives] are [a record of] people's suffering (*muʿanāt al-nās*).'[6]

'. . . civil marriage is requested by those who have no faith (*yu'minūn*) in the Church or the Qur'an or Islam . . . we accept freedom and the freedom of belief (*al-muʿtaqad*) . . . [T]he Church in general, and the Catholic Church in particular, do not object [against] those who want to exercise this right . . . but . . . if our brethren the Muslims do not consent [to it], then it is not possible that Christians [do so], because . . . [e]ither the Lebanese are equal in everything or they are not . . . Equality before the law requires that we stand by our Muslim brethren . . .'[7]

This is a collection of statements about Catholic marriage. It articulates a constellation of religious and secular concepts, attitudes, and practices, that suggest a specifically Lebanese Christian and Catholic sensibility or form of life (or a swathe of it). The picture of marriage it renders is of a nexus of religious doctrines, moral-juridical categories, medical procedures and technologies, political contingencies, and normative assumptions (e.g. about the human body). As in any such nexuses, marriage is prone to crises, and the likelihood is always present that a crisis lead to a breakdown. Once it becomes clear that the crisis is not resolvable, the prospect of annulling the (Catholic) marriage appears on the horizon.

[4] Ibid.

[5] Ecclesiastical judge at the Maronite ecclesiastical courts, answering my inquiry about divorce.

[6] It is these words that the same ecclesiastical judge used to justify his refusal to grant me access to the court's archives. They are records of 'people's suffering' and suffering is not, one is expected to conclude, a matter for public display.

[7] The Maronite Patriarch's discourse during the polemic that followed the President of the Republic's 'proposal for a civil law of marriage' in 1998 (Sunday sermon, *Annahar*, 23 March 1998, p. 5).

A marriage would be annulled when an examination of the conditions that bring it into being and ensure its persistence, and in which the crisis is rooted, shows that the conditions are defective. As long as the marriage is doing more or less well (e.g. the crisis is latent, or it is worked through with more or less success), the conditions of marriage remain implicit in it; a terminal crisis and the subsequent examination that precedes the annulment of a marriage would make them explicit. Accordingly, an analysis of the examination makes explicit the nexus of agencies and powers, institutions and authorities, and assumptions and norms that are constitutive of Catholic marriage in general, and, in the Lebanese legal arrangement, of the ways in which marriage functions as an articulation of the religious and secular (legal), ensures the mutual availability of the religious (the Christian) and the law, and marks the difference and distinctiveness of a Christian form of life (or sensibility).

Maronite Catholic ecclesiastical courts in Lebanon annul marriages for a variety of different reasons. Some marriages are nullified due to 'psychological incapacity linked to natural incompatibility between the spouses' characters, making it impossible to undertake the burdens of marital life'.[8] The wife may also be found to have been 'incap[able]', at the time she consented, 'to assume the essential duties and obligations of matrimony'.[9]

Sometimes the court declares the marital bond null and void 'on grounds of extreme fear borne by the husband', or his 'incapacity to assume the burdens of marital life'. In some cases, the court's decision to annul a marriage is followed by an injunction, 'prohibit[ing]' the spouse 'from marrying again before the competent ecclesiastical authority gives [him or her] permission to do so, on the basis of the opinion of a psychiatrist (*ṭabīb nafsāni*)',[10] or 'before receiving the parish priest's authorisation, on the basis of a medical report showing that [she or he] is capable' to do so.[11]

What is the relationship between Maronite (Catholic) marriage and medical discourse (practice)? What does a Maronite marriage and medical

[8] MUFIC, Decision No. 173/92, 27 April 1993 (George and Katia). Abou Eid (ed.), *Al-Qararat al-Kubra*, 41: 2–153.

[9] MUFIC, Decision Issued 5 August 1988 (Eleanor and Sami). Abou Eid (ed.), *Al-Qararat al-Kubra*, 7 (Beirut), pp. 53–93; p. 93.

[10] MUFIC, Decision No. 50, 10 February 1988 (Salwa and John). Abou Eid (ed.), *Al-Qararat al-Kubra*, 8 (Beirut), pp. 1–35; p. 35.

[11] MUFIC, Decision Issued 5 August 1988 (Eleanor and Sami), p. 93.

discourse (practice) have in common? How come Maronite ecclesiastical courts in Lebanon decide to annul a marriage only after the spouses had gone through a thorough medical examination and been given a diagnosis? What is it about medical discourse and Maronite marriage that enables ecclesiastical judicial authority to justify the conclusion it draws that a marriage is null and void? How does 'the law' figure into all of this? What is the support on which this convergence of positive law, Maronite marriage, and medical discourse (practice) rests?

Answer: the person or, more exactly, the person's body (what this is will become clear later). For the Maronite marriage is a Catholic marriage and, therefore, a Holy Sacrament of the Church. Two persons – bodies – enter into union with each other through a blessed act of mutual consent. Consent is an act of will the validity of which presupposes that it is given by a 'normal' person – that is, a person who is sound in mind and body. Once consent is given, and the covenant in which it joins a couple is blessed, it is absolutely irrevocable. It is possible, however, to annul a marriage: an ecclesiastical court declares it non-existent.

For a marriage to be annulled, the act of consent on which it has been based must be ruled defective. The causes of a defective consent reside in the person or, specifically, the person's body, and if it could plausibly be shown that the person is ill and incapable, therefore, of issuing an act of will (consent), it follows, then, that the marriage never took place – that is, it is null and void. The means by which a body could plausibly be said to be incapable of issuing a valid act of consent that binds a person to another in a sacred union is medical discourse, conveyed to the ecclesiastical court by medico-legal experts.[12]

A Very Short Introduction to Modern Catholic Marriage

Catholic marriage acquired its 'modern' cast with the Second Vatican Council, which sought answers to urgent questions about 'the ultimate

[12] The practice is common to Catholic courts elsewhere, including the Roman Rota. See John T. Noonan Jr, *Power to Dissolve: Lawyers and Marriages in the Courts of the Roman Curia* (Cambridge, MA: The Belknap Press of Harvard University Press, 1972).

destiny of reality and of humanity'.[13] The latter were felt to be going though a 'crisis' that threatened the 'human person', 'marriage and the family' and 'human society'. It was in response to the crisis that the Church strove to cast Holy Matrimony as a 'community of love' and an 'intimate partnership of married life and love', introducing thus a vocabulary that was absent from the Canon Law of 1917, effective at the time.[14] Marriage remains the result of an act of consent, but the sense of the latter shifts from contract to covenant.[15]

Whereas consent in the Code of 1917 meant a 'union of the flesh', it now involves the whole person. It constitutes a relationship of 'mutual help and service' between spouses 'through an intimate union of their persons and . . . actions'. A man and woman consenting to marry consent to 'mutually bestow and accept each other' in a binding 'relationship'.[16] An act of consent is an act of exchanging 'a gift of two persons' – and not just a unity of the flesh – through which the spouses are joined together in an 'experience [of] the meaning of their oneness'. The new definition presupposes an adjustment of the concept of the person, or a shift in emphasis on which of the features that are constitutive of personhood enter into the conjugal experience. The person who enters into a marriage does so not only as 'flesh' (no matter in what sense this is taken), and does so not for the sole aim of exchanging (sexual) rights to the body (as stipulated in the Code of 1917). 'The person', rather, is now the phenomenological end of marriage, and not only the means for other – social or biological – ends.[17] The person who enters a marriage does so not just as flesh or an instrument of the flesh, but as a self, a subject of experience and meaning. Conversely, marriage in the 'modern' definition is a meaningful experience of personhood as a whole and, in a sense, an experience of wholeness.

[13] *Gaudium et Spes* (henceforth, *GS*) §4, §77 and §82, respectively. The document is available at http://www.vatican.va/archive/hist_councils/ii_vatican_council/documents/vat-ii_const_19651207_gaudium-et-spes_en.html (retrieved 18 March 2011).

[14] *GS* §47 and §48.

[15] William LaDue, 'Conjugal Love and the Judicial Structure of Christian Marriage', *Jurist* 34 (1974): 36–67; p. 37.

[16] *GS* §48.

[17] *GS* §46.

If Christian marriage presupposes a Christian (concept of the) person, who wills freely an act of consent to enter into a marriage, then how different is the Christian person from the secular subject of 'civil marriage' – the sovereign individual, immediately present to her 'self', in full possession of her body, and to whom the world is, in virtue of that body, always accessible?[18] A hint towards an answer is to point out that the Christian person's world consists, among other things, in the exhortations and recommendations of the Pastoral Constitution (i.e. by the Church), which belong to the Catholic constellation, give substance and sense to the nexus of marriage, and structure the Catholic's expectations as he or she makes the decision to consent to it.

Thus, love is the 'appropriate enterprise of matrimony'.[19] Love, or, specifically, 'authentic conjugal love', as opposed to 'mere erotic inclination' and romantic feelings, is permanent and oriented towards the other – another person, that is, rather than one's own self and body. It 'fortifies' the 'Christian spouses', 'suffuses their . . . lives with faith, hope, and charity', and enables them to 'energetically acquit themselves of' their duties.[20] Love is 'the animating energy . . . which reveals itself through various signs and expressions' of affection. While 'eminently human', dispensed by the 'affection of the will', love is also 'blessed' by 'Christ the Lord', 'wells up . . . from the fountain of divine love'. Indeed, it is 'structured . . . on the model of His union with His Church', 'caught up into divine love', 'governed and enriched by Christ's redeeming power and the saving activity of the Church'.[21]

The Council seems to suggest that love is a natural disposition – that is, an essential disposition of human nature. The interweaving of marriage, love, and the person, and its grounding in '(human) nature', makes it possible to assert the continued relevance and force of 'the natural law argument for marriage', despite the latter's 'modern' Catholic rehabilitation.[22] This carries

[18] A civil law of marriage (or a law of civil marriage) does not exist in Lebanon. Several attempts have been made in the past to pass one. It is a recurrent topic in Lebanese politics, waxing and waning depending on the conjunctures and priorities that prevail at a certain time. Abillama, 'Contesting Secularism'.

[19] *GS* §49.

[20] *GS* §48.

[21] LaDue, 'Conjugal Love', p. 41.

[22] Gary J. Quinn, 'A New Look at Christian Marriage', *Journal of Religion and Health* 10, 4 (1971): 395.

judicial consequences, for it provides the basis for a solution to the 'problem of incorporating the findings of modern psychology and psychiatry into [the Catholic] legal system' and, crucially, to articulate Catholic marriage and secular positive law, and find reasons for annulling marriages.[23] The connection between Catholic marriage and the secular law could now be found in the idea of a freely willed act of consent and an appeal to a naturalistic concept of the body, the two constituents of the Catholic person.

This conception made its way into the new Code of Canon Law of 1983.[24] The act of consent remains in the new code an act of the will, and its validity still depends on several conditions already present in the earlier code, such as non-ignorance of the essence of marriage and its ends, knowledge concerning the person, and the alignment of the 'internal consent of the mind' and 'the words and signs used in celebrating marriage'.[25] However, in the new code, the act of consent no longer consists in the renunciation of the flesh, but in the mutual donation of selves.[26] 'Matrimonial consent is an act of the will by which a man and a woman mutually give and accept each other.' It is a covenant 'by which a man and a woman establish between themselves a partnership of the whole life', for 'the good of the spouses' (in addition to, and no longer solely for, 'procreation' and the duty of seeing to the 'education of offspring').[27]

Once it is admitted that marriage is a 'covenant based on an interpersonal relationship instead of [a contract based] on a merely physical one, the door is opened to the possibility that one of the parties is unable, for

[23] Charles Donahue, 'Comparative Reflections on the "New Matrimonial Jurisprudence" of the Roman Catholic Church', *Michigan Law Review* 75, 5/6 (1977): 994.

[24] The Code was promulgated on 25 January 1983, and came into force ten months later on 27 November. Interestingly, the Lebanese government issued Legislative Decree No. 78, on 9 September, 'imposing a pre-marital medical certificate', which 'includes the results of clinical, microscopic, and radiological tests defined by a decision issued from the minister of public health'. See Al-Zein, *Qawanin wa Nusus wa Ahkam* (Christians).

[25] Code of Canon Law (henceforth, CCL) 1983, nC1096 §1, nC1097, and nC1101 §1, respectively. The 1990 Code of Canons of the Oriental Churches adopts the same definition of consent as the Code of Canon Law of 1983, but underscores the 'irrevocability' of the covenant that results from it.

[26] Donahue, 'Comparative Reflections', p. 999.

[27] CCL 1983, nC1055.

psychological or other relevant reasons, to undertake to form' it.[28] The passage from the claim that marriage is an interpersonal relationship, to the hypothesis that the cause of its failure resides in one of the parties is made through the idea that a person who consents to it must be capable of it. According to the Code of Canon Law of 1983, 'incapable of contracting marriage' are 'those who lack sufficient use of reason', 'suffer from a grave defect of discretion of judgment concerning matrimonial rights and duties', and 'are not able to assume the essential obligations of marriage for causes of a psychic nature'.[29] If it is found that either spouse or both of them suffer from one or a combination of those 'impediments' to marriage, this then gives an ecclesiastical court reason to consider the prospect of declaring a marriage null and void.

Symptoms of Suffering, Signs of Crisis

The Catholic concept of marriage as just summed up figures into a case of annulment along with and at the same point at which the facts are collected and laid out. In a sense, it is constitutive of the facts, determining the very construction of 'a case'. Catholic marriage structures the perception through which a couple's conjugal life and its vicissitudes appear, it gives form to the narrative in which they are made recognisable to the ecclesiastical judiciaries and available to their judgment – and, importantly, the secular, positive law (and, through it, the Lebanese state). Each case is an articulation of the personal and medical, the 'mental' and physical, the experiential and diagnostic, and the sacred and profane, the two terms of each couple mutually reinforcing each other.

Salwa and John, for example, met and became friends as members of an apostolic movement. Their friendship developed into mutual love sealed in a marriage 'crowned by the child Richard'. John, however, had shown signs of illness prior to the wedding, having collapsed a year earlier, and suffered regular stomach aches afterwards. The gastrointestinal specialist who examined him suspected a neurological cause and referred him to a neurologist. The results of the neurological examination coming back negative, the couple saw no impediment to the marriage and went ahead with the wedding. John's suffering continued to

[28] Eileen F. Stuart, *Dissolution and Annulment of Marriage by the Catholic Church* (Sydney: Federation Press, 1994), p. 79.

[29] CCL 1983, nC1095.

disturb the 'peace of common life', terminating it with a 'permanent separation' two years later.[30]

The troubles of another couple began during the period when they were still getting acquainted with each other. The man discovered that 'his future wife was reluctant to have an explicit physical relationship'. He 'immediately took her to [a] doctor . . . a specialist in this matter'. They later visited a 'specialist in psychiatric medicine' who, after learning about 'Eleanor's condition was reluctant to encourage them to get married'. The marriage did not succeed, because the wife 'kept refusing [to have sexual intercourse] with her husband, despite her previous promises . . . to control her reservations and fears'.

The couple consulted a 'gynaecological surgeon . . . to carry out a "vaginal widening" operation . . .' in order to 'end the organic tensions and facilitate quick physical intercourse'. Things kept getting worse until the wife could no longer live with her husband 'under the same roof . . . making sure that [another] person' was present. Further medical intervention included 'artificial insemination', which failed, and a visit to a 'sexologist' whom she saw 'only once'. 'Moral and spiritual consultation' led to no positive result either. As described in the case transcript, after continued efforts on the husband's part, the wife finally stopped seeking assistance and 'expressed her ultimate intention, which . . . she would repeat during every attempt to have sexual intercourse to put an end to her legal relationship with [him]'.[31]

In the third case, George and Katia were married after a period of 'mutual liking lasting around a year and a half prior to the wedding'. George asked Katia to quit a job she had at the time and take up another before they married, 'feel[ing] relieved' when she agreed to do so. He apparently ignored his friends' and relatives' 'warnings about the negative consequences of his marrying a girl characterised by an authoritarian impulse'. They saw that the couple was incompatible, due to her 'masculine tendency to take initiative', considering that a woman who had 'surrendered her femininity' would be difficult to live with for a man 'known not to forfeit his masculinity so easily'.[32]

[30] MUFIC, Decision No. 50, 10 February 1988 (Salwa and John).

[31] MUFIC, Decision Issued 5 August 1988 (Eleanor and Sami).

[32] MUFIC. Decision No. 173/92, 27 April 1993 (George and Katia).

'Two weeks prior to the wedding, the husband' had not 'noticed anything worthwhile', but when 'something strange [and] worthy of interest' occurred, he offered her the choice of either accepting him as 'the man of the house . . . in which case we continue our journey', or to 'think about it for a week' and then decide. Katia took the time to think things over, but then 'the mother interfered', persuading her to change her mind and consent to the marriage, 'declaring', he claimed, 'whatever you [i.e. the husband] say'. The marriage soon began to fall apart, and when the 'interceding relatives' attempted to 'reconcile' the spouses, they failed to convince them to assume their 'common responsibility to save' it. 'Neither the man could surrender his role in his quality of man and head of household, nor could the woman curb her authoritarian and independent impulses.'[33]

In a more recent case, the facts of the case begin with the priest's blessing of Elie's and Eliane's wedding on 11 February 1996, and the remarks that the couple had subsequently given birth to two children. They met 'at a neighbours' . . . while [the husband] was paying them a visit'. He liked her and began courting her, 'putting on display . . . all [his] good qualities in order to convince her to marry him'. He 'promised her a happy life and a separate house on a lot which his brother-in-law' was developing. He even 'showed her the deed of sale and took her to examine the apartment in which she will reside once they are married'. Only a few people were invited to the wedding, which was 'quickly' done 'upon the request of the groom, under the pretext that he was mourning a relative'.[34]

The husband's 'truth' and that 'of his promises, which had no connection whatever to the truth, began to appear immediately after the marriage'. The wife 'found out that the deed . . . was forged, and that he had sold his car to pay for the wedding expenses'. Their 'differences . . . were exacerbated by the husband's neglect and irresponsibility', and when he 'hit her', she 'left the conjugal home and [went to] stay at her parents''. On 6 October 2009, she petitioned the 'Maronite Unified First Instance Court . . . to declare the marriage annulled'. Eliane gave two reasons why the marriage was null and void (or ought to be declared so): 'dissimulation

[33] Ibid.

[34] MUFIC, Decision No. 253/2009, 23 March 2011 (Elie and Eliane).

leading to an error in the quality of the husband's person, and his inability to bear the basic responsibilities of marriage, due to causes of a psychological nature (*li asbāb dhāt tabīʿa nafsiyya*)'.[35]

The causes of a marital breakdown are causes of a crisis in the interpersonal relationship and, therefore, methodically sought in the spouses themselves (and their bodies, in so far as they are 'persons'). The causes are not evident in the facts of the case. They figure in them only as symptoms which, at a first moment in the elaboration of a case, elicit 'suspicions (*irtiyābāt*)'. The latter are then formulated in a series of questions that 'specify the subject of the conflict' or crisis and serve to guide the subsequent examination. What the court wants to know, once the facts have been established, is whether they (or what they might contain, implicitly or explicitly) could be accounted for in terms of one or more of the causes, stipulated in the Code of Canons, that make a marriage null and void. More exactly, what it wants to do is secure a plausible (or persuasive) connection between the facts and the causes stipulated in the Code – bearing in mind that the facts of a case, as already told, lend themselves to this purpose.

Despite the irreducible singularity of each case, it is constructed in such a way as to enable the court to interrogate it through a combination of the three causes of annulment stipulated in the Code.

The court questions the claims about the marriage of George and Katia: 'Was the marriage void . . . due to simulation of consent or of the permanence of the bond on behalf of the wife before the marriage?' or 'Was the marriage void due to psychological incapacity linked to natural incompatibility between the spouses' temperaments, making it impossible to carry out the burdens of conjugal life?' In this case, evidence of simulation is sought in the dissimulator's statement, which discloses her or his 'motivations', since simulation consists in either 'a partial [or incomplete] action' or an outright 'act of lying'. Consent to marriage must be an authentic expression of a person's intention the disclosure of which is the aim of the judicial examination.[36] If the dissimulator is not available, the court infers her

[35] Ibid.

[36] '[T]he exchange of reciprocal consent considered a single unified action unifying the respective intention of both [spouses]' (MUFIC, Decision No. 173/92, 27 April 1993). '[T]here [is] a substance to marital consent beyond the ceremonial words of acceptance' (Noonan, *Power to Dissolve*, p. 82).

intention from her 'qualities' and 'psychological state . . . regarding the commitments and mutual responsibilities of interpersonal communion' at and before the time she gave consent.[37]

In order to do so in the case of Elie and Eliane, the court asks whether 'the marriage [was] void due to the wife's incapacity to assume its essential obligations and duties', where 'the notion of incapacity includes . . . both anatomical and psychological aspects?' In George's and Katia's case, in contrast, the court asks if 'the nullity of the marriage [is] proven . . . due to' three (or a combination of three) possible causes, all residing in the husband's person: (a) his 'grave mental illness, which disables him from bearing the serious responsibilities of marriage'; (b) 'an error in his essential attributes'; (c) 'unfulfilled consent on [his] part'. With the problem traced back to the relationship between the spouses, and probable causes located in one of them, the court proceeds with its examination, asking the spouses to give an account of their own experiences of the marriage and, specifically, of themselves in it. It will become clear in the following passages that the word 'experience' is to be taken in a specifically sensory and emotional sense that lends itself to medical, psychological or psychiatric discourses and their categories.[38]

What a Marriage in Crisis Feels Like

John provides a detailed description of his sensations and sentiments during his breakdowns, when he was 'exposed to aches in his stomach'. He 'felt as if he was suffocating' (the literal translation of his words is, 'as if a tightness of breath lay on my chest') and feverish ('accompanied by sweat on my brow'). The court cites a passage from the medical report in which John speaks to the doctor about 'an increased internal tension of an emotional or other origin', after which 'I feel like a muscular spasm and trembling throughout the body, a feeling of suffocation [and] light-headedness'. This is followed by 'a total loss of my forces, without loss of consciousness'. He becomes 'flabby, incapable of talking', although still able 'to hear what happens around me'.

According to his wife, Salwa, 'sexual relations were "normal (*tabīʿiyya* , also, natural)" as far as she is concerned', a claim with which the husband had 'agreed in his first interrogation'. He later changed his mind apparently, claiming that

[37] MUFIC, Decision No. 173/92, 27 April 1993 (George and Katia).
[38] Ibid.

'marital relations were not [so] harmon[ious]' as to make it possible for him to say 'that the couple became one body (*jasad wāḥid*)'. Complete carnal union was not accomplished, according to John, because of 'a lack that made both of them uncomfortable with the physical relationship'.[39]

In Eleanor's and Sami's case, she also 'complained about a real difficulty to accept a physical relationship' with her husband. When asked to describe their sexual relationship, he tells the court, in graphic detail, 'I tried . . . to initiate penetration . . . even superficially, by means of the genital organ and finger'. At first (this had taken place before the wedding), she 'would adamantly refuse because we were not yet married', but, as he later found out, the real reason was that she 'was suffering from vaginismus'.

According to Sami, he and Eleanor had been in 'an intimate relationship two months after they met, which continued until five months after the wedding'. However, it seems to have involved no sexual intercourse. The relationship was not reciprocal, however, for although he admitted his complete love for her, she 'was incapable of offering him sincere and spontaneous love . . . with no psychological inhibition (*inkimāsh nafsāni*)'. He thought that 'she kept [herself] at the receiving end, as if by propriety . . . because she was careful to keep me as her life companion'.

But then, in regards to her personal history, he hints at Eleanor's sexuality, which he attributes to a series of traumatic events. He singles out the loss of her father while she was young, her mother's second marriage, and her relationship with other women. Moreover, she had also witnessed her friend getting an abortion, which 'shocked her' and added to the 'deep hatred of men' that she had held in her since 'seeing her father abusing her mother, and her brothers-in-law abusing her sisters'. The first night after the wedding Eleanor 'confronted the husband with a total rejection, yelling, "impossible . . . impossible . . . it is a nightmare for me"'.

The active medicalisation of Eleanor's sexuality, which had already begun before her marriage, continues with the administration of a variety of different sorts of psychotropic drugs, both oral and intravenous. The purpose of that treatment was to get her to have intercourse with her husband, by first helping her relax and, ultimately, 'anaesthetising' her. Sami, who had lost patience with 'the phase of superficial fondling on the level of the "clitoris"

[39] MUFIC, Decision No. 50, 10 February 1988 (Salwa and John).

decided that it was time 'to try proper union (*al-jimāʿ al-ṣaḥīḥ*)'. She would consistently refuse: 'her blood pressure would fall', she would complain of 'a severe headache, her heart rate would rise, and she would feel sick and nauseous'. She agreed eventually to undergo a procedure to 'widen the vaginal opening [and] the hymen', which, according to the doctor, was 'hard'. She was more 'accepting of intercourse' after the procedure, but 'with increased reluctance, effort, and disgust . . . until all contact' between them 'ceased completely'.[40]

Eleanor keeps refusing intercourse, 'preferring immediate and direct divorce' instead.[41] In support of his assertion that she was incapable of 'proper physical relations Sami claimed that 'she is known that her favourite friends before and after the marriage were women and girls'. She would 'avoid being present with him alone', and the only period of time they did spend together lasted 'almost one year . . . while her aunt and sister lived with us under one roof in her paternal house'. Eleanor told the court that 'she could not "bear this situation"'. Her claim that her husband 'raped me brutally with his finger', and her complaint that he had 'request[ed] that she sleep on top of him and copulate with him unnaturally' under the pretext that 'his genital organ was sprained', were dismissed by the court.

The first claim was refuted by the doctor's description of her sexual anatomy, which justified for the court the husband's behaviour as 'positive and legitimate'. Regarding the second claim, the court explained the virtues of the position the husband had proposed, which 'encouraged the woman to take the initiative and to be the actor . . . [thus] help[ing] the anxious wife control her fears'. This position implied 'a familiar and ordinary erection . . . rather than a "sprained organ"'. The court ends with a lesson about male genital anatomy, 'preordained by God to fulfil its function' – 'on condition of the other party's cooperation'.[42]

Not all accounts the spouses give of their marital experience are as long or detailed, and not all are focused on sex and sexuality. In the case of George and Katia, the husband complained about her character (or person), claiming that he 'noticed, just two weeks before the wedding, the wife's authoritarian

[40] MUFIC, Decision Issued 5 August 1988 (Eleanor and Sami).

[41] Ibid.

[42] Ibid.

tendency'. The experience – his experience – seems to be told as a narrative of increased isolation and violence, in which Katia's hostility against him escalates gradually as their life becomes more secluded. Their troubles begin as early as the wedding, when Katia refused to invite her husband's aunt. The husband's efforts to persuade her otherwise seem to have provoked her, for, as he describes it, she 'lost her temper', going about 'yelling and screaming'.[43]

Their marriage deteriorates further in the following months due to Katia's 'authoritarianism and stubbornness', and her 'refusal to concede any of her convictions [beliefs]'. (The husband describes his wife's gesticulations to be 'similar to [those] of a traffic policeman'.) The final breakdown follows when she turns away 'even from preparing food . . . and [from] other domestic work', and with their 'complete disconnection from any social relationship with the outside'. At this point, they 'agreed to put an end to this tragic situation'.[44]

Elie's wife's statement describes their trajectory since 1995, when they first met. A few years later, she began to realise that he had been making empty promises and lying to her all along. After the household's financial collapse (which 'compelled her to find employment as a hairdresser'), her husband began to 'react with anger' to some of her questions 'about the house' he claimed he had been building for them, 'and go about breaking' things 'around their [rented] residence, hitting her occasionally'. It is at this point that Elie 'started taking psychotropic drugs', as she said in her statement, adding that she 'does not know if he used to do so in the past' or not. She became pregnant around that time, Elie 'spen[ding] most of his time at home, claiming sometimes to be working with his brother and not getting paid'.

Moreover, Elie 'begins to feel jealous of and for her, accusing her . . . of having affairs' with other men. 'His mental state' became much worse; he began to complain that 'he was having a nervous breakdown and . . . needed to be hospitalized'. Her descriptions suggest that Elie was also suffering from substance abuse. She 'was giving him psychotropic drugs', 'he drank liquor', and she saw 'some *ḥashīsh*' on him once, which, he told her, was 'to treat his toothache'. She eventually learned from him that he used to use drugs before

[43] MUFIC, Decision No. 173/92, 27 April 1993 (George and Katia).
[44] Ibid.

their marriage, but that he no longer does, a claim she doubts 'because the signs on his face seemed to show something bizarre'.

The wife explained that Elie 'suffers . . . from psychological problems', describing what appear to be psychotic episodes: 'He would wake up at night screaming that he is the chief (*al-zaʿīm*), and that he would do everything in his power to make people hate' her. His behaviour became increasingly erratic, angry, and violent, going as far as to 'hit her and the two children, smashing the icon of the Virgin, tearing her prayer books, breaking the mobile phone . . . threatening her with a rifle and that he would mutilate her face . . .' The final separation took place in July 2009 when 'at her birthday, he insulted her and hit her and then broke down crying asking for forgiveness'.[45]

What a Crisis in Marriage (or Marriage in Crisis) Looks Like

Witness accounts are a combination of observations of the couple's conduct and character, and conjecture about their psychological or mental states. According to Eleanor's mother, she was 'devoted to Saint Rita and is honest', while Sami was 'known for his devotion to the saints and his religiosity . . . and [was not] dishonest'. The wife's sister confirms 'Eleanor's sincerity and her devotion to Saint Rita', pointing out that 'Sami practiced regularly his devotional acts . . . and the sacraments'. However, she also 'noticed that . . . he twisted certain things in his interest'.

The descriptions can be graphic. Witnesses speak about – seem to be well-acquainted and involved in – the spouses' intimate life. They are witnesses to their intimacy. The ecclesiastical court – as well as all involved – are pulled in two directions: on the one hand, a definition of marriage the truth of which resides in the 'personal' or intimate; on the other hand, a judicial requirement that truth be established on the basis of a forensic investigation and recognition. The tension between the two would perhaps be not so disturbing if annulment were not the only recourse to dealing with the suffering that accompanies a dysfunctional marriage.

Witnesses seem to be well acquainted with the spouses' intimate life, not only as observers, but as participants as well to an extent. Their accounts

[45] MUFIC, Decision No. 253/2009, 23 March 2011 (Elie and Eliane).

of what they 'know' about the marriage are moral or ethical accounts of the spouses: their personality or character, their conduct and actions, their piety or religiosity. Eleanor's mother seems to know that that her son-in-law 'would insist' that he 'put her "finger" on Eleanor's vaginal opening to ease the conjugal relationship *(al-ʿilāqa al-zawjiyya)*'.[46] Eleanor's sister, Giselle, pointed out that 'the man possessed books and information about sex thanks to which he acquired masculine vigour . . . after my sister left for Canada'. The sister's observation did not escape the attention of the ecclesiastical judge who then asked her how she was so well-informed about her brother-in-law's 'acquiring masculine vigour?'[47] Giselle's husband, George, provided the answer, by claiming that it was Sami who had told him so, after 'testing himself with another woman'.[48] Another witness, one of several who do not seem to have any kinship with the spouses, 'admitted that the physical union happened after the surgery', a claim which another witness corroborates.

The witnesses on the husband's side testify to the contrary, asserting that the wife refused to have intercourse with her husband. His maternal aunt claims that 'everything was failing between the couple, especially since the wife . . . neglected the affairs of her household and refused to stay with her husband alone in one house to avoid an intimate relationship'. Sami's cousin, her son, knew about the failure of the marriage 'directly [because the couple] declared [it] before him and his wife'. He 'imagined that Eleanor's difficulties were identical to the ones his wife had had and eventually overcome, giving birth to three children'. This 'encouraged' Eleanor to 'return to her marital household', which she did, but with no similar result. The cousin's wife also testified that Eleanor 'refused any sexual relationship with Sami and any other man'. Even the husband's maternal uncle intervened to 'encourage' Eleanor who, 'in a private [conversation]', had told him that she 'refused all of Sami's display of generosity and his cajoling of her and her family because all of it might end . . . with a request for intimacy'.[49]

[46] MUFIC, Decision Issued 5 August 1988 (Eleanor and Sami).

[47] Ibid.

[48] Ibid.

[49] MUFIC, Decision Issued 5 August 1988 (Eleanor and Sami).

The circle of witnesses is as wide for George and Katia. George's parents 'noticed [during their] first visit to the wife's parents' that [she] was very strong and controlling of men, just like her mother', and that 'her father kept silent and would never say a word'. The husband's colleague also 'noticed, as others had, that [Katia] was [the center of] everything, and that she was [always] the first to initiate conversation'. She even 'drew his attention to' this fact, just as other witnesses had 'warned him of the consequences of marrying a woman whose conduct indicates her authoritarianism and her incompatibility with him'.[50] The husband's colleague, while noticing some aspects of the wife's conduct, 'knew well [the husband's] unique qualities'. His sister 'said of him that he is of superior morals, gentleness and conscience'. The former 'knew that he was not of weak character'.

The witnesses on his side all confirmed the wife's independence, authoritarianism and obduracy on the basis of their perceptions of her conduct. 'She behaved obsessively and with impatience', observed the husband's father; his sister noted that the wife 'was independent in her behavior'; the wife 'could not perform any role' that went against 'her basic authoritarian and selfish character', states a colleague of the husband's; the brother-in-law 'noticed immediately that [things were] not right' when, while they were first introduced, she 'greeted him' and went back to 'stay in her room'.[51]

According to one witness, Katia made explicit her desire to end the marriage, threatening to 'throw herself off the balcony' if any member of her family interceded between her and her husband. What all the witnesses also emphasise was the total breakdown in the familial and, more generally, the social relationships as a result. The accounts mention the tension between the couple and the tyranny of the wife, specifically, whom George's father compared to someone who had had 'a couple of bottles of *'araq* to drink'. Her father, in contrast, is 'a well-meaning and forgiving man', unlike 'her mother and aunts', from whom she had acquired her traits.[52]

The three different accounts which Eliane's sister, neighbour, and friend in turn give about her husband Elie display the same features as the ones in

[50] MUFIC, Decision No. 173/92, 27 April 1993 (George and Katia).

[51] Ibid.

[52] Ibid.

the preceding cases. They combine a close knowledge of the spouses and their conjugal experience with a strong inclination for ethical or moral judgments, occasional appeals to a pop-psychological vocabulary, assumptions about gender roles ('the man of the house') dampened by the acknowledgment of the need to work (Eliane's neighbour suggests that she find a job).[53]

The spouses' and witness accounts in the preceding two sections bring to light that part of the Catholic constellation I mentioned at the beginning of this chapter that is the community of kin, friends, and neighbours in which marriage is embedded. Together with the married couple, who experience marriage from the inside, as it were, the community is also a source of insight into the couples' interpersonal relationship, albeit 'from the outside'. (This distinction may be called into question, as at times it seems that the marriage and the community belong to a single continuum.)

While both perspectives are valid – in the sense that they are taken into account in the ecclesiastical inquiry – and incorporated into the process of drawing a more complete picture of the marriage, they do not constitute the final word on the crisis that traverses it or the definitive grounds for its annulment. Critically, the way the ecclesiastical judicial process is organised and the cases described suggest that there is essentially in the marriage – in marriage, as such – something that necessarily escapes both the immediate experience of its subjects and the observations of the community. As the next section makes clear, it is in this 'something' that the crisis is rooted and its causes sought out, and for that, the ecclesiastical judiciaries summon the medical experts.

Psychopathologies of Married Life

In the cited (and somewhat fragmented) form in which they occur in case transcripts, the reports of medical (medico-legal) experts are a mixture of behavioural observations, comportmental evaluation and psychological explanation. They display an effort towards systematic analysis. They do, however, occasionally make loose correlations among phenomena, as does the 'psychiatric specialist' in Elie's case, who considers that his 'non-appearance at court is a reflection of' his 'neglecting his responsibilities', since 'attendance [at court]

[53] MUFIC, Decision No. 253/2009, 23 March 2011 (Elie and Eliane).

is an obligation' that, moreover, 'is connected' in his case 'to his future and that of his family and children'.[54]

This is not, strictly speaking, a psychological proposition, but the observational basis of the expert's second hypothesis about Elie. The psychologist is suggesting that his non-appearance could also be a reflection of a general disposition or 'a style of dealing . . . with situations which he rejects, in the sense that he avoids them and by doing so undermines' any possible outcome that might seem to go against his desires or interests. This, in turn, 'reflects a childish manner of conducting [himself] since he believes like a child that no one would see him if he shut his eyes'.

Another series of actions on Elie's part that exhibit his general disposition is his 'rushing of the wedding', for the sake of which he had sold his car and borrowed money. This, according to the expert, 'reflects his inability to delay gratification', which 'indicates his emotional and psychological immaturity' and tendency to act spontaneously 'without considering the consequences'. He also 'has a tendency to display violent reactive behaviour when confronted with or asked to fulfill his promises, or when opposed', and 'to flee from confronting reality by taking refuge in psychotropic drugs'. Finally, the husband's 'inability to keep a job or employment' indicates that he is 'incapable of settling and committing to his duties', thus 'preventing his wife and family from feeling settled and secure', while putting him in a state of constant 'worry and anxiety' that erupts in 'episodes of breakdown'.

The impression which the medico-legal report makes of Elie is that of a man 'who suffers from a psychological disturbance (*yuʿāni min iḍṭirāb nafsi*)' that 'prevents him from committing to his duties and responsibilities', and is 'especially' lacking in 'capacity to enter and sustain a mature interpersonal relationship (*ʿilāqa shakhṣāniyya*)'. The psychiatric diagnosis of Elie's 'personality (*shakhṣiyyatihi*)' is of someone who suffers from 'psychopathic paranoia' and 'psycho-affective immaturity'. He is stubborn, refuses to admit that his conduct is 'ineffective' and contrary to 'social expectations', inclined to 'hostility' and the passing of 'false judgments on the basis of . . . preconceptions and passions' instead of 'factual events'. He is 'skeptical of the truth' and reluctant

[54] The doctor's full report was apparently attached to the case record, but it is not published. In the Arabic text, no distinction between 'psychology' and 'psychiatry' is made, the word '*nafsi*' used to refer to a class of scientific diagnosis of the subject's 'mental health'.

to 'confirm' it. He 'search[es] instead for evidence' in 'his private thoughts and unrealistic imaginings', which he does not submit to 'critical self-examination'. He is incapable of 'admit[ting] to himself and the other the extent to which he is responsible for the problems he faces'.[55]

The crisis in the marriage of George and Katia is rooted in their 'incompatible temperaments (*tanāfur al-ṭibāʿ*), according to the expert's opinion as the ecclesiastical court understands it, which means that their 'personalities (*shaksiyyatahuma*) have nothing in common'. Therefore, their mutual consent to marry, in so far as it is 'considered a single act that unifies their intention' and the founding act of their marriage, is invalid. For the consent to be found defective, however, their incompatibility must first be established. The ecclesiastical court, having listened to spouses and witnesses, turns now to the reports of the psychologists and medical doctors.[56]

The court's suspicions about the wife are initially aroused through its reflection on the kind of trouble that begins to appear between the spouses after their wedding. Witness accounts reinforce its doubts, but it is only the psychiatric assessment of the spouses that describes them plausibly enough to enable the court to proceed with an annulment. Witnesses identify the signs of incompatibility between the spouses but, in order to conclude that simulation took place, following which only it can declare the marriage null and void, the ecclesiastical court must have a more credible, 'scientific', account of the wife's intentions prior to the wedding: her 'intention – at least implicitly and within herself – regarding her commitment to a marriage lasting a lifetime'. Who Katia – the person who knowingly gave the consent – was, at the time of her giving consent, must be established. The establishment of her identity, however, is in the given context dependent on her knowledge of the Maronite (Catholic) doctrine on marriage and its consequences (legal and non-legal).

[55] MUFIC, Decision No. 253/2009, 23 March 2011 (Elie and Eliane).

[56] MUFIC, Decision No. 173/92, 27 April 1993 (George and Katia). The court quotes the following Rotal reasoning, which I translate in full from the French citation: 'Their consent does not correspond to a criterion of validity . . . nullity can be legally recognised . . . from the fact that at the moment of exchanging consent, each spouse was not conscious of the intentions and tendencies of the other, and that they were not capable of reciprocal adaptation due to the abnormality of their characters.'

Katia's intentions seem obvious from the facts (her actions): knowing the meaning of a 'Christian or Maronite marriage', she rejected one of its necessary tenets, namely, 'harmonious existence with her husband'. Yet, she is not responsible – not in a legal or moral sense – since her 'motive' is determined by the structure of her personality. Her intention to discontinue the marriage is not duplicitous, for by her very 'psychological constitution (*takwīniha al-nafsi*)' she could not remain in the marriage. She consented to the marriage on the basis of a 'misunderstanding', according to the psychologist, who attributes that misunderstanding to 'a virile character inherent to [Katia's] personality'.[57]

To answer the question regarding the 'natural incompatibility between the spouses' temperaments', which entails a 'psychological incapacity' that 'makes it impossible to carry out the burdens of conjugal life', the psychologist carries out a comparative examination. The report 'describe[s] in detail the upbringing of both spouses' on the basis of interviews with the husband, 'a scientific ability test', and witness statements. George is 'a womanly man indulging rapidly in domination and the attainment of Platonic (*ʿudhri*) goals', while Katia is 'a manly woman'.[58]

The report attributes this difference to the family in which each was brought up. George was raised as an only child among sisters and 'received the affection of his mother, who knew how to circumvent the interference of his father in his conduct', while the wife grew up in a household in which her mother had 'the last word'. 'Each personality', continues the expert, 'developed in a family milieu that reinforced its independence', is 'structurally different from the other . . . and cannot meet and understand [the] other'.

Since 'their emotional immaturity' has 'turn[ed] into psychological incapacity to accept the other as is, it was impossible for them to bear the burdens of a settled and stable conjugal life'. The court takes this diagnosis to mean that 'it was impossible for the husband to surrender his role as head of the family', while the wife 'held on to her role and her peculiar character, i.e., the manly woman, and her obstinate authoritarianism'.[59]

[57] Ibid.

[58] Ibid.

[59] Ibid.

Regarding the case of Eleanor and Sami, in order to conclude that their marriage is null and void, the court must in contrast know if the marriage took place 'according to custom and law' and, therefore, if 'cohabitation . . . including physical [sexual] acts' were possible.[60] The court is particularly interested in the history of 'the physical and psychological' problem between them, if it existed prior to their wedding, and if it 'could be treated or heal'. If not, the ecclesiastical court would consider the marriage 'decided but unconsummated'.

The Annulment of Marriage and the End of Suffering

The examination must make it clear whether the marriage was consummated or not, and this requires a detailed description of 'the muscular and neural cramps in the region directly surrounding the vaginal entry'. For this, the ecclesiastical court 'lack[s] the [direct] psychiatric expertise' that would provide it with the 'appropriate details and scientific analyses of the conditions which the defendant went through'. In 'compensat[ion]', the court carries out its diagnosis by drawing analogies with 'specimens' described in a medical textbook, from which it cites extensively.[61] The doctor who wrote the textbook 'ascertain[s] that the mere refusal of the physical relationship on the part of a healthy woman puts the aforementioned genital area in a physical and repelling state of revolt'. The court infers from its interpretations of the cases described in the textbook to the case in hand, suspecting that Eleanor suffers from 'psychic vaginismus' and 'functional impotence', the latter being 'a form of' the former.[62]

The condition is described as 'a state of anxiety' that involves 'memories of suffering endured during attempts at sexual intercourse'. When it takes the form of functional impotence, it 'consists in spasmodic, painful, and involuntary contraction of the muscles of the "pelvic floor" that block almost completely the vagina constituting . . . an obstacle to entry by the

[60] MUFIC, Decision Issued 5 August 1988 (Eleanor and Sami).

[61] The title of the book is *The Impotence of the Woman, Organic and Functional.* Its author is a certain 'Doctor Lotario'. The case transcript, which includes translated excerpts from it in Arabic and French, indicates that it was published in Rome in 1977. An internet search for the author's name and the title of the book yielded no result.

[62] MUFIC, Decision Issued 5 August 1988 (Eleanor and Sami).

penis'. Also observed are 'hyperaesthesia of the hymen and vulva . . . lesions and malformations', accompanied by psychological and somatic symptoms: irritability, anger, defensiveness, transpiration, crying, moaning, screaming, agitation, trembling, and so on. The court cites a list of techniques and treatments to deal with it: discernment, patience, scientific awareness, commanding authority, medicine, and psychotherapy, 'all together'.

Among them is masturbation. Eleanor had already told the court that it was the 'doctor . . . who had advised her [to practice] "the secret habit (*al-ʿāda al-sirrīyya*)"'. The court makes a short digression to explain that medical experts often suggest masturbation as a method of 'self-treatment', supplementing that with a detailed description of how it is performed: the 'introduction of the finger . . . to achieve . . . sexual relaxation through the excitation of . . .' The court explains that 'the husband may be invited to participate' in the procedure, 'as the doctors had advised her . . . in order to pave the way for an attempt at a natural physical relationship'. The court draws a distinction between two quite different uses of masturbation: as a medical technique and as a personal habit or practice. The two are not to be confused, for 'the secret habit', in opposition to the technique, is 'destructive of the will and is often the cause that destroys the family structure'. Eleanor had 'mistakenly described' what the doctor prescribed as 'the secret habit', and by 'admitting that she could not bear this situation' – viz. having her husband participate – could be said to have 'refused the simplest available means' to save her marriage.[63]

'Was the marriage void [then] due to the wife's incapacity to assume the marriage's essential duties and obligations?' Yes, decides the court, placing a conditional prohibition on the wife to marry again before receiving the parish pastor's authorisation, granted on the basis of a medical report showing that she is capable of assuming the burdens of marital life.[64]

John had already had several encounters with medical doctors before and after his marriage. He had 'succumbed to a sudden nervous stroke' once and 'been suffering [since] from [chronic] gastric pain'. He received medical attention, including an 'electroencephalogram'. The court goes into more details, citing excerpts of the medical report about 'wave points in the left

[63] Ibid.

[64] Ibid.

temporal lobe', 'electro-clinical crisis', and 'convulsions of the head and upper limbs'. The doctor's conclusion is that John is physically 'sound (*salīm*)', the court considering it 'difficult to conclude that he is epileptic'. The physical causes of his symptoms ruled out, 'the afflicted' nevertheless displays 'a violent tendency' – a symptom which witnesses are able 'to describe' – that justifies 'subjecting him to psychiatric expertise to determine its apparently psychological source'.[65]

The court 'presents John to the doctors'. The results of 'two styles of psychiatric expertise, the more important of which being [that of] the psychologist Herman Rorschach' compel the doctor to conclude that 'it is difficult to determine a well-defined psychological illness'. However, there are 'features . . . [of] a neurotic mental organization of the obsessive type' and 'indications . . . of a personality having paranoid inclinations'. From this the court infers, in a language that slides between scientific and moral categories, that 'the man's mental appearance (*al-maḍhar al-fikri*), in what regards his capacity to reason (*al-qudra al-al-ʿaqliyya*), was intact'.

However, the court adds, some 'lacunae remain, which it is appropriate to attribute to troubled reactions towards various degrees of responsibility'. 'It appeared from the tests' that 'the man tends towards introversion, and that a monomaniacal logic (*al-manṭiq al-haṣri*) dominates his relationship with others'. An introverted person, such as the defendant, 'is characterised by a relative difficulty accommodating a sudden external shock, be it psychological or physical'. This assessment opens up the path for the ecclesiastical court to issue a judgment on the person's qualifications to marry and to decide as a result to declare the marriage null and void.

The discourse – both clinical and juridical, as the distinction between the judge's and the doctor's voice often dissolves – moves in a series in which neurological, psychiatric, psychological and moral statements are linked by means of ambiguous connectors such as, 'reveals', 'there are indications', 'parallel', 'appropriate to ascribe', 'is inclined to', 'reflects' and so on. The ecclesiastical court leaps, for instance, from the observation that the man experiences anxiety to the prediction that it 'might hinder deep human

[65] MUFIC, Decision No. 50, 10 February 1988 (Salwa and John).

relations', or his 'attentive[ness] to neatness, obligations and cleanliness reveal the man's personality'.

The diagnosis gives the ecclesiastical court reason to be concerned about John's capacity to form an interpersonal relationship, but this is not enough to conclude that he is 'disabled', despite the 'sexual problems' he has as well. The court cites the doctor's summary of the 'results' of the examination: any psychological and neurological illness 'must be ruled out'. However, 'John has trouble with his environment – especially with his wife – because of his 'obsessive personality' and strict upbringing'. He suffers from 'behavioural problems (*troubles du comportement*) [and] a sentiment of inferiority', is 'neurotic . . . obsessive . . . and slightly paranoid'. His behaviour and sentiments are tied to a 'psychic structure', his obsession and neurosis are a 'type' of structure, his paranoia indicated by '"accessory" traits . . . (sthenicity, suspicion, psychorigidity, aggressiveness)'.

John has so far been considered normal clinically. The doctor noted that despite the 'difficulties regarding intimate relations between the spouses . . . Mr John . . . is qualified to take on the responsibilities of marriage . . .' Those difficulties are not 'proof that either party is unqualified, but an inevitable result of a marriage in which both parties unconsciously imagined to find through it solutions to their hidden psychological problems'.

The court sees a real or meaningful relationship between his symptoms and the failure of the marriage: 'different symptoms . . . constitute a real disability in the defendant . . . [which] appeared before the marriage . . . and led after a while . . . to the marriage's ultimate failure'. What 'led' meant, and how a disability leads to the failure of a marriage is not clear, but 'it is up to the judge to base himself on science and psychiatric expertise, in order to overcome [the difficulty to define the defendant's suffering] and decide what he sees to be applicable to the law (*al-qanūn*) and the facts'.

Accordingly, 'in the name of God the Almighty', the court declares that 'Salwa . . . and John's marriage is null due to the husband's incapacity to assume the burdens of marital life'. Moreover, he is 'prohibited to marry again until the competent ecclesiastical authority grants him permission . . . on the basis of a psychiatrist's opinion The latter should explicitly 'state (*yuṣarriḥ*) that John' is in possession of the 'capacity to assume the burdens of married life'.[66]

[66] Ibid.

Conclusion

The investigation of symptoms, which often includes detailed descriptions of the anatomy and physiology of the reproductive organs and techniques of erotic stimulation, is aimed to establish one thing and one thing only: knowledge of the person. This knowledge is not 'neutral', 'amoral', phenomenological or positivist (although it does contain elements of those), but is a knowledge of the person in so far as 'the person' is taken in the Catholic sense that resists its reduction to psychological and physiological processes (and, therefore, knowledge) and the 'naturalist' ontology they presuppose.

It is in this light that the spouses' accounts of their own experiences, the witness accounts of the spouses and their relationship, and the medical experts' diagnoses and reports acquire their sense and, importantly, their value within the whole – there is no obvious privileging of the latter as the exclusive source of certainty. Indeed, absolute certainty is expressly not sought out, and there is a tacit recognition that it is either not possible, or simply useless, for it does not account – not on its own at any rate – for a person's capacity to will freely an act of consent to enter into a union with another – a union the essential nature of which, moreover, escapes the certainties of medical expertise.

The person's 'body' – behaviours, anxieties, sensations, genitals, brain or nervous system – are all subjected to examination, diagnosed and evaluated by the medical standards of normality and pathology, with the sole aim of deciding a person's predisposition to assume the responsibility required to sustain conjugal life. The 'medical specialists['] . . . opinion [offers] the venerable judges the basic assistance to understand the nature of the ascribed ailment', but it is the ecclesiastical judiciaries who are to decide whether 'the . . . phenomenon constitutes the legally appropriate reason' to annul a marriage or not.[67] Medical knowledge belongs to a configuration of judgment that includes religious doctrine, moral theology and legal principle, each mutually supportive of the others, the whole finding its articulation in the ecclesiastical enactments through which a marriage is declared null and void.

Medico-legal expertise, despite the evidence it provides and the knowledge it contributes to, does not constitute a definitive basis for a decision. For psychological or physiological discourse to make any sense at all – to have any force – in the determination of the outcome of a case, the insight, knowledge and

[67] MUFIC, Decision No. 50, 10 February 1988 (Salwa and John).

authority of the ecclesiastical judge must supplement and, therefore, transform it, and subject its findings to a truth of an altogether different order. This truth is (resides in the Church's understanding of) the human person: 'the profound and constitutive unity of the person's human forces and his qualities', which are 'reason, will, body, soul, heart, and conscience'.[68] This informs the ecclesiastical method of judicial inquiry, which includes the description of facts, the parties' own statements, witness accounts and medical expertise. All enter into the ecclesiastical judiciaries' hearing of the case and impress on them an idea of the whole person on some of whose qualities their judgment falls.

It does not follow from this that marriage is 'personal', at least not in the 'psychological' sense of 'interpersonal,' or that whatever crisis befalls it is an 'effect' of psycho-physiological 'causes'. In the ecclesiastical understanding, the relationship between a pathological disposition and conjugal life is in some cases mutual. In as much as 'psychological incapacity' has 'effects on common conjugal life', the latter carries a certain degree of 'medical' or therapeutic power. 'Had she cooperated with her husband', the court says in one of the cases, 'she might have achieved control over her fears'.[69] That it is a Holy Sacrament of the Church and an interpersonal relationship does not isolate it from the world, or life in this world. Rather, 'the Church connects the fate of a marriage to public good and the salvation of souls', and it is this very connection between souls and the public, between salvation and the good – between, that is, the religious and secular – that opens it up to the world, exposes it to its demands, and makes it vulnerable to its forces.

[68] Ibid.

[69] MUFIC, Decision Issued 5 August 1988 (Eleanor and Sami).

4

CONDUCT AND JUDGMENT BETWEEN THE SHARIʿA AND THE LAW

'Similar attempts were made more than fifty years ago . . . on different occasions, and each time the Muslims would . . . stand' against them . . . For, 'a civil marriage law' would entail the 'suppression of the *sharʿīyya* courts' . . . this matter is 'absolutely not open for discussion' and 'better be withdrawn once and for all' and 'forever' . . . it is a matter of 'being or not being . . . the *sharʿīyya* courts are 'an institution deeply rooted in our Lebanese and Arab history (*tārīkh*)' . . . 'established during Ottoman rule in Lebanon' and 'are part of our heritage (*turāth*)' . . . any proposal that would 'separate us from our heritage, history and civilization' will be rejected . . . 'Muslims do not bind (*yulzimūn*) any member of the communities (*ahl al-milal*) in Lebanon with any of their rules . . . to submit the civil marriage law proposal to a 'referendum . . . will lead to submitting larger issues to a referendum, such as [the country's] independence, finality, and system of government' . . . civil marriage was a 'calling (*daʿwa*) for secularisation' . . . 'Lebanon will be neither a place for the corruption of religions and morals', nor 'a springboard for the corruption of its Arab milieu (*bīʾa*) and the mounting of aggressions against its eternal heritage (*mawārīth*) . . .'[1]

[1] These words are by the mufti Qabbani during the polemic of 1998 about the President's proposal of a civil marriage law (from *Assafir* and *Annahar* newspapers in 1998). The position was repeated in February 2019: 'The media office of the Dar [al-Fatwa] has ascertained, in a statement on its Facebook page, the position of the Mufti of the Republic, Abd el-Latif Derian, and

> Several members of the same family stood together before the judges, the siblings in disagreement about the value of their mother's support. Three judges sat behind the bench, a chief judge (*qādi sharʿī*) in the middle, and a consultant judge (*mustashār*) on each side. To their left sat a representative of the prosecutor general of the Lebanese Republic, to their right the court reporter. Around this raised circumference stood the state's armed security guards and other courtroom employees. The room remained silent until the judge announced the decision, when a complaint was heard from one of the defendants. The judge checked it promptly, asserting firmly that the verdict had already been read, and that, therefore, no more complaints could be heard. Instead of disappearing into silence, the murmur turned gradually into a discourse that conveyed neither anger nor threat, but rather a timid and reverential appeal. His repeated attempts having failed to silence the subject, the judge stood up frowning, and pounding the table below him with his hand ordered the man, 'Quiet! You are talking to the law!' Seeing that the defendant did not – could not – contain himself, the prosecutor stepped forward, threatening the man with incarceration, as two of the security guards moved towards him. This, together with his siblings' urgings managed finally to keep him quiet and bring the session to an end.[2]

> 'Marriage (*al-zawāj*) in Islam between man and woman is the basis and nucleus of the family (*al-usra, al-ʿāʾila*) . . . and in marriage the woman bears children, so this nucleus and family grow and expand, and ties (*al-ʿilāqāt*) develop in the family, at first between the man and woman . . . Islam set up this foundation on spiritual tranquility (*al-sakan al-nafsi*),

of Dar al-Fatwa and the Shariʿa Council, and the Council of Muftis, which has not changed, saying, "[the position] has been known for years as an absolute refusal (*al-rafḍ al-muṭlaq*) of the project of civil marriage in Lebanon and opposing it because it goes against (*yukhālif*) the rules (*aḥkām*) of the benevolent Islamic shariʿa . . . [as well as] the provisions (*al-aḥkām*) of the Lebanese Constitution in what relates to the obligation to respect the personal statuses applied in the religious courts of the Lebanese in its Article 9, and therefore it is not possible to promulgate it at parliament without seeking the opinion and position of Dar al-Fatwa and the rest of the religious authorities (*al-marājiʿ*) in Lebanon".' https://www.bbc.com/arabic/interactivity-47294464 (accessed 2 January 2023).

[2] Fieldnotes, 2007. The setting is the Higher Sunni Shariʿa Court. For an ethnographic account of the latter, see Clarke, *Islam and Law*. His discussion of the '*shaykh* as judge' is especially illuminating, pp. 107, 115, *et passim.*

complementarity (*al-takāmul*), affection (*al-mawadda*) and compassion (*al-raḥma*) . . . between the couple (*al-zawjayn*), and this is the meaning of Almighty God's saying in the Noble (*al-karīm*) Qur'an: {And of His signs is that He created for you from yourselves mates that you may find tranquility in them; and He placed between you affection and mercy. Indeed, in that are signs for a people who give thought}; and in this sense as well is Almighty God's saying in the holy Qur'an: {O mankind, fear your Lord, who created you from one soul and created from it its mate and dispersed from both of them many men and women And fear Allah, through whom you ask one another, and the wombs. Indeed, Allah is ever, over you, an Observer}; and in this sense as well is Almighty God's saying in the holy Qur'an: {O mankind, indeed We have created you from male and female and made you peoples and tribes that you may know one another. Indeed, the most noble of you in the sight of Allah is the most righteous of you} . . . And when the children grow up and a tie develops between them and their parents, Islam based the ties between them on honour (*ikrām*), care (*iḥsān al-muʿāmala*) and civility (*adab*) on the part of the parents towards their children in accordance with the prophet Muhammad's (SAW) venerable hadith, "Be kind to your children, and perfect their manners." So did Islam base the children's treatment of their parents on reverence (*al-birr*), loyalty (*al-wafā'*) and charity (*al-iḥsān*), and God Almighty in the holy Qur'an enjoined children with this saying, {and to parents, good treatment. Whether one or both of them reach old age [while] with you, say not to them [so much as], "*uff*", and do not repel them but speak to them a noble word} {And lower to them the wing of humility out of mercy and say, "My Lord, have mercy upon them as they brought me up [when I was] small"} {Your Lord is most knowing of what is within yourselves. If you should be righteous [in intention] then indeed He is ever, to the often returning [to Him], Forgiving}.'[3]

The first of these three fragments is composed of a series of statements made by the Mufti of the Republic of Lebanon explaining the reasons

[3] An excerpt from an interview I had with the Mufti of the Republic on 15 May 2007. The verses are, in succession: Verse 21 from Sura Ar-Rum, https://tanzil.net/#30:16; Verse 1 from Sura An-Nisa', https://tanzil.net/#4:1; Verse 13 of Sura Al-Hujurat, https://tanzil.net/#49:13; Verses 23–5 of Sura Al-Isra, https://tanzil.net/#17:23. All are from the English Sahih International translation. For the hadith, see: https://sunnah.com/ibnmajah:3671.

why Muslims in Lebanon have been, and will remain, opposed to the proposition that a Lebanese law of civil marriage be passed. The mufti's words draw a direct link between the prospect of such a law and the destiny of the shariʿa courts in the country. They give voice to the sentiment that the shariʿa courts have always been, and will remain, vulnerable to the state's legislative (secular) power. The mufti's words stress the vital connection between the shariʿa courts and the identity (existence) of Muslims in the country *and* the Lebanese state. What is clear is the prominence which, through marriage and its consequences (the family), the shariʿa courts have in the life of ordinary Muslims – what is clear is that the shariʿa courts, through marriage and its consequences (the family), *do* occupy a place in the life of Muslims. The mufti's words are a statement about the mutual dependency of the Lebanese legal arrangement – in so far as it guarantees the persistence of the shariʿa (and, generally, the religious) courts – and the coexistence of Muslims and Christians in Lebanon.

The second of the three fragments describes an event in a courtroom at the Sunni shariʿa courts in Beirut. It draws a picture of what the mufti wishes to convey in the preceding fragment, namely, the function which the shariʿa courts have in the network of relations among ordinary Muslims, the shariʿa judiciary, and the Lebanese state and, thereby, in the constitution of a sensibility (form of life). The event described offers insight into the distinction between the shariʿa and the law (and, more generally, of the religious and secular), and the way in which it enters into the constitution of an Islamic sensibility. In the first place, there is neither opposition or mutual exclusivity between, nor confounding of, the shariʿa and the (positive) law. They remain distinct, but are joined together through (in) the Sunni courts, which are, in the Lebanese legal arrangement, their privileged (authoritative) articulation.

As the judge's exclamation puts it forcefully, he is a shariʿa judge *and* a representative of 'the law', he *is* a shariʿa judge and a *representative* (representation) of 'the law', and is authorised, *therefore*, to back up his commands with a threat – always present – of state-sanctioned violence. A markedly different sensation accompanies the counterpart utterance, 'You are speaking to the shariʿa' is near to being nonsense, forced – as if something about it is out of place or as if '*al-qānūn*' lends itself to 'thingness' or 'objectness' – to *positivity* – to having and being in place, in ways that are just not quite so for '*al-shariʿa*'.[4] The Sunni courts articulate the shariʿa and the positive law and their ontological difference; and, arguably, it is that ontological difference that makes the joining, the articulation, possible.[5]

The scene in the courtroom is an episode in a sequence of events that are the consequence of an act that would have taken place earlier – they would have begun with a marriage. As the mufti explains in the third fragment, marriage is the origin – 'the nucleus' – of the family, which then 'grows' and 'expands' and becomes more complex as 'ties develop' among its members. Apart from this description of the genesis of filial and affinal ties from the primary tie between a man and a woman, the mufti's account is also a description of the ties themselves: what they consist in, what sentiments sustains them, and what qualities of life they foster in, and what characteristics they acquire through, a family. It is there, where 'spiritual tranquillity' is condition and horizon, that they are learned, as they become embodied in the attitudes and actions of the members of a family towards each other. The mufti's words suggest that what qualities the ties acquire are dependent on the conduct of parents and children, and the answer to what constitutes proper or appropriate conduct resides in the shariʿa (as does the mufti's account).[6]

The three fragments together offer to view a picture of a constellation of interconnected and mutually supportive concepts, practices and attitudes that are constitutive of a distinctive sensibility (or form of life). That sensibility (form of life) is characterised by a distinctive attitude towards the Lebanese state, its location in time and space, and of the significance of the legal arrangement that supports it (indeed, an attitude informed by the claim that the existence of the legal arrangement and of the Lebanese state are interdependent). It involves an acquiescence to the principle of coexistence in Lebanon, and the limits it imposes on the shariʿa's reach *and* on the scope of secular positive law. It is informed by a conception of marriage and the

[4] Compare the sensation of waiting 'before the law'.

[5] This difference is captured in Agrama's comparative ethnography of the personal status courts and fatwa council in Egypt. Agrama, *Questioning Secularism*.

[6] For an account of the conceptual transformations that turned 'the family' into the ethical locus of Muslim life and *shariʿa*, see Asad, *Formations of the Secular*. See also Clarke, *Islam and Law*.

family as webs of active and affective ties that are conducive to a divinely sanctioned form of life, ties which the conduct of husbands and wives, and of parents and children, sustain with the guidance of divinely revealed precepts which, in turn, are cultivated through the conduct of conjugal and familial life, where discord or dispute is to be settled in accordance with the shariʿa and (as) Lebanese law.

This chapter is an account of a Lebanese Sunni Muslim sensibility (form of life) as it is construed through the Sunni judicial process of settling conjugal and familial disputes – that is, the ways in which a case proceeds – in shariʿa courts. The form of life or sensibility which the judicial process articulates is of Muslims as subjects of law, that is, who make claims (of right) before the law in terms that matter to the law, on the basis of a narration of events and actions that matter to the law as well, in so far as they are legally accountable. Muslims figure in the judicial process as legal subject and as Muslims. They belong to a religious tradition – the divinely revealed and discursively transmitted precepts by which, in what pertains to the web of conjugal and familial relations in which they are embedded, their conduct is conducted and judged. It is in accordance with that tradition that judgement, as a modality of conduct, is conducted, in conformity with legal principles conducive to coexistence and the respect of jurisdictional boundaries that it requires. The judicial process itself is a distinctive articulation of the religious and secular, of ensuring the mutual availability of the religious and secular.

Muslims as Muslims, Muslims as Subjects of Law

Muslims stand before the shariʿa judge as Muslims whose marital and familial lives are guided by the shariʿa. In so far as the shariʿa judge is *also* a representative of 'the law', they stand before him as legal subjects as well. They are natural, human persons who are endowed with a body, which, as the second fragment above shows, may be subject to the violence of the state. Moreover, they are legal subjects in so far as they are, in the judicial scene, the subjects of claims and actions – claims and actions that are attributable to their person and for which they are legally accountable. Muslims are legally justiciable, their claims are verifiable by legally prescribed methods, and their actions are legally (and morally) judgeable.

The legal subject presupposes the legal process, the first part of which comprises the presentation of facts that constitute a complaint, and from which a case could be made.[7] The facts are of two kinds: the claims proper, which are claims of right, and the actions which the claimants had performed prior, which may have led to it, or may constitute the grounds or reasons for judgment and ruling (the confirmation or denial of certain claims). The facts are typically presented in chronological order, claims of right – for example, over custody, support, or inheritance – made by spouses or various members of a family against each other, or, if they are appealing, against a lower court. In this respect, there is nothing remarkable about the shariʿa judicial process.

Case #1: *ḥaḍāna*, Single Shariʿa Judge in Tripoli, Decision No. 275, 1985: A man approaches the court with a claim of custody (*ḥaḍāna*) over his daughter, countering his former wife's claim for an increase in the amount of money he has been giving her for support (*al-nafaqa*). Apparently, the husband had left both his wife and child without providing either of them with any support for several years. The judge rejects the father's claim to custody over his daughter, ruling that she be kept instead with her mother.[8]

Case #2: *taslīm awlād*, Single Shariʿa Judge in Tripoli, Decision No. 659, 1986: A man complains before the Sunni judge against his daughter-in-law, asking the court to have her hand him his grandchildren (*taslīm al-awlād*), and to drop the support it had imposed on him to pay the mother for the children's needs. The father had disappeared and left the children with their mother, which had at the time given the court reason to impose the payment of support on the grandfather, 'for their food, clothing, dwelling and the rest of [the children's] needs . . . as an indictment of their father'. The grandfather and the mother admit during the trial that they had agreed that she keep the children with her on condition that she accept a 75 per cent reduction of the support money. He had already petitioned the same court, was refused, and sentenced instead to paying the children's support. He approached the court again thirteen days later with a petition for custody and a release from the obligation to pay support.

[7] The presentation of cases is a procedural requirement stipulated in the Law of Shari'a Courts. Clarke, *Islam and Law*, p. 35.

[8] Single Shariʿa Judge in Tripoli (henceforth, SSJT), Decision No. 275, 13 June 1985. Badawi, Hanna (ed.), *Al-Huquq al-Lubnaniyya wa-l-ʿArabiyya*, 1–4 (Beirut, not dated): 42–5.

Since the children had already attained the shariʿa age of custody, the grandfather should have taken the children without bargaining. When the grandfather approaches the court with a request to ratify the agreement, the court rules to compel him to pay support in full, on the basis of a comparative assessment of his and his daughter-in-law's character.[9]

The two preceding cases involve two principals, making a claim against each other, the decision issued confirming on claims as it denies the other. Some cases are more complex and protracted, for they bring together (against each other) several members of 'extended' families, over two or three generations, dealing with problems that result from accumulated actions over a long period of time. Complaints are sometimes made before one court by the same claimants as their case is still being reviewed by another court.

Case #3: *ṭalāq*, Single Shariʿa Judge in Tripoli, Decision No. 18, 1994: In a dispute over inheritance, several members of a deceased man's family approach the court with a request to distribute his inheritance. The claimants petitioned the court to include their father Saleh's second wife, Manal, 'in order to confirm his repudiation of her'. Two of Saleh's children from Maysa, Saleh's first and current wife, agree with their step-siblings' request, on condition that their mother also be included. The second (repudiated) wife Manal asks the court to include Maysa (the current wife) in the case in order to annul her (Maysa's) marriage with the deceased. She argues that Saleh, who was suffering from 'death-sickness' (*maraḍ al-mawt*) and in no state to divorce her, was coerced by his children (from Maysa) to do so.[10] Manal's aim is to exclude Maysa and have the court designate her (Manal) as sole heir. The judge confirms Saleh's divorce from Manal and denies Manal's claim that Saleh's and Maysa's marriage is void. However, contrary to the heirs' wishes,

[9] SSJT, Decision No. 659, 18 December 1986. Hanna (ed.), *Al-Huquq*, 1–4 (n.d.): 38–41.

[10] 'The illness which it is generally feared will lead to death and which is connected to the fact of death.' Mohammad Abu Zahra, 'Family Law', in M. Khadduri and H. J. Liebesny (eds), *Law in the Middle East* (Washington, DC: The Middle East Institute, 1955), pp. 132–78; p. 162. See also Hiroyuki Yanagihashi, 'The Doctrinal Development of "*Marad al-Mawt*" in the Formative Period of Islamic Law', *Islamic Law and Society* 5, 3 (1998): 326–58.

he includes Manal among them, deciding to grant Manal and Maysa an equal share of the inheritance, distributing the rest among the children.[11]

While the cases that are heard by the shariʿa judiciary are disputes over personal or familial rights, they bring occasionally to view some of the claimants' intentions. Saleh – who is now dead, present but not, technically, a claimant in this case – abused his shariʿa right to divorce; his children 'coerced' him to do so in order to dispossess his wife, an instance of what in a civil case might be considered legal fraud. The complexity of a case is increased when an appeal is made against lower instances, or as sometimes happens, other jurisdictions are involved.

Case #4: *tafrīq*, Higher Sunni Shariʿa Court, Decision No. n./a., 2014: A woman petitions the Higher Sunni Shariʿa Court to appeal the decision of a lower court authorising an agreement for a *khulʿ* between her and her husband, and have her give him back 75 per cent of her dower (*al-mahr*).[12] The decision had declared them divorced as a consequence of the *khulʿ* and had her 'pay 75 per cent of the fees and costs' of the proceedings. The woman appeals the lower court's decision of *khulʿ* that had assessed her responsibility at 75 per cent. She wants the Higher Sunni Shariʿa Court to rule in favour of 'separation (*al-tafrīq*) with full responsibility falling on' her former husband, the defendant, and 'to have him pay all costs and fees, plus damages (*ʿiṭl wa ḍarar*)'. The man appeals the lower court's decision before the same court, asking the latter to declare that 'the main cause of the discord between the two of them is the illness of the wife', and 'her behaviour on Facebook, which is contrary to the shariʿa'. In addition, he wishes the Higher Sunni Court to quash the lower court's decision for 'neglecting' to consider 'his claim that she had prevented him from exercising his shariʿa right to sexual intercourse [with her], her bad behaviour, and her lies', and for

[11] SSJT, Decision No. 18, 20 January 1994. Hanna (ed.), *Al-Huquq* 7, 13–15 (October 1994): 26–31.

[12] See Wael B. Hallaq, *Shariʿa between Past and Present: Theory Practice and Modern Transformations* (Cambridge: Cambridge University Press, 2009), pp. 283–286 for '*khulʿ*', and p. 77 for '*mahr*'.

'ignoring' his request to call into question 'the [medical] reports'. The man asks the Higher Sunni Shariʿa Court to rule that his former wife 'was alone responsible for the discord between them, decide on the *khulʿ* in exchange for all of his shariʿa rights and the entire dowry, and have her pay all of the fees and costs, as well as damages'. After several claims and counterclaims, the court decides that the former spouses are responsible in equal measure.[13]

Case #5: *ḥaḍāna*, Beirut Sunni Shariʿa Court, Decision No. n./a., 2018: A woman petitions the court 'to make a decision that would assert her right of custody over her son and oblige the father', the defendant, 'to surrender him to her'. She also wants the court to grant her custody over him and 'permission to take him to her place of residence in Dubai'. The father had changed his place of residence, moving to Lebanon, where he is receiving treatment for cancer, while the mother had filed a similar claim of custody before the shariʿa court in Dubai, the execution of which is still awaiting decision by the Lebanese civil courts. In the preceding case, the father counters the mother's claims with a petition to the court to deny the mother's custody and declare him instead sole custodian over their son. The father justifies his claim by accusing the mother of 'being unqualified (*ʿadam ahliyyatiha*) by shariʿa and law to' fulfil her duty as custodian. The father claims that, in contrast, 'he is in full possession of the conditions specified for custody by shariʿa', adding that there is 'evidence that the son's *maṣlaḥa* and benefit (*manfaʿa*) will be secured if he remained with him'. The court decides to deny the mother's claim and grant it the father, 'allowing the boy for his own *maṣlaḥa* to remain with his paternal grandmother [who had earlier asked the court to include her as a third party to the case] in Lebanon'.[14]

Claims and counterclaims, as well as the narration of the actions leading up to the case in hand are made in terms of legal and shariʿa categories – for example, *ḥaḍāna* (custody), *nafaqa* (alimony), *irth* (inheritance) – and concepts such as *maṣlaḥa* (interest), *ahliyya* (qualification), *masʾuliyya* (responsibility) –

[13] Higher Sunni Shariʿa Court (henceforth, HSSC), Decision No. n./a., 14 *rabiʿ al-awwal hijriyya* 1435, coinciding with 15 January 2014 *miladiyya* (case transcript downloaded from al-Mustashar online database).

[14] Beirut Sunni Shariʿa Court (henceforth, BSSC), Decision No. n./a., 22 *shaʿbān* 1439 *hijri*, coinciding with 8 May 2018 *milādi* (case transcript downloaded from al-Mustashar online database).

that point to the stipulations, provisions or precepts that apply and constitute a legal and a shariʿa argument.

Webs of Relationships

The categories or concepts are articulations of law and shariʿa. However, they pertain specifically to that web of relationships which marriage and the family constitute – relationships between persons (husband and wife, parents and children, and so on), and between persons and things or between persons and persons through the transmission of things (succession, inheritance of mobile and immobile properties). Muslims appearing before the shariʿa judiciary do so in so far as they are embedded in such relationships, which, given possession of certain 'personal qualities', they are expected to sustain (or, in so far as they are before the judiciary, might have actually undermined).

There is judgment in this formulation: a normative conception of conjugal and familial relationships and of the 'qualities' of the persons that are embedded in them are subject to evaluation that would give reasons for judicial decisions. Thus, the categories and concepts are presupposed in the shariʿa judicial process and perform the work of ensuring the availability of the shariʿa (and the law) in judicial reasoning (and, as described in the subsequent section, in Muslim life).

> Case #1: *ḥaḍāna*, Single Shariʿa Judge in Tripoli, Decision No. 275, 1985: 'Referring to the considerations of the books of the *madhhab*', the judge points out, 'we see that the point of the matter (*madar amr*) of the child's custody . . . is to ensure his *maṣlaḥa*, such that wherever his interest is, he must be'. Moreover, the 'jurists (*al-fuqahāʾ*) [have extended] the rights of *ḥaḍāna* to women . . . in accordance with a scale of priorities'. Yet, in order to 'ensure the child's *maṣlaḥa*', he adds, they 'went beyond the texts' to stipulate 'several exceptions'.[15]

> Case #2: *taslīm awlād*, Single Shariʿa Judge in Tripoli, Decision No. 659, 1986: The grandfather 'does not have the right to surrender his right (*lā yamluk al-tanāzul ʿan*)' to *ḥaḍāna*. However, the judge decides to keep the children

[15] SSJT, Decision No. 275, 13 June 1985.

with their mother, since according 'to the books of the *madhhab* . . . we see that . . . the right to the child's custody . . . [is] aimed to [ensure the child's] *maṣlaḥa*'; 'wherever his *maṣlaḥa* is guaranteed, he must remain'.[16]

Case #5: *ḥaḍāna*, Beirut Sunni Shariʿa Court, Decision No. n./a., 2018: The judge reasons as follows: 'custody lawsuits . . . concern the *maṣlaḥa* of the [children in question] first and last', and this principle dictates the judge's duty, which is to 'assess only [their] *maṣlaḥa*'. The court, 'with the authority (*wilāya*) it legally [*al-qānūniyya* and not, notably, *al-sharʾiyya*] possesses to care for and protect the rights of the children, must take any measure it finds necessary [to secure] the *maṣlaḥa* of the child'.[17]

In Arabic, the word '*al-ḥaḍāna*' is derived from the three-letter root '*ḥḍn*', from which '*al-ḥiḍn* ' is derived, the noun that designates the region of the body beneath the armpit, lap or bosom. The noun '*al-ḥiḍāna* ' means the carrying of the child in one's lap and, figuratively, the raising of the child ('*al-tarbiya*'). This meaning is close to the shariʿa concept, which is to 'have custody over the child according to the shariʿa', that is, 'to raise him, by doing what is good for him (*ʿamal mā yaslaḥ lahu*)', to 'take charge of his affairs' – in short, to ensure his *maṣlaḥa*.[18] According to Hallaq, 'Mothers have an unqualified right to custody over their minor children'. However, if the mother is for some reason or other not available, then 'custody rights pass [first] to: the mother's mother, the fathers' mother, the fathers' full sister, his half-sister on the mother's side, the maternal aunts, etc.' There is no consensus about 'the age at which the mother's custody over boys must terminate, seven or nine years being generally the Hanfite position'.[19]

The concept of *maṣlaḥa* in the *fiqh* goes back at least to the earliest systematic attempt to define it by the jurist Abu Hamid Muhammad al-Ghazali in the eleventh century CE. For al-Ghazali '*maṣlaḥa* was God's purpose . . .

[16] SSJT, Decision No. 659, 18 December 1986.

[17] BSSC, Decision No. n./a., 8 May 2018.

[17] Wael B. Hallaq, *Shariʿa between Past and Present: Theory Practice and Modern Transformations* (Cambridge: Cambridge University Press, 2009), p. 287.

[19] Imam and al-Shafiʾi, *Masaʾil al-Ahwal al-Shakhsiyya*, p. 489.

in revealing the divine law'.[20] It consisted in whatever ensured 'the five elements of [human] well-being, namely, their religion, life, intellect, offspring and property'. Muslim reformers of the nineteenth and twentieth centuries redefined *maṣlaḥa* to respond to the challenges of secularisation and the secular state. Being a manifestation of God's wisdom behind the shariʿa, so they reasoned, *maṣlaḥa* could be taken as the criterion 'in deciding cases [that] correspond to the spirit' of the shariʿa if a clear provision is not immediately available in the sources.[21]

The judge traces the line of references in accordance with Article 242 of the Law of Shariʿa Judiciary, which stipulates that the 'Sunni judge issues his rulings according to the preponderant opinion of the *madhhab* of Abu Hanifa, except in those matters [*al-aḥwāl*] which the [Ottoman] Law of Family Rights . . . stipulates', in which case he 'applies the stipulations of that law'.[22]

> Case #2: *taslīm awlād*, Single Shariʿa Judge in Tripoli, Decision No. 659, 1986: The judge, seeking a shariʿa understanding of *ḥaḍāna*, finds reasons in 'a return to the considerations of the books of the *madhhab*', specifically, 'a text which we quote in order to perceive the scope of the vast authority that is placed upon the judge (*al-sulṭa al-mulqāt ʿala ʿātiq al-qāḍi*) in this field'. The judge selects the text from a book by 'Ibn Abidin . . . in the chapter on

[20] Felicitas Opwis, '*Maṣlaḥa* in Contemporary Islamic Legal Theory', *Islamic Law and Society* 12, 2 (2005): 182–223; 188. '*Maslaḥa*, although it is not mentioned in the Qurʾān, has become synonymous with God's purpose in revealing His law to humankind. The purpose of the divine law is understood as attaining the well-being (*maslaḥa*) of humanity in all their mundane and otherworldly affairs. In its relationship to what is referred to as the purposes of the shariʿa (*maqāṣid al-sharīʿa*) *maslaḥa* is one of the main procedural vehicles to address legal change. It can be used as a tool of finding new law when the authoritative texts are silent and of adapting existing law when circumstances call for it.' Felicitas Opwis, *Maṣlaḥa and the Purpose of the Law: Islamic Discourse on Legal Change From the 4th/10th to 8th/14th Century* (Leiden: Brill, 2010), p. 2.

[21] Opwis, '*Maṣlaḥa* in Contemporary Islamic Legal Theory', 198–9.

[22] Article 242 of the Law of Shariʿa Courts issued on 16 July 1962. Al-Zein, *Qawanin wa Nusus wa Ahkam* (Muslims). The translation is Clarke's with slight modifications (Clarke, *Islam and Law*, p. 37). In addition, there is a series of texts on specific issues: 'The Will (*al-waṣiyya*) According to the *ḥanafi madhhab*', 'Inheritance (*al-irth*) According to the *ḥanafi madhhab*', and 'Interdiction (*al-ḥajr*) According to the *Majallat al-Ahkam al-ʿAdliyya*'. The rules on will

custody (*fī bāb al-ḥaḍāna*)', citing verbatim the passage in question.[23] 'There is no doubt (*lā shakka*)', he asserts, 'that', according to Ibn Abidin, 'safety from contagious and complex diseases is one of the branches of the condition of capacity (*min shuʿub sharṭ al-qudra*)'. He then cites another passage from Ibn Abidin's '*ḥāshiya* (gloss)' – 'copied from the *Khulasa* and others (*naqlan ʿan al-khulāṣa w ghayriha*)' – on another book, '*Al-Durr al-Mukhtar*'.[24]

Case #3: *ṭalāq* ('divorce'), Single Shariʿa Judge in Tripoli, Decision No. 18, 1994: The judge argues as follows: 'Before entering into the discussion of the claims and sayings of the . . . parties', the judge 'must (*yajduru bina*), in regard to the mentioned issue, return to the considerations of the books of the *madhhab*'. The judge seeks in 'what is written' in them 'the dominant opinion

and inheritance are two separate texts, taken from *Kitab al-Ahkam al-Sharʿiyya fi al-Ahwal al-Shakhsiyya ʿala Madhhab al-Imam Abi Hanifa al-Nuʿman* by Muhammad Qadri Pasha (Al-Zein, *Qawanin wa Nusus wa Ahkam* (Muslims), p. 190 n. 1, and p. 196 n. 1). For Qadri Pasha and his effort to codify the shariʿa, see Tarek Elgawhary, *Rewriting Islamic Law the Opinions of the ʿUlamāʾ towards Codification of Personal Status Law in Egypt* (Piscataway: Gorgias Press, 2019), pp. 58–69. According to Hallaq, 'The transposition of Islamic law from the fairly independent and informal terrain of the jurists to that of the highly formalized and centralized agency of the state found manifestation in the compendium entitled *Mecelle-i Ahkām-ı Adliye* (Ar. *Majallat al-Ahkām al-ʿAdliyya*), produced by a committee headed by the Shariʿa jurist Ahmet Çevdet Pasha who . . . won the debate against the powerful Westernizer Ali Pasha' (Hallaq, *Shariʿa between Past and Present*, p. 411). The translation of '*al-ḥajr*' as 'interdiction' is Hallaq's (p. 239, and n. 4).

[23] Born in Damascus in 1198 H/1784 CE and died in 1252 H/1836 CE, Muhammad Amin Ibn Abidin stood at the threshold of the nineteenth century 'modernizing' reforms of the Ottoman Empire. Haim Gerber, *Islamic Law and Culture, 1600–1840* (Leiden: Brill, 1999), p. 20. His work 'earned him the undisputed title of being the last great traditional jurist of the Hanafite school' (ibid., p. 26). Ibn Abidin relied in his fatwas on a chain of texts that reach back to the sixth/twelfth century, a substantial number of them being those of Ottoman muftis (ibid., p. 61). See also Wael B. Hallaq, 'A Prelude to Ottoman Reform: Ibn Abidin on Custom and Legal Change', in Israel Gershoni, Hakan Erdem and Ursula Woköck (eds), *Histories of the Modern Middle East: New Directions* (Boulder: Lynne Reiner, 2002), pp. 37–61.

[24] SSJT, Decision No. 659, 18 December 1986. Muhammad Ibn Ali Ibn Muhammad al-Husni, known as 'Ala' al-Din al-Hafsaqi (1025–1088 H/1616–1677 CE); see https://al-maktaba.org/book/21613. Shams al-Din Muhammad Ibn Abdallah Ibn Ahmad, al-Timurtashi (939–1004 H/1532–596 CE); see https://shamela.ws/author/1217 (last accessed 30 May 2023).

> (*arjaḥ al-aqwāl*') of the *madhhab* of the *imām* Abu Hanifa, which is 'applied in our Sunni shariʿa courts'. The plaintiffs' claim is made up of two interconnected problems: Are Saleh and Manal to be considered divorced? Is Manal to inherit?[25] The judge proceeds to enunciate 'the shariʿa principles (*al-mabādiʾ*), rules (*al-qawāʿid*), and foundations (*al-usus*)' of marriage.[26] According to the judge, a consensus (*ijmāʿ*) exists in Hanafi jurisprudence that if a man divorce his wife irrevocably (*ṭalāq bi-l-baynūna al-kubra* or 'major separation') 'in order to evade' the obligation of leaving her a share in the inheritance, 'she would still inherit'.[27] However, two conditions must be satisfied: first, that he repudiate her 'without her request or consent while [he is] in a state of death-sickness', and, second, 'as long as she is still in her waiting period (*al-ʿidda*)'.[28]

According to '*fuqahāʾ al-madhhab*', the school's jurists, 'who had defined the concept of death-sickness', it is a condition in which the person 'is incapable of conducting his immediate affairs outside the house, such as going to the mosque, to his store', a condition that 'does not worsen during a year or more, and [in which] there is no risk of his imminent dying despite his sickness being linked to death'. In cases like this, the judge explains, the 'legislator (*al-shāriʿ*) treat[s] [the husband] contrary to his intentions, as long as the effects of marriage persisted'.[29]

> Case #3: *ṭalāq*, Single Shariʿa Judge in Tripoli, Decision No. 18, 1994: A second set of principles is derived from 'the concept (*mafhūm*) of the marriage contract'. He cites two definitions, one by an anonymous jurist, the other by '[the author

[25] SSJT, Decision No. 18, 20 January 1994.

[26] *Al-nikāḥ*, or marriage, 'is a sanctified social and legal institution'. Hallaq, *Shariʿa between Past and Present*, pp. 271–80.

[27] Ibid., pp. 280–3, '*ṭalāq*'.

[28] '[T]he principle of *ʿidda*, a waiting period imposed on divorced women.' It is the 'postponement of the irrevocable dissolution of the marriage until three menstrual cycles had been completed or, if the woman were pregnant, until the birth of the child. During this period, which allowed for reconciliation between the spouses, the husband was obliged to provide both domicile and financial support for his wife. Furthermore, a divorced woman with a child was to suckle it for a period of two years, and the father was required to provide for mother and child during this same period.' Ibid., pp. 32–3.

[29] See footnote 10, above, on 'death-sickness'.

(of)] *Sahib al-Kanz*', both of whom identify the marriage contract as an instrument that permits (*yaḥull*) mutual enjoyment (*al-mutʿa, al-istimtāʿ*, or pleasure).[30]

However, the judge points out, '*fuqahāʾ al-madhhab*' had 'given it an imprecise definition', specifically 'in respect of its most important purposes and functions'. The judge adjusts this definition of marriage, appealing first to a verse from the Qurʾan about the 'affection (*al-mawadda*) and compassion (*al-raḥma*)' that reside in marriage, before calling upon '*al-fuqahāʾ al-muʿāsirīn* (the modern jurists)'. The judge singles out '*al-ʿallāma* Mohammad Abu Zahra', who had 'noticed this lack among the predecessors (*al-farīq al-salaf*)', and whose correct definition of marriage is similar to the one which the 'Syrian Law of Personal Status' (No. 59 of 1953) adopts, as its 'First Article stipulates with more precision'.[31]

The judge explains that marriage has 'higher purposes, among which procreation and the preservation of the human kind', as well as 'emotional and spiritual attributes, such as 'finding . . . in the partner spiritual companionship (*al-uns al-rūḥi*)'. The judge points out that marriage is 'a contract' that enables 'intimacy (*ʿishra*) between a man and a woman . . . the accomplishment of what human nature needs, [and] their life-long cooperation, and assigns to each [their] rights and obligations'.[32] In addition, the judge cites the first article of the Syrian Law of Personal Status, which stipulates that marriage is 'a contract between a man and a woman . . . for the purpose of founding the bond of common life and procreation (*nasl*)'.[33]

[30] The two definitions are cited in the court transcript without reference to title or author, except for the enigmatic 'according to *sahib Al-Kanz*', who, it turns out, is Al-Nasafi, the author of the *matn Kanz al-Daqaʾiq*. I owe Nada Moumtaz the author's name and the title of his *matn*.

[31] Mohammand Abu Zahra (1898–1974), 'professor of Islamic Law at the University of Cairo, Egypt, and author of several works in Arabic on Islamic Jurisprudence'. Khadduri and Liebesny, *Law in the Middle East*, p. xvii (see note 10, above). 'The Syrian Law of Personal Status' (No. 59 of 1953).

[32] Cited in the transcript without information about the source.

[33] A judge argues in another divorce case that marriage performs the biological function of ensuring the persistence of 'the human race (*al-jins al-bashari*)', appealing to 'the value of the human being (*al-insān*) [who] cannot be sold or bought', whose 'humanity is invaluable, and whose freedom sacred in Islam'. HSSC, Decision No. 169, 9 January 1992. Hanna (ed.), *Al-Huquq* 1–4 (n.d.): 50 (not discussed elsewhere in this chapter).

Case #3: *ṭalāq*, Single Shariʿa Judge in Tripoli, Decision No. 18, 1994: The judge suspects that Saleh's intention to divorce the second wife, Manal, and remarry Maysa (his first, former wife) is to disinherit the former and make the latter and his children from her sole heirs. The judge wants to know, in the context of what he calls 'this charade', 'the wisdom (*al-ḥikma*) concealed behind the marriage contract'. The divorce is in conformity with the law and shariʿa, and so is Saleh's last marriage to Maysa. However, it is Saleh's intentions, which the judge calls into question through an examination of the difference between the shariʿa definition of the concept of marriage and the circumstances of Saleh's three marriages. The judge finds Saleh's use of marriage as a means to disinherit Manal and make Maysa and her children his only heirs reprehensible. It is on that difference that the court's judgment and subsequent decision hold, namely, 'to consider Saleh divorced from his wife Manal . . . with the intention of disinheriting her' and 'to count her among his shariʿa heirs contrary to his intention (*raddan li qasdihi ʿalayh*)'. 'Since', he says, 'when he [the husband] intends (*qaṣad*)' to dispossess his wife, 'the legislator (*al-shāriʿ*) treats him against his intention'.

Judging Conduct, Conducting Judgment

Norms of conduct are embedded in conjugal and familial relationships and enter into the transactions that secure them. They structure the claims and counterclaims which a couple or members of a family bring before the judiciary, and enter into the latter's assessment of the facts of the case (the claims and the actions of the principles in a case) and the passing of judgment and ruling. The judiciary attends to the principals' conduct (at least in some cases), finding in it reasons to settle disputes or make a decision.

Case #1: *ḥaḍāna*, Single Shariʿa Judge in Tripoli, Decision #No. 275, 1985: The judge singles out the fact that the husband 'had turned his back' on his daughter, refused to pay her maintenance, and neglected his shariʿa and legal duties. 'It did not cross [the husband's] mind (*ghāba ʿan dhihnihi*) that the place to keep a child is the household', which he had abandoned once he left his wife. The wife, in contrast, is 'borrowing [money] to spend on herself and daughter', to ensure the latter's 'private schooling and [medical expenses]'. She 'consented to remain under his *ʿiṣma* [right to initiate divorce] while still young', and did not seek 'separation' even though he was absent all that time. A letter from the husband's family, signed by a coroner and a shariʿa judge, favoured explicitly the wife over their own son – and over any other agnate – making it plain that they wanted to 'save this girl [the daughter] and keep her away from trouble'. It is clear, the judge concludes, that she is 'a good (*ṣāliḥa*) mother, a loyal and reasonable (*ʿāqila*) wife from whom we must not take the child away'. In a remark addressed to the husband, the judge explains that 'the Islamic legislator (*al-shāriʿ al-islāmi*) . . . decree[s] a right to a human being (*haqqan li insān*) in exchange of an obligation (*wājib*) he imposes on him'. The husband cannot simply ask for his right to keep his daughter without providing support. Moreover, to take charge of a child is to aspire to 'charity (*al-birr*) and piety (*al-taqwa*)', and avert 'evil (*al-ithm*) and enmity (*al-ʿidwān*)'. The judge decides to keep the daughter with her mother for otherwise she will end up 'in the hands of an insensitive (*mutalabbid al-hiss*) father, in the custody (*ḥuḍn*) of her stepmother (*ḍurra li wālidatiha*) in a foreign country which [threatens] her conduct and creed'.[34]

Case #2: *taslīm awlād*, Single Shariʿa Judge in Tripoli, Decision No. 659, 1986: According to the judge, the grandfather, being the shariʿa and legal guardian, may not surrender 'his right' of guardianship, which is precisely what he tried to do in his agreement with the child's mother. The agreement which the two of them had signed is thus defective in some of its 'fundamental conditions'. This gives the judge the right to reject it in order to prevent a 'wrong and render justice (*dafʿan li-l-ḥayf wa taḥqīqan li-l-ʿadl*), in the interests of the minors', and in accordance with 'the Law of the Shariʿa Judiciary'. The judge notes that the mother was under '*ikrāh maʿnawi* (emotional duress)' when entering the agreement, because she wanted to keep the children. In contrast, the grandfather aimed to avoid paying the support that is 'imposed [on him] by a binding court ruling'. If implemented, the agreement would not only reduce the children's access to the 'necessities of livelihood . . . such as food, clothing, shelter, education, and medical care', it might force the mother to beg ('*madd yadaha*', lit. extend her hand) in order to provide for her children, exposing them 'to ethical harm (*ḍarar adabi*)'. The fact that the mother admitted that 'she was poor and owned nothing' reinforced the judge's opinion of the grandfather as 'unreliable (*ghayr ma'mūn*)'. The latter 'expressed his readiness' to take custody of the children only 'when their mother asked him for their support and . . . after a decision was issued against him' by the

[34] SSJT, Decision No. 275, 13 June 1985.

first instance judge. 'What motivated (*dafaʿa*) him', concludes the judge, 'was nothing but his concern to avoid paying for support'. The judge decides that he 'should not compel (*ʿadam jawāz ilzām*) [the grandfather] to take charge of his grandchildren because he lacks the two conditions of capability and trustworthiness', and that 'the children must remain with their mother . . .' The woman's 'concern for [the children] was demonstrated by the fact that she had accepted the aforementioned agreement' only because 'she did not want to [lose them] even if that required her to seek the charity of others'.[35]

Case #3: *ṭalāq*, Single Shariʿa Judge in Tripoli, Decision No. 18, 1994: The problem begins when Saleh dies while the court was still considering his petition to the court to confirm his divorce from his second wife, Manal. Saleh had divorced his wife Maysa at a time when they had already had several children.[36] The same year, he married Manal, who gave birth to three children before he was struck by a disease that affected his brain and lungs. He then divorced Manal through the intermediary of his son – who held power of attorney over Saleh's affairs (*wakīl*) – and remarried Maysa, the son's mother. The judge argues that Saleh's financial conduct is sound, but finds fault in his attitude towards marriage. The judge asks, rhetorically, 'Did he, Saleh, divorce his second wife and remarry his first shortly before he died in order to satisfy a sexual impulse (*al-watar al-jinsi*)', or for 'the sake of having children?' Was it a 'desire and yearning to start a new page of companionship, friendship and peace . . . or a wish that his divorcee of yesterday become his mermaid in the other world?' In his overview of the facts, the judge wondered about the deceased's conduct. 'Rather than be placed on the right path (*al-ṣirāṭ al-mustaqīm*) as he gets ready to leave on the path to the other life, to better prepare for his meeting with his Lord (*rabbihi*)', Saleh chose instead to 'divorc[e] his wife during his death sickness in order to exclude her from his inheritance', and marr[y] his divorcee to replace her'. His marriage was 'based on a questionable power of attorney' and a 'medical report confirming his capacity to marry' ten days before he died. The judge does not question the deceased man's piety as such – he died 'having completed his religious duties (*wājibātihi al-dīniyya*)' – but what was reproachable was his conjugal or marital conduct.[37]

[35] SSJT, Decision No. 659, 18 December 1986.
[36] SSJT, Decision No. 18, 20 January 1994.
[37] Ibid.

Case #4: *tafrīq*, Higher Sunni Shariʿa Courts, Decision No. n./a., 2014: The court is called upon to decide on 'the degree of responsibility (*mas'ūliyya*) which each party bears for the conflict between them'. The wife complains 'against her husband's *sū' ʿishratihi laha* (bad company)' and his threats to dispossess her of 'her salary and jewlery'. He 'slandered her', and when they went to 'her parents' house' with the intention of seeking their help 'to solve the problem between' them, 'had left her there and did not bring her back to the marital household'. In his counterclaim, the husband 'denied that he had mistreated his wife', or that he slandered her (*'naʿataha bi ṣifāt ghayr akhlāqiyya'*). Moreover, the husband accused his wife of concealing from him 'a longstanding disease (arthritic rheumatism)', about which he 'learned . . . after the wedding'. The problem is not the fact of her disease, or her keeping it from him, but the fact that 'the medication to treat [it] is very costly' and that the disease 'impacts [her capacity] to bear children', for there is a 'probability' that they acquire it during pregnancy. The husband claimed that his wife 'cheated and tricked' him, especially since 'once her health improved, she would leave the house' to spend time 'at places of entertainment . . . and cafés, and to attend . . . weddings and parties' in which men and women comingled. He 'showed' the court 'pictures of her, asking to make her fully responsible' for the separation. 'It is clear', the judge states, that 'the plaintiff's pretext that his wife's health had caused a repulsion between them' demonstrates a lack of 'seriousness' on his part to 'hold onto his wife'. If he was, 'he would have sought to her reconciliation or ask her back to live with him'. Instead, 'he took another wife, which increased the hostility between him and his [first] wife'. The judge concludes that the two 'have not shown any seriousness in [reaching] mutual understanding and reconciliation, each proceed[ing] instead to seek separation and [make the other fully responsible]', deciding that they 'bear responsibility together in equal measure (*munāṣafa*)' for 'the interruption of their marital life'.[38]

Case #5: *ḥaḍāna*, Beirut Sunni Shariʿa Court, Decision No. n./a., 2018: The judge singles out two reasons why the child's *maṣlaḥa* dictates that he remain with the father. First, 'the paternal grandmother's place of residence . . . is with his father', and, second, the grandmother has 'made a commitment (*taʿahhud*) to provide her grandson with the necessary nurture, care, and supervision'. The

[38] HSSC, Decision No. n./a., 14 *rabiʿ al-awwal* 1435 *hijriyya*/15 January 2014 *milādiyya*.

judge grants the grandmother 'her request for custody . . . despite [the child's] exceeding the age of seven years', in order to 'protect his *maṣlaḥa* from harm [*ḍarar*] if he were to be surrendered to a custodian [his mother] who is incapable of providing him with the Islamic religious and moral upbringing'.[39]

The judiciary attend as well to their own conduct, for it informs their assessments of the facts of a case, it places limits on the methods they employ to interpret legal and shariʿa texts, and figures in the constitution of their judicial authority.

Case #2: *taslīm awlād*, Single Shariʿa Judge in Tripoli, Decision No. 659, 1986: It is the aim of achieving justice (e.g. securing the child's *maṣlaḥa*) that guides the judge's approach to 'the understanding of the texts (*taḥmilu ʿala fahm al-nuṣūṣ fahm yasīr fi ittijāh taḥqīq al-ʿadāla*)'. The judge reaches out to Ibn Abidin, who writes that 'the mufti must have the insight (*al-baṣīra*) to consider what is 'best (*aslah*)' (e.g. for the child). The discretion a judge is granted places his 'conscience (*ḍamīr*) . . . under divine censorship (*al-taghallub ʿala ẓāhir al-nuṣūṣ*)'. His 'conscience may be swayed', which is likely 'when the heart weakens and piety is lacking', misleading the judge to circumvent 'the literal sense of texts (*al-taghallub ʿala ẓāhir al-nuṣūṣ*)' with 'stratagems (*ḥiyal*)' that subvert the dominant interpretation or correct doctrine. It is not sufficient for the judge to be pious and possess knowledge. The decision he makes does not depend only on his insight into a person or his relationship with God, but is anchored in a tradition to which he belongs. Thus, the judge appeals to Ibn Abidin to be with 'us' in the present, he reminds himself (and his listeners and readers) as he reads him, that 'the law (*al-qānūn*) is not safeguarded by its guardians, but by the purified hearts in the depths of which the fear of God has settled'.[40]

Judicial conduct is not just a matter of the judge's authority and piety, and has implications beyond the case proper, for it bears on the validity of the

[39] BSSC, Decision No. n./a., 8 May 2018.

[40] In a case I do not discuss in this chapter, the judge speaks about being 'honest and inspired (*nazīh wa mulham*)', in possession of 'a living conscience (*damīr ḥayy*), radiant sentiments (*wujdān muta'alliq*), fine sensibilities, and a sense of the divine supervision over him'. SSJT, Decision No. 459, 1992. Hanna (ed.), *Al-Huquq* 1–4 (n.d.): 56.

ruling. Thus, it could be a cause of conflict between shariʿa and the positive law, and a reason, thereby, for the imposition of a legal sanction against the shariʿa judiciary (e.g. an appeal before the civil courts that would result in the defeat of a shariʿa ruling).

Authority, Textual Consistency, and the (Islamic) General Interest

There is more at stake in the conduct of the shariʿa judiciaries and their attitudes towards the legal and shariʿa texts than the soundness or validity of their rulings in conjugal and familial disputes. The cases discussed in the preceding sections suggest that the shariʿa judge occupies a prominent place in the life – the conjugal and familial life, at least – of ordinary Muslims, and his conduct matters in so far as he is the authoritative connection between the latter and the shariʿa (and law), or as the authority through the agency of which Muslims on the one hand, and the shariʿa and law on the other, are made mutually available. Apart (though not disconnected) from this, however, at stake in the shariʿa judge's conduct is the Islamic general interest, and, beyond it, the general interest.

The decisions of the first instance court may be appealed before the Higher Sunni Shariʿa Court (last instance), and it is the prosecutor general at the Higher Sunni Shariʿa Court who decides whether a case is to be appealed or not. The prosecutor general examines a demand to appeal a case and offers an opinion about it before transferring it to the Higher Court if it fulfils the conditions. The prosecutor's role is regulatory, having 'the sole objective of preventing unsound reasoning (*ijtihād khāṭiʾ*)' on the part of lower instance judges, and to make sure that they 'apply the texts correctly'.[41]

The 'settled application of texts 'serves the general interest (*maṣlaḥat al-muslimīn al-ʿāmma*) of Muslims'. Textual consistency implies Islamic general interest because inconsistencies entail a conflict with the state and other

[41] PG, Decision No. 423/94, 3 March 1994. Abou Eid (ed.), *Al-Qararat al-Kubra*, 36 (Beirut), pp. 156–9. For a description of the office and funciton of the prosecutor general at the Sunni courts in Lebanon, see Clarke, *Islam and Law*, p. 111.

jurisdictions (e.g. ecclesiastical tribunals), and thus leads to having the shariʿa judge's decisions quashed by the Court of Cassation. There is a specific configuration of authority, text and interpretation that secures the general interest of all Muslims. The general (public) interest of Muslims is opposed to 'personal interest (*al-maṣlaḥa al-shakhṣiyya*)', and the function of the prosecutor general is to 'guarantee the proper application of shariʿa and legal rules in order to achieve the Islamic general interest (*al-maṣlaḥa al-ʿāmma al-islamiyya*) [rather than] anyone's personal interest'.

The coexistence of Muslims and Christians in Lebanon constitutes the context in which the Islamic general interest acquires some of its characteristics. The two are interconnected and mutually supportive. The Islamic general interest resides in taking into account the requirements which the coexistence of Muslims and their Christian compatriots imposes on them (both). A presupposition of coexistence between Muslims and Christians is that they are distinct from each other and distinctive, from which follows that their distinctiveness be preserved, and a certain degree of distinction between them be maintained.

This is guaranteed by each community's 'religious laws of personal status'. In addition to the difference which 'religion proper' – that is, beliefs, rituals – makes, a community's 'religious laws of personal status' secure not only the difference in the way each community organises the marriages of its members (and some of its results), but the place which marriage (and its results) occupies in what counts as 'religious' – the interconnections, if any, between marriage and what counts as 'religion'.

The shariʿa judiciary occupies a pivotal place in the articulation of the sensibility of Muslims in Lebanon in its threefold capacity as participant in the Lebanese legal arrangement and one of the Lebanese state's formal institutions, as the official and authoritative repository of shariʿa (and legal) knowledge, and as guarantor of the shariʿa's continued relevance to (presence in) Muslim life.[42] The shariʿa judiciary performs a mediating function between Muslims in Lebanon and the Lebanese state to which they belong (according to the mufti above, as a prerequisite to their belonging to it), between them

[42] It does not follow from this that it is exclusive or uncontested.

and the shariʿa as 'discursive tradition', and between the latter and the positive law (and the Lebanese state).

Conclusion

How the Sunni shariʿa judiciary in Lebanon performs this mediating function was the focus of this chapter. It pursued the judiciary's efforts through the judicial process to bring together accounts of people's problems, the legal stipulations that apply to and guide their resolution, the shariʿa concepts that it mobilises to respond to them, the sense and judgment of the kinds of actions or conduct that translate them, and the kinds of relations they put into play (among Muslims, between them and the law, between them and God, and so on).

The practice of shariʿa judges, circumscribed legally within the limits of their jurisdiction and the positive law, is informed by the shariʿa. Conversely, it ensures as well the continuity and relevance of the shariʿa. It is through sharʿi judicial practice that 'Islamic' concepts are mobilised, authorised and enacted to give coherence to a changing sensibility (form of life) in a changing world. In the words of a Sunni shariʿa judge, 'The conditions . . . are in continuous change and transformation (*fi tabaddul wa taghayyur mustamir*), which entails a change in the causes (*al-asbāb*) of the rules (*al-aḥkām*)'.[43]

Thus, it matters for the mufti to emphasise what marriage is 'in Islam', that it is between 'a man and a woman', and that it is 'the basis and nucleus of the family' in which a Muslim is born and raised as a Muslim. What this consists in, however, is not just the holding of beliefs, or the participation in 'ritual', but the acquisition of qualities or attributes – 'spiritual tranquility', 'compassion', 'reverence', 'respect', 'civility'. These virtues sustain and accompany the 'relations' that develop and grow out of marriage – in a movement initiated by marriage. They are expected of a Muslim, they enter into his or her conduct, and constitute the basis on which moral and judicial judgments are made.

They are enacted through judicial practice and embodied by the shariʿa judge who, in virtue of the disposition they inform, is guided to read carefully and interpret truthfully the shariʿa and legal texts, to apply their norm and

[43] BSSC, Decision No. n./a., 8 May 2018. See footnote 13, above.

rules judiciously, and to rule justly. As some of the cases analysed above suggest, a shariʿa judge's authority encompasses a discretion to appeal to and make use of concepts, some of which he might have to redefine or correct – and do so within constraints that protect against arbitrariness. Some of these concepts he derives directly from the texts of antecedent jurists (his predecessors), while others are, strictly speaking, of the positive law.

'The law', 'the person', 'shariʿa', 'judge', 'public order', as well as 'marriage and its results', articulate Muslims in Lebanon and the Lebanese state. They are links in a single chain, or elements in a web of relations that join Muslims in Lebanon together, to the Lebanese state, and to fellow Christians. They enter into the constitution of a Lebanese Muslim's sensibility – of what it is to say 'Muslim in Lebanon'. It does not follow from this, of course, that there is consensus among Muslims about it.

PART III

DISPASSIONATE BODIES

5

OFFENDING THE RELIGIOUS

In the early months of 2018, the judge of examination of North Lebanon 'ordered three young men accused of offending the Virgin Mary to memorize verses that glorify her in the Qurʾanic Sura Al Imran . . . as a condition of their release'. According to the judge, the offenders would by doing so 'learn forgiveness among religions and the love that Muslims have for Mary, instead of the ugly ideas which extremists sow in their minds'.

On Friday, April 27, 2018, 'the examining judge in Mount Lebanon . . . ordered the release of "A.Gh." under the condition that [the latter] be obliged to memorise a Qurʾanic verse from "Sura Maryam", granting [him] until Monday' to appear again before the judge in order to prove that he has 'memorised the aforementioned verse'. A.Gh. was arrested 'after a quarrel . . . with a group of young men . . . during which [he] proceeded', according to the news report, 'to denigrate the divine dignity (*taḥqīr al-ʿizza al-ilāhiyya*) and offend the monotheistic religions (*taʿarrada li-l-diyānāt al-samāwiyya*), which is considered an infraction (*jurm*) of incitement to communitarianism (*ithārat al-naʿarāt al-tāʾifiyya*)'.[1]

[1] National News Agency, '*Qararan bi Ikhla' Sabil Mawquf*'; Lebanon24, '*Mujaddadan . . . Qadi Ulzim*'; Rita al-Khoury, '*Min Jadid, Qarar Qada'i Jari*'; Rashid Saʿid Qarani, '*Qadi Ya'mur Muttaham*'. It is not clear if the phrases 'the divine dignity', 'the Abrahamic religions' and 'incitement to communitarianism' occurred in the judge's decision or if they were the reporting agency's addition. I will exclude them from this analysis.

The incident that led to the young men's arrest in the first case had taken place in the city of Tripoli, fifty miles north of Beirut and a forty-five-minute drive to the northern Lebanese border with Syria. The second largest in Lebanon and home to around half a million Sunnis, ʿAlawis and Christians, the city had around the same period witnessed several heavy rounds of armed combat between the first two communities. The judge's order was the first of its kind in Lebanese case law and drew the attention of Lebanese officials. The prime minister at the time commended the judge in a 'tweet', expressing his appreciation of her wisdom.[2]

The Lebanese as well as the Arab press (e.g. in Iraq and Egypt) wrote about it, many (in Lebanon, mostly) impressed, others puzzled, some dismayed. Given the ambiguity of the case, the reactions are not surprising: young men are arrested for offending a personage whom Christians consider sacred; the young men turn out to be – or are identified by the judge to be – Muslims; instead of handing down on them their due punishment in accordance with Lebanese criminal law, a 'Christian' (as an Arab newspaper stressed) judge releases them on condition that the young Muslim men memorise verses from the Qurʾan; the judge justifies her order to spare the young men by her intention to set an example of 'forgiveness among religions', asserting that Muslims have a love for Mary, and that they could find evidence of their love for her in the Qurʾan; finally, that having learned love and forgiveness, they would be led towards a moderate Islamic path.

In the second case, the quarrel took place in the area around the southern town of Rmeileh, home to a population of Sunnis, Shiʿa, Druze and Christians twenty-three miles south of Beirut, the capital city of Lebanon. The area had been in the news when a series of armed conflicts broke out between supporters of a self-proclaimed Sunni militant shaykh and supporter of the Syrian opposition on the one hand, and members and supporters of the Shiʿi Hizballah on the other.[3]

Criminal law, the Virgin Mary and Qurʾanic verses interpenetrate in the office of a judge of examination – a functionary of the Lebanese state – setting

[2] This chapter is a slightly revised version of Raja Abillama, '"The Love That Muslims Have for Mary": Secularism and Christian–Muslim Coexistence in Lebanon', *Comparative Studies of South Asia, Africa and the Middle East* 42 1 (2022): 51–62. Duke University Press.

[3] The conflicts in both regions had some connection with the Syrian civil war.

a stage for the dissemination and circulation of ostensibly religious references across the borders that (are supposed to) keep separate people's private beliefs and public authority, Lebanese Christians and Lebanese Muslims, religious education and penal procedure. This religious performance in a judge's office would seem to be in line with the Lebanese Constitution, according to which the Lebanese state, 'in rendering homage to God Almighty', has a duty to 'respect all religions and creeds', 'guarantee . . . the free exercise of all religious rites', and ensure 'that the . . . religious interest of the population, to whatever religious sect they belong, shall be respected'. The two cases would seem to be in that same spirit: the Lebanese state, through the intermediary of its judges, rendering homage to the divinity.

The idea of 'Muslim–Christian coexistence' enters into the judicial decisions as a structuring principle: it is that which the words of the accused are deemed to violate, and it is that which the judges' task is to protect. Muslim–Christian coexistence is constitutive of a world in which reasons are sought, and actions are singled out and judged. It is with Muslim–Christian coexistence in sight that the judges prescribe the reading and memorising of the Qur'anic verses, and pursue instead of punitive violence the path of mercy. Christian–Muslim coexistence is the context in which '(the Virgin) Mary' acquires its distinctive, secular sense, as the common symbolic mediator between Christians and Muslims and the object of their affective, political and economic investment.

In what follows, I discuss first the idea of 'Muslim–Christian coexistence' in the context of 'the national process of interfaith dialogue' in Lebanon, where 'dialogue' is the discursive form in which 'coexistence' is put into practice, and the medium in which it is performed. I then turn to an account of the Virgin Mary's apparition to a Muslim boy in a Christian village in a predominantly Muslim region of northern Lebanon, examining specifically the state's response and people's attitudes towards it. In the third section, I turn to the Lebanese Penal Code and its criminal taxonomy in the framework of which the words against Mary are identified, investigated and judged.

I take up the project of Penal Code reform in Lebanon in the fourth section, to which the two cases apply – specifically the judges' decisions to release the accused, opting not for punishment, but education. Reforming the punitive sensibility and the idea of coexistence between Christians and Muslims converge: the offenders are reformable in so far as they are legal subjects and predisposed to learn the truth (of religion), a truth which, once learned, is constitutive of a sensibility or disposition conducive to maintaining Muslim–Christian coexistence.

Coexistence and/as/in Dialogue

In February 2010, the Lebanese prime minister announced the government's decision to mark 25 March, the Day of the Annunciation in the Christian calendar, as the 'National Day for Christian–Muslim Dialogue' and celebrate it as an official holiday.[4] Until then, official holidays in Lebanon were either 'civic' national holidays (e.g. Independence Day) or religious – Islamic (e.g. *Al-Fiṭr* and *Al-Aḍḥa*) and Christian (e.g. Christmas and Easter). They all are official holidays and observed, at least by public institutions. With the National Day for Christian–Muslim Dialogue/Day of Annunciation the government has inflected the secular, national calendar, with a new kind of experience. Henceforth, the Lebanese would celebrate a time that is neither exclusively religious – Muslim *or* Christian – nor, strictly speaking, 'civic'. On the National Day for Christian–Muslim Dialogue, Muslims and Christians in Lebanon would be celebrating the articulation of two distinct religious traditions around the now explicitly common figure of Mary, and a new, national, secular time. With the National Day for Christian–Muslim Dialogue/Day of Annunciation the government altered the sense of the Day of the Annunciation, of the Annunciation, and of Mary.

The suggestion to mark the day of the Annunciation as the National Day for Christian–Muslim Dialogue was made two years earlier by Shaykh Mohammad Nokkari, secretary general of Dar al-Fatwa in Lebanon and chief of staff of the office of the Mufti of the Lebanese Republic.[5] Nokkari made the suggestion at a meeting on 25 March of the previous year – the Day of

[4] Henri Chamussy, 'Le dialogue islamo-chrétien au Moyen-Orient', *Confluences Méditerranée* 66, 3 (2008): 179–90; Claire Grandchamps, 'Lebanon: the Only Country in the World to Have an Islamic-Christian National Day', *L'Orient-Le Jour*, 26 March 2019, https://www.lorientlejour.com/article/1163467/lebanon-the-only-country-in-the-world-to-have-an-islamic-christian-national-day.html.

[5] It would seem that Nokkari's status as a '*shaykh*' is not certain. Chamussy considers him to be one. However, Nokkari has apparently no training in shariʿa (he has a doctorate from the Sorbonne), and his appointment at the shariʿa courts seems to have been a source of controversy (Nada Moumtaz, personal communication, 20 April 2020).

Annunciation – at a Jesuit school located on the hills that surround Beirut's eastern suburbs called '*Notre Dame de Jamhour* (Our Lady of Jamhour)'. The meeting included Christian and Muslim representatives (the school's rector for the former, an advisor to the Shiʿi Higher *Jaʿfari Shariʿa* Courts and the Sunni Nokkari with a delegation from Al-Azhar University for the latter).[6]

Such initiatives of 'Christian–Muslim dialogue' have been a recurrent feature in Lebanon since the mid-1960s, carving out a space of discourse and practice in the country between the 'private' space of 'religion proper' and the 'public' space of ('sectarian') politics.[7] They seem to have begun in 1965, with two series of lectures entitled 'Lectures on Islam and Christianity in Lebanon' and 'Lectures on Justice in Christianity and Islam'. The two lecture series brought together a number of high-profile speakers such as Sayyid Moussa al-Sadr (Shiʿi), Father Georges Khodr (Greek Orthodox) and Father Youakim Moubarac (Catholic). In the years preceding the armed conflicts of 1975, the Mufti of the Republic, Shaykh Hasan Khaled at the time, organised a series of conferences, continuing throughout the Civil War, in which the 'spiritual leaders' of the two communities would engage in 'Christian–Muslim dialogue'.[8] It, and it would seem that, since the very beginning, the dialogue between Christians and Muslims was a dialogue between their religious or spiritual

[6] Chamussy, 'Le dialogue islamo-chrétien'.

[7] For a comprehensive list of initiatives of dialogue, see Ahmad bin Abd al-Rahman bin 'Uthman al-Qadi, *Daʿwa al-Taqrib Bayn al-Adyan: Dirasa Naqdiyya fi Daw' al-ʿAqida al-Islamiyya* (Riaydh: Dar Ibn al-Jawzi, n.d.), 1349ff. Jordan, Palestine, Tunisia, the Sudan and, more recently, Qatar have also seen similar initiatives and in some cases the establishing of institutions of 'interfaith studies' (e.g. the Doha International Center for Interfaith Dialogue); see ibid., pp. 1375–409. 'Interfaith relations' have become a global concern after 9/11; ibid., p. 1410. A recent example is the 'Document on Human Fraternity' signed by Pope Francis and Sheikh Ahmad el-Tayeb, the Grand Imam of al-Azhar, during a summit in Abu Dhabi in February 2019. Al-Qadi's book, provides a detailed description of the history and conceptual underpinnings of 'interfaith' initiatives. It also makes a case against the very concept of 'inter-religious *rapprochement*' from a particular strand of Islamic thought.

[8] Pope Paul VI, 'Declaration on the Relation of the Church to Non-Christian Religions', *Nostra Aetate*, 28 October 1965, http://www.vatican.va/archive/hist_councils/ii_vatican_council/documents/vat-ii_decl_19651028_nostra-aetate_en.html. See also, Hughes, *Abrahamic Religions*.

representatives – a dialogue in which neither ordinary Muslims and Christians nor the professional politicians through which they secure their place in the Lebanese state would participate.

It was not fortuitous to pick 1965 to initiate a process in which Muslims and Christians would begin to consider in dialogue their attitudes towards each other. It was the year of the Second Vatican Council, during which Pope Paul VI, in a statement on 'The Relation of the Church to Non-Christian Religions', declared that 'the Church regards with esteem also the Moslems', who 'adore the one God . . . also honor Mary, His virgin Mother . . . at times . . . even call[ing] on her with devotion'.[9] There is more to the connection between Vatican II and Christian–Muslim dialogue in Lebanon than coincidence, via the French Catholic orientalist Louis Massignon and his student and secretary, the Lebanese priest Youakim Moubarac, who was a speaker in one of the two series of lectures in 1965. Massignon was a decisive influence on the Council's views on Islam (and the third 'Abrahamic religion', Judaism), and it was through his efforts that the matter of the Church's repositioning was placed on its agenda.[10] In 1966, Moubarac took part (with the same organisation that had organised the first series of lectures) in a project that sought to lay down the bases of an 'Islamic–Christian dialogue'.

An explicit objective of that project was to elaborate an alternative to the model of 'separation of religion and the state' that was propagated by 'secular nationalist ideologies'. The aim of dialogue was not to seek '[ways] to separate Islam and Christianity [on the on hand] from political society in Lebanon [on the other], but to think of ways they could cooperate, and ways they could be the basis of the political . . . while avoiding the commingling of religion and the state . . .'.[11] Thus, the project seemed to stand in opposition to secularism as it was at the time conceived, namely, as a feature of nationalism and as a principle of separation. However, that opposition presupposed a questionable conceptual opposition between 'separation' and 'collaboration', the latter

[9] Hughes, *Abrahamic Religions*, 60ff.; Neal Robinson, 'Massignon, Vatican II and Islam as an Abrahamic Religion', *Islam and Christian–Muslim Relations* 2, 2 (1991): 182–205; Sidney Griffith, 'Sharing the Faith of Abraham: The "Credo" of Louis Massignon', *Islam and Christian–Muslim Relations* 8, 2 (1997): 193–210.

[10] Cited in al-Qadi, *Daʿwa al-Taqrib*, p. 1352.

[11] In 1969, 1971 (two), 1973, 1975, 1977, 1981 and 1984.

seeming to grant some relevance to religion in the postcolonial state, while preventing the drift towards a theocracy.

Despite their opposition to secularism (as separation), the Muslim and Christian participants in the dialogue would seem oblivious to three facts. In the first place, in their proposal, Christians and Muslims are joined together as *interlocutors* – an eminently *secular* articulation of Muslims and Christians (and an alteration of what it is to say 'Christian' and 'Muslim' in Lebanon). Moreover, the presupposed, tacit distinction between Christians and Muslims as communities (or identities) on the one hand, and religion (i.e. beliefs, rituals, doctrine, and so on) is a *secular* distinction (that maps neatly onto the distinction between private and public). Finally, that the search for what is common between the communities to serve as the basis of the political would suggest a search for a Lebanese version of the principle of overlapping consensus – a *secular*, liberal political principle.[12]

The year the Civil War ended, in 1990, a semi-official Islamic–Christian National Dialogue Committee was established by the spiritual leaders of the major officially recognised communities of Muslims and Christians in Lebanon.[13] The Committee included lay representatives of the Maronite (Eastern Catholic) Patriarchate, the Sunni Muslim Dar al-Fatwa, the Armenian Catholics of Cilicia, the House of the Unitarian Druze *Ṭā'ifa* (*Bayt Ṭā'ifa al-Muwaḥḥidīn al-Durūz*), the Greek Orthodox Patriarchate, and the Supreme Islamic Shiʿi Council According to its 'Unified Working Paper', the Committee is '[g]uided by the process of national understanding' that began with the signing of 'the Document of National Understanding' by the warring parties in 1990, which put an end to the Civil War and parts of which were subsequently incorporated into the Lebanese Constitution.

[12] Critics of 'sectarianism' are in agreement with that which they criticise. They both presuppose the separation of 'properly religious' beliefs and doctrines on the one hand, and religious identity (or 'the religious sect') on the other. This *secular* distinction in other national contexts is supposed to be the basis of the plural liberal state – the kind of state they dismiss in Lebanon as 'sectarian'.

[13] Among the many organisations, institutes and committees that came out of that effort were the Institute of Islamic–Christian Studies, established in 1977 at the Jesuit Université Saint Joseph in Beirut, the Islamic–Christian Dialogue Committee of the Higher Shiʿi Islamic Council, established in 1993 under the auspices of the *Jaʿfari* mufti shaykh Mohammad Mahdi Chamseddine, and the Center for Christian and Islamic Studies, established in 1995 at the Greek Orthodox University of Balamand in North Lebanon.

According to the paper, Muslims and Christians in Lebanon are engaged in a common project, 'to build their state', which is to be 'republican, parliamentary, [and] democratic', whose Muslim and Christian citizens enjoy 'complete equality in rights', and which is 'committed to the principle of freedom of religion, thought, and information . . .'[14]

The 'formula of coexistence' is the principle that gives the Lebanese state intelligibility and the reason of its existence, that without which both are called into question. It is the result of a 'human agreement which unites around it the Lebanese in their various spiritual families', it is 'Lebanon's greatest, value', its 'mission to the world', 'a pattern of life', 'a relationship of continuous dialogue between the Christian and Islamic worlds', and 'a link of continuity to enrich the values imprinted on human character by these two divinely revealed messages'. In the Committee's reasoning, Lebanon is especially well positioned to perform that role because it (already) is 'a human terrain for freedom and dialogue between the followers of the divinely revealed religions, a land of life shared by Christians and Muslims'.[15]

An Apparition of the Virgin Mary

This conjunction of geography and the two monotheistic religions is what gives a distinctive sense to the Lebanese state and what justifies its existence as a distinctive entity. It is the source of its identity as a mission and model of coexistence, a message to the world. This missionary vocation of the Lebanese Republic was reiterated by Pope John Paul II in an exhortation to 'the faithful in Lebanon'. The exhortation was delivered on 10 May 1997, as 'the Post-Synodal Apostolic Exhortation: "A New Hope for Lebanon"', and was published during the Pope's visit to Lebanon.[16] It reaffirmed the

[14] Islamic–Christian National Dialogue Committee, *Unified Working Paper*, n.d., http://www.chrislam.org/actions.html (last accessed April 2022; the website seems to have been taken down).

[15] Ibid.

[16] Pope John Paul II, '*Une Espérance Nouvelle*'. The visit took place two years after the closing of the synod, 'Special Assembly for Lebanon – Christ is Our Hope: Renewed by His Spirit, in Solidarity We Bear Witness to His Love', 26 November and 14 December 1995. Several Catholic synods in – and for – 'the Orient' have been held since the first half of the eighteenth century. See Elias Atallah, *Le Synode libanais de 1736*, 2 vols (Paris: Letouzey et Ané, 2001).

positions of the Church announced during the Second Vatican Council, namely, that 'the Church regards with esteem also the Muslims', who 'adore the one God', 'submit to Abraham, with whom the faith of Islam takes pleasure in lining itself', consider 'Jesus . . . [whom] they revere . . . a prophet', and 'also honor Mary, His virgin Mother . . .'[17] An occasion to spread this message and put to work the common devotion to Mary became available a few years afterwards.

On 21 August 2004, in a Christian village in the predominantly Muslim Shiʿa northern part of the Bekaa Valley, it was reported that a Sunni Muslim Jordanian boy on a visit to the village with his father and his father's friend, a native of the village, saw the statue of Mary move and smile to him inside the village church.[18] The claims were soon confirmed by other visitors, who saw the Virgin, covered with 'aromatic oil', move 'her eyes . . . as if to make the sign of the cross'. Then, 'a prayer' is heard 'from the boy's lips' asking the Virgin to 'restore peace, love, and freedom on the face of the Earth . . .'[19] News of 'Mary's apparition' spread beyond the confines of the village, turning it into a centre of transnational pilgrimage for both Christians and Muslims. By one estimate, it attracted an estimated million visitors between 2004 and 2006.[20] It would seem that public authorities were involved in organising some of these pilgrimages, the president of the Lebanese republic at the time 'order[ing] the renovation and widening of the road that led to the village', the Ministry of Interior 'open[ing] a civil defense post', and the Ministry of Public Works erecting 'fountains and public restrooms and order[ing] the construction of a large parking lot' – a remarkable care granted a region consistently neglected by the Lebanese state since its creation in 1920. There was additional investment in the village by the parliamentary representatives of

[17] Under the heading, 'The relations [of the Catholic Church] with the faithful of the monotheistic religions, and particularly the Muslims'.

[18] The Catholic Maronite Church was 'hesitant to recognise' the apparition. Emma Aubin-Boltanski, 'La Vierge, les chrétiens, les musulmans et la nation', *Terrain* 51 (2008): 9.

[19] The prayer is cited in full in Aubin-Boltanski, 'La Vierge, les chrétiens, les musulmans', p. 3.

[20] For a full ethnographic account of Mary's apparition on which the analysis in this section is based, see Aubin-Boltanski, 'Fondation d'un centre de pèlerinage au Liban', *Archives de sciences sociales des religions* 151 (2010): 149–68, and 'La Vierge, les chrétiens, les musulmans'.

the region who were keen to secure their re-election in 2009. As a result of all of this, 'the village [today] sports' basic amenities such as 'sidewalks and public lighting'.[21]

It is remarkable that it took (what for many is) a miracle to mobilise the Lebanese state to act with such decisiveness as it is that the historical suspicion of, and sometimes active resistance to, the state's attempts to assert its sovereignty over that part of the country were now surrendered. This could be another example of cynical reason, or 'sectarian' politicking by the Lebanese state and local and regional strongmen taking advantage in this case of a spontaneous and popular manifestation of faith. What is undeniable is that Mary's apparition yielded an attempt to rearrange the Lebanese territory (e.g. connecting the village to other parts of the country), to alter the demographic composition (e.g. drawing visitors to it), and to redistribute resources (e.g. renovation of infrastructure). This could very well be the local, Lebanese version of a more widespread phenomenon – religious tourism as a strategy of development – and there is in this respect nothing extraordinary about it.[22] Religious tourism is a stark reminder that the religious and secular need be neither opposed to each other nor mutually exclusive, and that, as has been repeated often by scholars of secularism, the two are often mutually reinforcing. What is interesting in Mary's apparition is the insight it offers into Lebanese secularism, that is, the idea of Muslim–Christian coexistence, having (the Virgin) Mary as its symbolic and affective *datum*. (The *secular* sense of 'apparition': what makes its apparition with Mary is the coexistence of Christians and Muslims as a founding principle of the Lebanese state.)

This assertion of the Lebanese state's sovereignty over territory, population and resources is one perspective on the workings of coexistence. The way the latter enters into the structuring of a sensibility is another. This is not to be taken in the sense of a 'top-down' imposition of a concept of coexistence on

[21] Aubin-Boltanski, 'Fondation d'un centre de pèlerinage', p. 152.

[22] Fatima, Lourdes, Medugorje, Mexico (the Virgin of Guadalupe) are the more prominent examples. The articulation of religion and development in religious tourism is not exlusively Christian (Catholic). Islamic examples would include the city of Karbala in Iraq, and Mecca in Saudi Arabia.

an otherwise 'ordinary' experience, but as a suggestion that the discourse of coexistence is rooted in ordinary language and the sensibility it articulates. The question of a Muslim and Christian experience in Lebanon is already constitutive of the experience – religious and otherwise – of Muslims and Christians, and of the identities – religious and otherwise – through which that experience is mediated. As one Shiʿi woman, for long deeply devoted to Mary, wonders, 'Our Lady of Beshouat [the name of the village], everyone in Lebanon loves [her], why then not have her portrait here in my living room?' Or, the Christian man who, when asked about the purpose of his visit, 'pointed with his finger at a Muslim family [sitting] next to the church, answered, "I am expecting that the Virgin show us that we can live together"'.[23]

A theme subtends Mary's apparition, namely that Muslims and Christians honour her. This theme was taken up again by the judge of examination, who made the decision to release the Muslim men accused of offending Mary on the basis of the claims that 'Muslims [and Christians] have a love for' her. The apparition would seem to validate this claim by providing it with tangible evidence: Mary appeared to a Sunni Muslim after all, in a Christian Catholic village among a constellation of Shiʿa villages, and the pilgrims attracted to the site of her apparition were Christians and Muslims. That Muslims have a love for Mary, her apparition in the plain of the Bekaa would reinforce a narrative of Christian–Muslim coexistence, a narrative that has long been in the making in Lebanon.

Considered in the light of the 'formula of coexistence', the government's effort to develop the village and its surroundings, just as it could not be said to be merely instrumental, is not to be dismissed as merely symbolic, but as the geographical inscription of coexistence in the land on the surface of the earth. In the same vein, the proclamation of the Day of the Annunciation as the National Day of Islamic–Christian Dialogue, like all 'national holidays', incorporates Mary into the national calendar, inscribes her in secular time. It joins together an abstract principle – the formula of coexistence – the Lebanese state, and the religious sentiments of the faithful among Muslims and Christians who have 'a love for the Virgin Mary', and whose feelings are now the object of the state's concern. What is said about her (or done to her various manifestations

[23] Quoted in Aubin-Boltanski, 'La Vierge, les chrétiens, les musulmans', p. 13.

or representations, such as a statue), how what is said is said, and in what circumstances or context it is said, are now matters of state and the objects of its coercive power.

Offending the Religious Sentiment

The nexus of the passions that accumulate around the Virgin Mary is now constitutive of (the state's) order *and* disorder, unity *and* disunity, stability *and* instability. Passions are bound to actions (including speech) – to what is said and done, and the manner in which what is said and done is said and done. In so far as they are so, the passions now concern the state, for they come to be vital to it and must be placed under its surveillance, identified, evaluated, sanctioned, and, if possible, prevented.[24] The Lebanese Penal Code anticipates this and provides mechanisms by which dangerous acts – for example, injurious words against Mary – would be considered criminal and punished. The Code includes a chapter on 'Crimes against Religion and the Family', in which, under the heading 'Of Misdemeanors against Religion', it is specified that what is to be protected is 'the religious sentiment (*al-shuʿūr al-dini*)'.

In a section entitled 'Of Misdemeanours (*al-jinaḥ*) against the Religious Sentiment', the Code sanctions the person who 'blasphemes (*man jaddafa*) in public against the name of God', 'defames religious observances that are performed in public' (or 'incites' to doing so), 'disrupts the performance of rites , ceremonies, or rituals', and 'demolishes, destroys, vandalises, desecrates, or pollutes' religious structures.[25] Persons who are guilty of any of

[24] Criminalising offences against religion is not unique to Lebanon. British law sanctions 'offences against religion and public worship'. While French law contains no specific provisions against 'blasphemy', it does sanction certain kinds of offensive speech (e.g. against 'believers'). There is an exception, however, in Alsace-Moselle (see '*La répression du blasphème*, LC 262, Janvier 2016', *Revue internationale de droit comparé* 68, 1 (1997): 233–38). In 2018, the European Court of Human Rights upheld a ruling against a defendant 'for disparaging religious doctrine', considering that 'the domestic courts had comprehensively assessed the wider context of the applicant's statements, and carefully balanced her right to freedom of expression with the rights of others to have their religious feelings protected, and to have religious peace preserved in . . . society.' European Court of Human Rights, *E.S.* v. *Austria* (Application no. 38450/12), https://hudoc.echr.coe.int/eng#{"itemid":["001-187188"]}.

[25] Aref Zaid al-Zein, *Qawanin wa Nusus al-ʿUqubat fi Lubnan* (Beirut: Manshurat al-Halabi al-Huquqiyya, 2009), p. 79.

those misdemeanors are punishable by between a month and three years in prison and/or a fine. An offence against the religious sentiment would take place in 'actions and gestures', in 'a public place, a place accessible to the public (*al-jumhūr*)', or while 'exposed to view, or witnessed' by someone else as a result of a 'mistake on the performer's part'. An offence could also be committed by 'speaking or screaming', directly or through 'mechanical means' in such a way that 'it is heard by a bystander'. Lastly, apart from the body and its gestures, actions and voice, an offence could be committed by means of textual and non-verbal signs, such as 'pictures, drawn or photographic images, films . . . and symbols' of various sorts, 'if displayed in public . . . or exposed to view or sold . . . or distributed to one or more persons'.[26] There is in the Code no account of what 'the religious sentiment' consists in, what sort of thing it is, how it is to be separated from other kinds of sentiment, and so on. Nor is there an account of what it is in or about an action, word, sign or gesture that would constitute an offence against the religious sentiment.

Apart from crimes against religion, the Penal Code contains two additional categories of crime that are closely – and ambiguously – connected to them. The first category, which includes crimes that 'threaten the aura of the state (*haybat al-dawla*) and the national sentiment', belongs to a family of crimes 'against the external security of the state', such as treason and espionage.[27] These involve 'calls that are aimed to . . . incite . . . doctrinal (or sectarian) tensions (*iyqāẓ al-naʿarāt al-madhhabiyya*)' in times of 'war or in expectation of its eruption'.[28] The second category falls under the family of 'crimes against the internal security of the state', specifically 'assaults that aim to incite a civil war or [*inter-*]*communitarian fighting*'. These are placed under the separate heading of '*fitna*', which, in turn, has the same status as 'terrorism', 'crimes against the Constitution', and 'crimes against national unity or that disrupt the peace among the elements of the nation'. They include 'action, writings, and discourse that are intended to, or from which results, the incitement of sectarian differences . . . or the provocation to a conflict among the *ṭawāʾif*'. Punishment for all of the aforementioned

[26] Ibid., p. 38.

[27] Ibid., pp. 49–50.

[28] Article 295 in ibid., p. 52. Emphasis added.

crimes varies between one to three years imprisonment, the payment of a fine, and a ban on the exercising of civil and political rights.[29]

The Penal Code offers to view more than a scheme of criminality and punitive retribution, but also the structure of 'the Lebanese public', into which the religious (e.g. symbols, acts of worship or ceremonies) enters in a constitutive capacity. The law is supportive of the structure of the public through its regulating of conduct in such a way as to avoid offences against religion that threaten to bring the religious passions violently into the open. 'Religion' and 'the public' (i.e. both the public sphere and the public space) are mutually dependent: to regulate what could offend religion is to temper the religious sentiment, achieved by regulating the relationship to things with which the religious sentiment is invested (the assumption seems to be that there are 'normal' religious sentiments that then could be stimulated by certain acts and made to deviate from that normality).

The coexistence between Christians and Muslims, taken in practice to involve a dialogue between the two communities, depends on making sure that certain conditions are found that would require a constant disciplining of the religious sentiment. 'Dialogue' is the practice by which such sentiments could be so regulated and a 'dialogical' sensibility cultivated. The law is another – working to condition the dialogical disposition by the quite different, but the equally constant, threat of violence. In the sphere of the criminal law, 'blasphemy' is a violation (against religion, rather than, as it could be within a particular religion, a sin) or even violence, not simply against religion, but against the law. Thus, criminal law presupposes a secular concept of 'blasphemy' when it considers it an act of violence that disrupts a particular notion of the public by 'causing' the outward expression of religious passions – a violence against the law met by the violence of the law.

It is the category of 'religion' that makes it possible to posit a distinct domain of beliefs, acts, gestures, sentiments and signs in which both Muslims and Christians participate. As the common essence in which Muslims and Christians participate, it is what makes it possible for them to carry out a dialogue that would ensure their coexistence. It stands opposed to 'sectarian differences' and 'communitarian impulses', the latter two being the basis

[29] Ibid., pp. 53 and 54.

of division, potential – and potentially violent – conflict, and threat to the nation state. While in the Code crimes that offend the religious sentiment, crimes that exacerbate (religious) sectarian differences, and crimes that arouse (religious) communitarian impulses fall under three distinct categories, and while the first is connected directly to the individual body, and the second and third are connected to the nation and the state, the distinction in practice between the three is not so obvious or easy to draw. It is plausible to think, especially in the context of Lebanon, that the religious sentiment (tied to embodied dispositions), religious schools or doctrines or 'sects' (as discursive or textual formations or traditions), and religious community (as a sociological and historical 'fact'), which in the logic of the Penal Code are kept apart, are interconnected.

It is plausible that an offence against the Virgin Mary, even if revered in both the Islamic and Christian traditions, be felt differently by Catholics, Shiʿa, Sunnis, Druze, Orthodox and Protestants who would react differently to the offence, and it is as plausible that different doctrines treat Mary differently. She might not hold the same place or possess the same status in different religious doctrines, a place or status that would involve different sorts of investment, involving, in turn, different sorts of sentiment, and different sorts of responses on the part of the individual or the community. While the Code makes it seem that the three kinds of crime are three distinct kinds of facts, connection between the three, movement from one to the other, is plausible. The three could be conceptualised as constituting a field of action, which would enable (and constrain) the making of certain kinds of claim and in which secular, judicial or legal power could decisively act, to decide on the connections among them, to join or separate them – in any case, to decide authoritatively.[30] Thus, it is in that field that an utterance or a gesture like the one against the Virgin Mary would be perceived and identified, its sense and force assessed, its subject judged and sanctioned.

The True Faith of Legal Subjects

Since the mid-1990s, there has been an effort to reform the Lebanese Penal Code, promulgated in 1943, the year of Lebanon's independence from the

[30] There have been cases in which a plaintiff makes the claim that an act is an offence against religion *and* an incitement to communitarianism or doctrinal tensions. See Chapter 6.

French Mandate. This effort is aimed to align the Code with contemporary changes in the attitudes towards crime and punishment: in the words of a member of the committee in charge of the reforms, '[i]n view of the evolution of the world [and] the needs and exigencies of society', which 'necessitate a modernized penal law, based on a revision of the notions of crime and punishment'. The inclination is to turn away from the notion of punishment as repression (or 'privations of liberty') in favour of devising measures to achieve the rehabilitation of the criminal within his social milieu. 'The idea is to achieve an equilibrium between the rights of man (human rights) and those of the society in which he lives.' The proposed reformed penal law would stipulate that 'for minor misdemeanors [that are] punishable by less than a year's imprisonment, it is henceforth permitted the judge to substitute . . . a sentence [imposing on the convict] non-paid work of social interest . . .'[31]

Another feature of the Penal Code reform is the office of the *qāḍi al-taḥqīq*, or the judge of examination, the scope of its powers and the symbolic value attached to it in the hierarchy of the state.[32] The jurisdiction and competencies

[31] https://www.lorientlejour.com/article/1058372/un-petit-pas-vers-la-modernite.html (last accessed 31 May 2023). The Lebanese reforms were proposed in explicit reference to the French *Code Pénal.*

[32] The office of the *juge d'instruction* is ambivalent, to say the least, and the dynamic of reforming it is shaped by this ambivalence. The *juge d'instruction* has been considered 'a model of justice that is aimed to reconcile the defense of the interests of society and the preservation of individual liberties' (Vincent Fontana, 'Clère (Jean-Jacques), Farcy (Jean-Claude) (dir.), *Le juge d'instruction : approches historiques*', *Crime, Histoire & Sociétés/Crime, History & Societies* 18, 2 (2014): 1, http://journals.openedition.org/chs/1500/). This ambiguity is due to the two different powers which the office carries: (1) the power to protect society and coerce individuals in the name of that protection (by the power of provisional detainment and autonomous jurisdiction over the criminal investigation); (2) the power to protect individual liberties. This tension has inhered in the office since its inception by Napoleon Bonaparte in the *Code d'instruction criminelle* of 1808. The office would seem to have its roots in the inquisitorial model of the *Ancien Régime*, 'the *Lieutnant criminel*', a function created in 1670. The latter was abolished and replaced by the former during the Revolution in order 'to guarantee the protection of individual liberties' (p. 2). The history of the *juge d'instruction*, especially since the late nineteenth century, could be characterised as one in which the scope of the powers of the office have been gradually reduced through liberal reforms that privileged the rights of the individual over the protection of society. In France, this tendency is further pushed forward by the promulgation of *Code de procédure pénale* of 1958 and continues in the twenty-first century (p. 4).

of the judge are detailed in Law No. 328 of 2 August 2001, Criminal Procedure, which replaced the previous law of 1948, promulgated five years following independence.[33] At stake in the passing of the new law and the debates in parliament that preceded it is the state's prosecutorial powers and individual liberties, the morality of crime and punishment, and political consideration that had to do with the securitised regime that was in place at the time.[34]

In the Penal Code, a crime against religion is construed as an action against 'things' marked as religious and causally connected to religious sentiments that would be aroused by the act, and the perpetrator is punished because their act was injurious to the religious sentiments. But, could not the act be prevented, and, if so, how? In a speech she gave at a celebration of International Women's Day in the city of Tripoli (where the young blasphemers were apprehended), Judge Jocelyn Matta, who set the precedent, shared her experience as a judge, explaining the case along the way.[35] Employing words that are evocative of the doctrine of the impossibility of erring knowingly and the words of Jesus on the cross ('Father forgive them they know not what they do'),[36] Matta told her audience, 'On the eighth of last February two young men in the prime of life appeared before me, their guilt being that they did not know what they were doing.'

She drew that conclusion on the basis of her 'sens[ing], while interrogating them, the state of ignorance (*al-jahl*) and disinformation (*al-taḍlīl*) that had driven them to commit something of whose consequences they were not aware'. Faced with 'several choices' on how to proceed, she found herself 'appealing to the principle that the truly faithful (*al-mu'min al-haqīqi*) carries in his heart a great respect for others', from which, reasoning by analogy, she extracted the proposition that 'a Muslim could not be a true Muslim without applying the teachings of the Noble Qur'an'. This enabled her to 'turn to the Qur'anic texts that honor the Virgin, [seeking] Sura Al Imran,

[33] http://ahdath.justice.gov.lb/law-nearby-penal-procedures.htm (last accessed 31 May 2023).

[34] https://www.legal-agenda.com/article.php?id=1325 (last accessed 31 May 2023).

[35] Mahkama, *Al-Qadi Jocelyn Matta: Dhahabt ila-l-Fikr al-Tarbawi wa Laisa-l-Jaza'i Faqat*, *Mahkama*, 3 September 2018, https://www.mahkama.net/?p=5965 (last accessed 31 May 2023).

[36] Luke 23: 34.

to remind those two young men that with such behaviors they are profaning Islam in the first place before profaning the statue of the Virgin Lady'.[37]

The judge's first premise is that a 'truly religious' or, particularly, 'a true Muslim', would not act to offend religion and the religious sentiment. The 'truth of religion' – any religion – includes its teaching 'a great respect for others', a precept which, once learned, becomes constitutive of the 'truly faithful'. The judge posits what she seems to believe is a universal principle – 'respect for others' – finding an 'Islamic' articulation of that principle in the Qur'an. A series of conceptual correspondences structure the judge's argument. The judge assumes that the defendents are 'Muslims' (could they have objected that they were not, or otherwise?), and, along with this, that religion (Islam) is relevant to them, or to their uttering the offensive words for which they have appeared before her. She seeks the truth in the Qur'an, which the judge considers to be the privileged site of the 'teachings' of Islam – not only does she consider the Qur'an a source of information ('teachings'), but also that it is *the* source of religious knowledge for Muslims (excluding, for example, the *sunna*). This series of assumptions is generic, in the sense that it applies to all 'religions of the book', is then subjected to epistemological assessment whereby its truth or falsity, and its essence, are determined. Two assumptions undergird the series: first, a liberal secular conception of religion that aligns religion, its truth, its text, and the individual subject; second, a sociological taxonomy that grounds action and judgment in two religious identities, 'Muslim' and 'Christian', the dyadic basis of Christian–Muslim coexistence.[38]

[37] Mahkama, '*Al-Qadi Jocelyn Matta*'. Matta said '*al-sayyida al-'aẓrā'*,' the Arabic name for 'Our Virgin Lady', which Arab-speaking Christians would typically use to refer to her with formal reverence. Note the difference in the *name*, or the form of address, in the two traditions, which would indicate a difference in the respective status of Mary in Islam and Christianity, and the respective Marian sensibility of Christians and Muslims. Neither the judge nor the protagonists of the 'National Day of Christian–Muslim Dialogue/Day of the Annunciation of Mary' seem to take this difference into account.

[38] The judge *assumes* that the accused are Muslims, and that their identity as Muslims matters to the case. This assumption is curious, since the categories of 'Muslim' and 'Christian' are only *legally* relevant in Lebanon in the context of personal status laws, which fall under the exclusive jurisdiction of the religious communities.

The judge's second premise has specifically to do with the law: what it is, what it does. She says, 'As a judge and a human being I am under the obligation of seeing to the application of the law, and, upon that, to approach the issue in a constructive and beneficial way.' To do so, she 'turned to article 111 of the Law of Penal Procedure which gave the judge of examination, whatever the kind of crime, [the authority] to substitute for the arrest of the defendant the obligation [to perform] a duty or several duties that [the judge] deems necessary, some of which article 111 enumerates'. This 'opened the door for [her] to appeal to educational thought (*al-fikr al-tarbawi*), and not just penal thought (*al-fikr al-jazā'i*)'. Matta concluded her speech by telling the audience that her 'experience as a judge was initiated by the persistent thought that everything evolves, so why then not the law as well? Why not approach the judiciary', she asked, 'from the educational and instructional (*tathqīf*) aspect' as well? For example, 'how could a young man, in the prime of life, be [taught] the thought that the idea of violence is first and foremost destructive of the one who is in possession of it?' With this conclusion, Matta wishes also to disconnect the law from its violence, offering instead a conception of law as 'construct[ive] of the human and the society together, though one must search for the means' to actually do so. An implication of this reformist conception of law, which considers law an instrument with which to reform persons (and society), is that crimes against religion could be dealt with not as mere violations met by the law's (or society's) counter-violence. Since they are acts that are rooted in conditions of ignorance, the law could be employed to eradicate their 'causes', by converting ignorance into true knowledge – ignorance of (one's own) religion into true religious knowledge.

The cases could be conceived differently, such that the same result – release and rehabilitation of the defendants – be obtained on different premises. The cases could be conceived in a way that makes no reference to Muslims and Islam, the Qur'an or the 'love for Mary'. Yet, those premises and references were made, and a case was constructed on their basis. So, what did the judge do by constructing her case that way? The case gives the idea of 'Christian–Muslim coexistence' a legal form, displaying as it does the function (or role, or 'mission') of Lebanese law to frame and uphold it, and cultivate the subjects that embody it. In this respect, the case is an enactment of Lebanese secularism; the assumption that there is a 'truth of religion' that is constitutive of it. It is constitutive of Lebanese secularism to be a 'true Muslim (or Christian)', that is, to possess a true knowledge of one's religion, a knowledge the source of which is a religion's 'primary text' (here, the Qur'an). That knowledge is ambiguous, however, both propositional (discursive) and embodied: the defendants are expected to know *that* 'Muslims honour Mary', a 'fact' sought and found in the Qur'anic text (the Qur'an *as* text), and are expected to acquire that knowledge by having it 'inscribed' in their memory, by way of reading and memorising specifically selected verses as if they were another set of signs of which the text is the exclusive repository. Lastly, they are expected – ordered – to demonstrate the newly acquired truth by reciting the memorised signs before a representative of secular power (the judge), who is authorised by that power to authenticate the fact that the defendants now know (the truth of/about their religion).[39]

In this ontological and epistemological identity is dissolved the difference between the Lebanese Muslim and Christian. It might seem that once the young men acquire the religious knowledge, once they are enlightened about their faith (and that of others), or once they are converted to the true faith, the possibility of uttering injurious words against religion in the future would be eliminated. However, there is another possibility here, one that would indicate the limits of legal reform: for the young men to acquire knowledge, to become aware, to be taken out of their ignorance, which is the cause, as the judge sees it, of their guilt, is not only for them to be redeemed (in both secular and religious senses), but also to be rendered responsible – legally responsible, that is, and, therefore, punishable in the future. What comes along with 'being truly religious' in a state consisting of Muslims and Christians coexisting is none other than the secular subject of law.

Conclusion

Thus, Christian–Muslim coexistence would call for a distinctive sensibility and a manner of conduct appropriate enough to secure its persistence.

[39] Compare with a Christian conception of the relationship between the religious text (scripture), reading as a disciplined activity, and the process of acquiring religious knowledge (Francis Jacques, 'Qu'est-ce qu'un texte religieux?' *Raisons politiques* 4, 4 (2001): 40–56), and with the 'ritual reading' of the Qur'an in the Islamic tradition (*The Islamic World: Past and Present.*).

The preconditions of both reside in the subject of law: the human person who, being essentially in possession of rational faculties and endowed with 'a body', and being cognisant of and responsible for its actions, is amenable to coercion and persuasion, to punishment and reform.

The religious community (or 'sect'), or religious (or 'sectarian') identity no doubt possess a prominent place in the organisation of coexistence. This prominence is regularly met by calls for the adoption and implementation of secularism, which would involve for its proponents an agreement among the Lebanese (individuals, or communities?) to separate religion and the state, and found Lebanese politics and legal institutions anew on secular foundations. Secularism would take away the reasons for fearing the 'religious other' in which are rooted the pull to privilege the religious community in public life, the identity it confers on citizens, and the divisions it creates among the Lebanese.

This presumed hold which religious communal identity possesses over the political imagination in the country has also been a concern among scholars of Lebanon.[40] Some consider 'sectarianism' (as it is termed in English) and secularism to be opposed, either mutually exclusive, or, in stronger versions, the one undermining the other.[41] Others, taking into account in their assessments the multidisciplinary recasting of secularism that has been taking place since the early 2000s, regard 'sectarianism' and secularism to be different, yet compatible or even mutually constitutive phenomena.[42]

[40] Melani Claire Cammett, *Compassionate Communalism: Welfare and Sectarianism in Lebanon* (Ithaca: Cornell University Press, 2014); Makdisi, *The Culture of Sectarianism*; Joanne Nucho, *Everyday Sectarianism in Urban Lebanon: Infrastructures, Public Services, and Power* (Princeton, NJ: Princeton University Press, 2017); Weiss, *In the Shadow of Sectarianism.*

[41] E.g. Farha, 'Stumbling Blocks to the Secularization of Personal Status Laws'; Mark Farha, 'Secularism in a Sectarian Society? The Divisive Drafting of the 1926 Lebanese Constitution', in Asli U. Bali and Hanna Lerner (eds), *Constitution Writing, Religion and Democracy* (Cambridge: Cambridge University Press, 2017), pp. 101–30.

[42] Lara Deeb, 'Beyond Sectarianism: Intermarriage and Social Difference in Lebanon', *International Journal of Middle East Studies* (April 2020): 1–14; Makdisi, *Age of Coexistence*; Maya Mikdashi, 'Sex and Sectarianism: The Legal Architecture of Lebanese Citizenship', *Comparative Studies of South Asia, Africa and the Middle East* 34, 2 (2014): 279–93; Maya Mikdashi, 'Religious Conversion and Da'wa Secularism: Two Practices of Citizenship in Lebanon', *Journal of Middle East Women's Studies* 11, 2 (2015): 254; Nada Moumtaz, 'From Forgiveness to Foreclosure', *The Muslim World* 108, 4 (2018): 593–612.

In both views, secular designates the domain of politics, specifically in what pertains to the state, the citizen, and their respective rights. This sense of secularism and the problems that accompany it is a feature of the modern state and, in this respect, there is nothing special about the Lebanese case.[43] 'Sectarianism' could well be the name of only one way in which secular and religious domains are formally separated, contested by another – call it secularism – in which the separation is construed differently, more in line with, say, the French or Turkish standard.

The analysis carried out in this chapter takes an articulation of 'the secular' as a substantive concept – in other words, a concept that is constitutive of the world or context in which the distinction between religious and secular or secularism and 'sectarianism', the standard by which it is made, and the decision to draw it would make sense to both Muslims and Christians. In that world, 'Muslim' and 'Christian', as well as 'religion', would accordingly acquire a distinctive sense, one that would orient them towards and guarantee coexistence of Christians and Muslims in Lebanon, where the sense of 'Lebanon' in turn is sought and found in 'coexistence'.

The judicial cases are enactments of 'Muslim–Christian coexistence', taken as a normative principle. It is the common basis that joins together to constitute a coherent, interconnected whole: a discursive practice ('Christian–Muslim dialogue'); Lebanese sovereignty and the construction of national spacetime; the identity of the Lebanese state; a sensibility that embodies it (*via* 'the love for Mary'); a knowledge of the truth of religion that sustains it (in virtue of the cognitive and moral capacities of the subject).

This context, this world or 'whole', calls for constant reinforcement and protection, which the Lebanese state is given to secure within the legal and moral framework of the Lebanese Penal Code. This exercise of state power belongs to that world, but is only one component of it among others. It is the vocation or 'mission' of the Lebanese state to secure that world of coexistence between Muslims and Christians, which, in turn, sustains and supports it – confers on it its unique identity, rendering it, thereby, recognisable by, intelligible to both Christians and Muslims.

[43] Mahmood, *Religious Difference*, p. 2.

6

THE RELIGIOUS OFFENDED

'In accordance with the directions of the mufti of the Lebanese Republic . . . the fatwa Secretary . . . has approached the Public Prosecution . . . with [a complaint] against . . ., who is claiming falsely that he is a divine messenger (*rasūl*) sent from heaven (*mursal min al-samā'*) with a divine message (*risāla samāwiyya*) . . . [the Secretary] has requested that the Public Prosecution . . . take the necessary legal action against [the aforementioned] on the basis of articles 317 and 474 of the Penal Code.'[1]

'[T]he Maronite (Catholic) Eparchy of Jbeil calls upon the competent authorities . . . to make sure that the concert be cancelled [for] the aims of the band . . . and the content of the songs they perform . . . offend the religious and human values and expose to profanation the Christian sanctities (*al-muqaddasāt al-masīḥiyya*) . . . to remove what must be removed and apologise . . . [as a display of] respect for the sentiments of the two religions of Christianity and Islam in Lebanon.' [2]

'[T]he determination of what [the freedom of religion] includes and what is excluded from it is not a mathematical affair, especially in artistic matters . . . [It is] often affected by . . . the degree of tolerance (*al-tasāmuḥ*) or intolerance (*al-lā-tasāmuḥ*) which a particular society has reached. . . . [I]n democratic

[1] https://www.alhurra.com/lebanon/2022/01/21/السلطات-اللبنانية-تلاحق-مدعي-النبوة-ضجة-بلغت-دولا-أخرى and https://m.facebook.com/ajmubasher/videos/-دار-الفتوى-اللبنانية-تحرك-دعوى-قضائية-ضد-نشأت-منذر-بعد-ادعائه-النبوة/615491012852176 (last accessed 1 June 2023).

[2] A copy of the eparchy's statement is available at https://www.facebook.com/jbeileparchy/photos/a.1030880813614439/2402703719765468/?type=3&theater. (last accessed 1 June 2023).

> systems, the the proper instance (*al-marjaʿ al-ṣāliḥ*) to determine if defamation of religion took place or not is the judiciary, [which does so] in a fair trial . . . [R]ecall again [the] three important rulings, which contain the fundamental [legal] considerations through which the principles of toleration and mutual respect triumphed over fanaticism (*al-taʿaṣṣub*), extremism (*al-tazammut*), and, importantly, excessive sensitivity (*al-ḥasāsiyya al-mufraṭa*) from which this or that group (*al-ʿiṣba*) might suffer'.[3]

The coexistence of Christians and Muslims in Lebanon implies the assertion that they share the same legal and political space, participate in the same historical time, as 'Christians' and 'Muslims'. Conversely, in so far as they do share the same spacetime, Muslims and Christians coexist. Their coexistence presupposes their distinctiveness and difference, and requires that their uniqueness and separation be guaranteed to a certain extent. It is expected that they maintain a relationship between each other and between them and others – those who claim no religion, or whose faith is not officially recognised in Lebanon.

This involves a certain degree of mutual accommodation, an art of conducting politics, and a consistent government (some would like to call this 'toleration'). These ensure that coexistence is not undermined by words or actions, signs and images that offend the sensitivity of Muslims and Christians, or defame what they count as religious. Coexistence is constitutive of a distinctive sensibility, one that is attuned to the enunciations and projections that threaten it – enunciations and projections that acquire their sense and force in virtue of their occurrence in a context of coexistence, or the sense and force of which reside in the fact that they occur in the context of coexistence between Christians and Muslims.

Thus, a text might be published or a film produced that contains material that runs the risk of offending the Christian or Muslim (and sometimes both),

[3] *Legal Agenda. 'Al-Mufakkara Tudhakkir bi Thalthath Ahkam Ra'ida Hawla al-Tasamuh al-Dini fi Lubnan: al-Din, al-Hasasiyya al-Mufrata, wa Hurriyat al-Taʿbir wa-l-Ibdaʿ'*. 30 July 2019. https://www.legal-agenda.com/article.php?id=5764 (last accessed 1 June 2023). The note includes a link to a newspaper opinion piece written by the director of the *Legal Agenda* in which he complains about the censoring of a film produced in Iran entitled, '*Al-Masīḥ* (Christ)', which was banned after the Catholic Church objected to it. Nizar Saghieh, 2009, https://www.al-akhbar.com/Opinion/107457/المسيح-يمثل-أمام-محكمة-متري---الراعي-الحساسي-ة-دائما-على-حق (last accessed 1 June 2023).

whose passions are structured in such a way as to be moved to commit acts that might unsettle coexistence. In some cases, the event triggers a standoff between the offending and offended parties, escalates into mutual accusations and denunciations, threats and counterthreats that draw – or are performed with the deliberate intention to draw – the attention of public authorities.

These are called upon and are expected to intervene in the dispute or take measures to settle the issue definitively and firmly in order to prevent outbreaks of violence (in discourse and practice), and ultimately the troubling of public peace, safety and security. Typically, a state organ (e.g. General Security) is called upon to mediate between the parties, finding ways to have the offended party retract the offence or censors the text or film (or other medium) in part or in full, or bans performance or projection.

A discourse often accompanies an event of this kind, the character of which depends on the speaker's position. The supporters of the offence (the author is not always invested, for various reasons, such as the lack of intention to offend in the first place, or disinterest in the polemic that ensues) describe it in terms of such ideas as freedom of expression or speech, artistic creativity and license, tolerance and the right to offend, while the offended party assert against the former their right to be offended and the freedom of religion. The event and the commentaries on it develop into a polemic that makes it difficult for the observer to distinguish the discourse on the values of a secular, liberal and democratic state, the conditions of the generation of the offending words and images, and the sentiments of the various parties.

A legal process is also initiated, with less noise, as some assume the task of reminding the public of the value of 'the rule of law', of impartiality of judicial authority and its capacity to deal with such cases justly. Sometimes, no public event or polemic need take place to set the legal machine in motion, but an indication from a suspicious organ of state – the censorship bureau, for example – to the prosecutor general, or a complaint by a concerned or offended citizen against a publication of some kind or another.

Lebanese law – the Penal Law, specifically, and the Law of Publications – prepares the ground for such occurrences. It provides the categories of crime by which prosecution is carried out, the rules to apply to cases as they occur, and the kind and intensity of the punitive responses to them. It is incumbent on criminal judiciaries to judge if a word or image falls within the scope of the crime as defined by the law, deliver a sentence, and, if guilt is established, mete out a punishment accordingly.

This chapter is an account of how this happens told through an analysis of three cases. One of the cases is considered extensively and in detail, while the other two are introduced towards the end. The account is focused on the judicial arguments, giving attention especially to the way certain concepts figure in it. After reviewing the facts of the case and the way it is set up, the chapter proceeds to discuss the concepts of defamation of religion, neutrality of the state, freedom of religion and public order, before considering the judicial discourse on religion or, more precisely, whether proselytism and conversion are essential features of the Christian religion or not. The chapter then considers the notions of ordinary human being and normal sensibility, suggesting, in reference to two additional cases, that judicial reasoning in such cases presupposes a shared (secular) aesthetic on which coexistence could settle.

Elements of Suspicion: Conversion, Proselytism, Conspiracy

In a typical fashion, the facts of the case are given the form of a long narrative. This case begins '[o]n the 2nd of June, 2003', when an 'express mail delivery company informed the General Administration of General Security (*Al-Mudriyya al-ʿAmma li-l-Amn al-ʿAm*, henceforth GAGS) of a video tape' a pastor wanted mailed to Sweden. The tape was then 'viewed' by 'agents of the Administration's Bureau of Information Affairs (*Maktab Shu'un al-Maʿlumat*, henceforth BIA)', who reported that it contained 'an interview' between the two defendants. It shows one defendant (henceforth, the Pastor) seeking 'to cast light on the reasons that led' the other defendant (henceforth, the Convert) 'to change his Islamic religion (*dīnihi-l-islāmi*) and embrace (*iʿtināq*) and embrace (*'iʿtināq*) the Evangelical *madhhab*'. The two men were then 'summoned for interrogation regarding what occurred in the aforementioned tape'.

Preliminary investigations 'revealed' that one of the defendants 'is an Evangelical pastor in charge of an Evangelical church' located in a neighbourhood in Beirut called 'Ashrafieh'. The Pastor 'works in the field of the Christian media (*al-iʿlām al-masīḥi*)', and he 'also arranges broadcasting programs for the Scandinavian Evangelical Ministry'. As for the Convert, he 'is a Palestinian refugee with an Islamic religious background (*dhū khalfiyya dīniyya islāmiyya*) residing in the refugee camp of Nahr al-Bared'. He is a student of 'the Wahabi doctrine (*al-ʿaqīda al-islāmiyya al-wahābiyya*) at the Bukhari Institute in the region of Akkar' in the north of Lebanon.[4]

The two men met there. The Convert was 'regularly present' in a 'village' there to pursue 'his religious studies', while the Pastor 'preached at the Evangelical church in the same region'. After some discussions between the two, the Pastor invited the Convert 'to participate in conferences and parties which the church organizes for its members in Lebanon'. The Convert accepted the invitation 'out of curiosity at first'. He went back to the church several times afterwards and 'listened to the sermons . . . until he was in the end convinced of the Christian calling (*al-daʿwa*)'. He then 'decided to change his religion (*taghyīr dīnihi*) and embrace the Evangelical *madhhab* instead'.

At the end of 2001, the Pastor and Convert 'met in a church located in the region of Jounieh', a town a few miles north of Beirut, 'the minister of [that] church' acting as intermediary. There, the Convert 'told [the Pastor] how he "accepted Jesus Christ as his Savior and became a brother of His in the Evangelical faith (*al-imān al-injīli*)"'. The two 'became closer' afterwards. The Pastor then 'took the initiative to introduce [the Convert] to . . . [an] Austrian minister and his assistant, [a] Swedish minister, while they were on a visit to Lebanon'. They 'had learned . . . about [the Convert's] personal experience and expressed a strong interest in him', asking if he would 'travel to Sweden to bear witness (*al-idlā' bi shahādatih*, also to give testimony) at a ceremony which the Evangelical Church organises there for its faithful'.

However, after the 'Swedish embassies in Lebanon and Syria rejected' the Convert's application for 'a visa', the Austrian minister gave him a call and 'asked him to collaborate with [the Pastor] in the recording of a videotape that summarizes the experience he went through in the path of embracing the Evangelical faith'. It was to be shown 'to the Arab faithful in Sweden'.

The video was completed 'at the Pastor's house'. It shows an interview between the Pastor and Convert in which the latter gives an account of 'the

[4] In 2007, the camp turned into a battlefield in the 'global war on terror' between the Lebanese Armed Forces and Fath al-Islam and was destroyed as a result. https://www.unrwa.org/where-we-work/lebanon/nahr-el-bared-camp (last accessed 1 June 2023).

circumstances and reasons that had led him to change his religion (*taghyīr diyānatih*)'. Answering the Pastor's questions, he tells 'of the change that occurred to his religious convictions (*qanāʿātih al-dīniyya*)' and makes 'comparisons between verses of the Noble Qurʾan and the Holy Bible'. He details as well the ways in which his 'view on many issues changed with his embrace of the Evangelical *madhhab* and the Holy Spirit's entry into his heart'.

The two 'confirmed in their initial depositions that they respected all religions, including the Islamic religion', which 'it was never their intention to offend by recording the videotape'. For, as they explained, they made the tape 'upon the wishes of the Austrian minister'. They had full knowledge that its 'purpose was . . . to cast light on the Convert's transformation' as 'he decided to leave his Islamic religion and embrace the Evangelical *madhhab*'. As additional evidence of their good intentions, they point out that the enterprise would have been unnecessary had the Convert been able 'to travel to Sweden to bear witness in person'. They assert that 'the tape will not be shown at all inside Lebanese territories'.

In this account of the facts, religion (proselytism, conversion, Wahhabi Islam, Evangelical Christianity, a convert, pastors, ministers, churches) figures in a context that gives it an ambiguous – and for the public authorities at the time, suspicious – cast. In the first place, the actors are not Lebanese citizens: one of them is a Palestinian refugee, the others are Europeans. Moreover, the Palestinian refugee is a Muslim studying 'Wahhabism', a word that has reflexively become associated with a secular and liberal idea of radical Islam. The pastors are European Evangelicals working among a majority Muslim population. While Protestantism is one of the officially recognised religious *ṭawāʾif* in Lebanon as the 'Evangelical Church', the pastors seem to be working on their own.

Moreover, the circumstances in which they met and the subsequent interactions among them give reason to suspect a behaviour that could be classified as 'conspiracy', a criminal legal category. The attempt to have the refugee travel to Europe under what might be a religious pretext reinforces judicial suspicion, at a time characterised by the generalised paranoia of the 'global war on terror', the contribution to which was the Lebanese state's surveillance of people's mail (among other things) and its subsequent destruction of the refugee camp in which the Convert resided.

Defamation of Religion, Neutrality of the State

The two men were arrested on 17 June 2003 in response to 'an indication from the government's agent (*mufawwad al-ḥukūma*) at the military tribunal'. They 'repeated their initial statements' before 'the military judge of examination'. The Convert 'made it clear that what he meant' when he said 'that he carried Satan (*iblīs*) inside him was that his conscience was heavy with sins. Neither was he referring to his own previous religion (Islam), nor did he have any particular religion in mind. In fact, he told the judge, with his conversion, 'he began to love all people no matter what their religion'. Moreover, he ceased 'believ[ing] in the usefulness of blowing himself up (*tafjīri nafsihi*)', and, thus, 'the message that he had intended to send . . . was a message of love and peace'. In other words, his was a true religious conversion, not fraudulent change of religion.

Three days later, the military judge declared his tribunal incompetent to hear the case and had 'the documents . . . transferred to the Public Prosecution of Appeals in Mount Lebanon, which decided . . . to release the defendants' on condition that they remain in Lebanon. The prosecutor general then 'filed a complaint against them before' the Single Penal Judge in Baabda on the 23 June 2003, for the two felonies (*jinḥatayn,* sing. *jinḥa*)' stipulated in 'articles 317 and 474 of the Penal Code'.[5] The defendants did not appear 'at the concluding trial' and were 'tried in absentia'.

The second part of the transcript, under the heading, 'On Law', elaborates a series of legal considerations that prepare the grounds for the court to issue a decision. The first legal consideration is the act of accusation. The prosecutor general accused the two defendants of committing two distinct crimes: 'defaming religious rites' and 'arousing communitarian impulses'. The prosecutor general attributes the felonies not to the Muslim's conversion to Evangelicalism, but to 'the recording [of the] videotape in which' he speaks about 'his decision . . . to change his original Islamic religion and embrace the Christian Evangelical *madhhab*'.

It is not clear from the transcript which part of this constitutes the crime: the act of recording, the testimony of the Convert, or the dissemination of information. Nor is it clear what the relationship is between the defamation of religious rites and the arousal of religious communitarian impulses. The dissemination is

[5] See Chapter 5.

particularly sensitive, for it makes public, introduces to the public, an image of the relationship between Muslims and Christians in Lebanon in which the latter work towards the conversion of the former, or in which Muslims appear to be targets of Christian proselytising. The Convert – a solitary Muslim – appears as if a victim who finds himself caught in a conspiratorial web of ministers and pastors, national and foreign. (That they are European evangelicals, while he a Palestinian refugee, and, on top of it, *a priori* suspect of terrorism – both parties eminently transnational – gives more reason to make the authorities anxious about public order and security.)

The judge specifies the aforementioned legal consideration by adding to the act of accusation the fact that the videotape was recorded, first, with the 'aim of showing it to an assembly of the faithful [belonging to] the Evangelical Church in Sweden' only 'after he [was] unable to travel to testify there in person, due to the [Swedish embassy's] refusal to grant him a visa'. This shows that the defendants did not record the interview with the intention of showing it in Lebanon, and, therefore, cannot be accused of arousing communitarian impulses, which is a crime in Lebanon only in so far as it is a threat to the Lebanese state (which is how it is classified in the Penal Code).

The second crime – the defamation of religion – is more general and only contingently connected to the first. It would be plausible to argue that the defendants could still be accused of defaming religious rituals, regardless of the jurisdiction in which the action is performed. However, the judge makes a connection between this possibility and a more fundamental question, namely – this is the second legal consideration – the freedom of religion. 'The legal matter the current case poses', explains the judge, consists 'in its essence' in figuring out if 'the actions . . . remained within the limits of the freedom of religion and belief (*ḥurriyyat al-dīn wa-l-mu'taqad*) *Liberté de Religion et de Croyance* [sic]', or if 'it constitutes in its essence (*bi māhiyyatiha*) a violation of the constraints which the Legislator had placed on that freedom, among which are . . . articles 317 and 474 of the Penal Code.'

The third legal consideration – in addition to character of the act of accusation, and the freedom of religion and belief – pertains to the method of reasoning to be employed in settling 'the matter that has been proposed'. It involves a survey of 'a range of general principles and legal norms enshrined in positive Lebanese and international laws' according to which the judge would be able to carry out 'the examination of the concept of freedom of religion and belief'. The law would enable the judge to accomplish this task with objectivity and fairness that is 'compatible with the state's required neutrality *vis-à-vis* that freedom'.

The judge defines neutrality by drawing a distinction between 'negative' and 'positive' neutrality. Negative neutrality is an articulation of an attitude. It consists, first, in the 'respect' the state holds 'for all religions', and second, in 'its impartiality towards each of them'. Positive neutrality turns on the individual and the state's active duty to 'secu[re] citizens the freedom to practice their religious rites'. Positive neutrality, however, is limited by the condition that the right to religious freedom be exercised without disturbing or 'violat[ing] the public order'. Thus, positive neutrality presupposes and depends on the degree to which a state (or a society) tolerates certain forms of religious expression.

A question recommends itself in this regard, especially in a state that takes as the basis of its public order a limited multiplicity of religions, what if a practice that is considered to be essential to one *madhhab* or religion offends the sentiments of another? In this particular case, the question is not mere speculation: what if Christian proselytising in a Muslim milieu offends Muslims? What if the zeal displayed by northern European Evangelicals in Lebanon offend Catholics? How then would the state conduct itself?

The judge makes an appeal to 'legal principles and norms', citing them 'according to the principle of the hierarchical ordering of legal norms'. The first source of those principles and norms, and the text from which the judge derives ultimately his authority, is the Lebanese Constitution, Sections B and E of the Preamble, and Article 9. Section E stipulates the principle of separation of powers, Section B the Lebanese state's 'commit[ment] to . . . the Universal Declaration of Human Rights'. According to Article 8, '[f]reedom of conscience is absolute . . . the State respects all religions and creeds and safeguards the freedom of exercising the religious rites . . . without disturbing the public order'.[6]

[6] Next in the hierarchy are the International Private Covenant for Civil and Political Rights (1966), the International Declaration to Eliminate All Forms of Extremism and Discrimination on the Basis of Religion or Belief (1981), the Arab Charter of Human Rights (1994), and the European Agreement of Human Rights (1950).

Freedom of Religion, Public Order

So, what is the freedom of religion and belief? The judge derives from those texts 'the principle that the human being (*al-insān*) is born free and is in possession of complete freedom to choose his religion and belief', It follows, therefore, that the Convert is well within his right to convert from Islam to Christianity. The judge continues, somewhat unnecessarily, to assert that the principle of religious freedom is 'derive[d] initially from the core (*ṣalb*) of the teachings of the Islamic and Christian religions'. As proof, he cites the titles of a series of verses from the Noble Qur'an, 'Sura Yunus . . . Sura Hud . . . and Sura Al-Baqara' and examples from 'the Holy Bible that confirm the freedom of God's people . . . frees them from sin . . . gives them the freedom of pursuing the way that leads to truth and eternal life', and so on.

Freedom, the judge explains, is composed of two parts, internal and external. Its internal feature part 'grants it a fundamental and absolute character (*liberté fondamentale et absolue*)'. This includes the 'freedom of every human being to choose his beliefs and religion . . . and . . . change his religion anytime he wishes'. The external feature of the freedom of religion and belief 'reveals itself usually when the freedom of religion is put into action'. It includes 'the human being's freedom to display his faith', which he could do through acts of 'worship and the exercise of . . . rites and rituals'. External freedom includes as well the freedom to 'work to propagate [the] faith to others (*propager sa foi*)'. The judge analyses external freedom further into two dimensions, 'individual' and 'collective'. The former is 'restricted to the conscience of each person, and . . . connected to his convictions, his comprehension of life, and his relationship with his God'.

The collective dimension of the freedom of religion 'deriv[es] from [the fact that] its practice surpass[es] the person and . . . those who share his faith and may bear on the other' when it takes place in public. It entails the 'recognition . . . of additional freedoms for groups', freedoms that 'deriv[e] from the freedom to display the faith'. One such additional and derivative freedom – 'perhaps the most important' – is 'the freedom to disseminate and communicate religious convictions (*liberté de diffuser et de communiquer des convictions religieuses*)'. This freedom to propagate the faith 'finds its roots in', and is encompassed by, 'the freedom of expression'.

Just as the principle that the human being is born free is intended to protect the Convert's right to convert, the judge's delineation of the 'collective dimension' of the 'external aspect' of the freedom of religion, would secure the right of the Pastor and Convert to proselytise. He points out that 'some opinions in comparative jurisprudence' would include within the freedom to display one's faith 'the right to try and convince others of one's [doctrines, *al-ʿaqāʾid*] (*droit de convaincre son prochain*) through teaching' or proselytising. The right to proselytise is the counterpart of the freedom of religious conversion ('to change . . . religion'), which without it would 'become pointless'.[7]

That the judge considers the propagation of faith an exercise of the right to the freedom of expression would place the two men's doing so using video as their medium under the protection of the Lebanese laws that regulate the media. Hence, the freedom of expression carves out 'a space for groups to establish schools, organise meetings and ceremonies, and distribute pamphlets and newspapers that have a religious character'.

There are limitations to that freedom, however. For, as the judge explains, recognising it 'as an acquired right . . . is aimed . . . to establish peace, harmony (*al-wiʾām*), and tolerance in society', not to encourage 'separation (*al-furqa*) or reinforce conflict among the various communal components of society'. Thus, the freedom of religion and belief is not a good or value (or end) in itself, but a means to a higher end – social tolerance, peace, and harmony – to which it is subordinated, its force determined within the bounds of a substantive context – Lebanese coexistence – which it is to support and sustain (or at least not undermine).

The only reasonable restriction on the freedom of religion and belief according to the judge resides in the public order. The public order 'constitutes . . . the only legal norm that could justifiably be imposed on any will, be it individual . . . or connected to the state'. The 'preservation of order is the public motive that justifies interference in any guaranteed right'. How does the judge define 'public order'? He draws a distinction between an 'objective' and a 'subjective' public order. The former is 'connected to the logic of

[7] The judge makes a reference to the European Court of Human Rights's ruling in the so-called 'Kokkinakis Affair'. See http://hudoc.echr.coe.int/eng?i=001-57827 (last accessed 1 June 2023).

the freedom of religion and belief', which 'constrains the citizen . . . and the state'. It constrains the first 'to respect the freedom of others and their beliefs' on the one hand, and the second, which is the very condition of freedom ('without which any freedom is unimaginable') on the other. Whereas the objective public order pertains to a universal standard, the subjective public order concerns the particular. It 'constrains the citizen to respect ethical values (*qiyam maʿnawiyya*)' such as 'diversity, coexistence, national consensus (*al-wifāq waṭani*)' – the values, that is, 'which distinguish Lebanon from its peers in the world'. Unlike 'public freedoms and human rights', those values are relative and contingent, dependent on specific times and places, because they are 'the product of the historical choice of a society'.

What it Is to Be a Christian: The Right to Bear Witness

The state's effort to constantly adjust the sense and scope of freedom of religion and belief to the changing character of the public order is what enables the state to 'justify' for itself 'its deviation from neutrality and intervene, in order to preempt the dangers of abusing this right'. At what point would the exercise of the freedom of religion and belief constitute an abuse? If it is exercised 'with the intention of infringing on the general interest (*al-maṣlaḥa al-ʿāmma*) or the rights of others'. It is *the intention* to do so that matters: the Convert's intention, as he himself describes his reference to 'the devil inside him', was in no way intended to offend Muslims.[8] At what point would the state's interference be excessive? When it 'lead[s] to evacuating from [the freedom of religion] its true meaning'. How is the 'true meaning' of religious freedom to be determined?

The third part of the ruling is a presentation of the judge's reasoning and decision. Implicit in the judge's reasoning, however, is a claim about what 'Christianity' consists in, and what it is to be a Christian.[9] Both reasoning and decision are based on material contained in the 'documents on file', viewings of 'the video tape which the defendants had recorded', and

[8] The judge does not explain if there is a difference between 'public order' and 'public interest' (*al-niẓām al-ʿām* v. *al-maṣlaḥa al-ʿāmma*) and, if so, what it is.

[9] Cf. Winnifred Fallers Sullivan, *The Impossibility of Religious Freedom* (Princeton, NJ: Princeton University Press, 2005).

'reflect[ion] . . . on' what they said 'during the investigation'. The judge 'drew a firm conviction that the actions attributed' to the two defendants 'cannot be counted as a crime'. For in neither did they overstep the limit 'of their right to display their faith and disseminate their religious conviction in complete liberty', or 'violate . . . the public order or encroach on the rights of others'.

In the first place, the Convert, 'as any citizen or foreigner residing on Lebanese territories' – the Convert is a Palestinian refugee, not a Lebanese citizen – 'has the full freedom to choose the religion that meets his convictions'. Therefore, the Convert has 'the right to change his original religion and adopt the Evangelical *madhhab*'. He also has a right to 'display his new faith through worship', 'the practice of rites and rituals', and 'the communication of its doctrines and beliefs to others, within the limits of the law'. Among these rites and rituals is 'testimony (*al-shahāda*) *le Témoignage* [*sic*]', which the judge asserts is a 'recognized right in the Christian religion . . . and is considered one of the means of proselytizing and propagating the Christian faith since old'. It is 'one of the aspects of the Christian faithful's practicing his religion . . . to bear witness to the existence of God . . . and transmit to others his experience of applying Christ's Word among his family and community at all levels'. This is what the Convert 'did and said in the videotape'.

Moreover, the contents of the videotape are a 'strictly personal approach' on the part of the Convert 'to the transformation . . . of his religious convictions'. It is a narrative about 'two distinct periods of his life': as a Muslim, and, after his conversion, as an Evangelical Christian. According to the judge, from this autobiographical structure, it is 'logical' that the Convert draw comparisons between the two religions. In his videotaped testimony, the Convert adopts an approach to his experience in which he 'carried out a modest comparison between verses of the Noble Qur'an and other [verses] from the Holy Bible'. His comparison 'might have been based on faulty understanding on his part of the righteous Islamic religion', but, 'without any doubt', it 'was devoid of any insulting or offending expressions made out of disrespect [to or entailing the] defamation of Islam'.

The judge's words articulate the intelligibility of a religion – the ways in which it is construed – and the religious sensibility that predetermines the threshold of tolerance and predisposes an individual to be offended, or take up what is said about their religion as defamation. 'Therefore', the judge concludes, with the normal citizen as his benchmark, 'it could not be said that' the Convert transgressed either the 'limits of the freedom to express publicly [his] faith, which is legally permitted', or the limits of another 'person's freedom to persuade' others.

In addition to considerations deriving from the essence of the Christian faith, and those deriving from the Convert's attitude towards his conversion – the spirit in which he bears witness – the judge proceeds to account for the two defendants' intentions. He points out that they 'have ascertained more than once . . . their full respect of the Islamic religion and of Muslims . . . and denied categorically that by recording the videotape they intended to defame Islamic worship (*al-shaʿāʾir al-dīniyya*) or incite people to do so'. Regarding the last claim, the judge points out that 'the videotape was made to be shown in Sweden, and was not shown in Lebanon at all'. It could not be claimed, therefore, that the two men had 'any intention to arouse communitarian or *madhhabiyya* impulses (*ithārat al-naʿarāt al-ṭāʾifiyya aw al-madhhabiyya*), and incite conflict among the *ṭawāʾif*'.

Finally, the judge saw that 'the defendants, in their recording of the videotape . . ., have exercised their acquired right to display their religious convictions in all freedom'. They neither 'overstepp[ed] the limits of the public order by arousing communitarian impulses', nor did they 'violate the rights of others by defaming their religious rituals'. It is, therefore, 'necessary to cease the prosecution against them for the felonies or articles 317 and 474 of the Penal Code', which are designed 'to protect the religious freedom of every individual and curb him from transgressing his right to use it to excess', as they are not applicable in this case.

The Ordinary Human Being and the Normal Religious Sensibility

A final consideration takes the judge's argument in a direction beyond the law, strictly speaking, to bring to view the normative anthropological foundation on which the judge erects his legal edifice. So far, the judge has asserted that the 'human being is free to display his faith and propagate his religious convictions'. He has also asserted that freedom of religion is to be exercised in such a way as to not 'disturb the public order'. Public order would be threatened by actions that 'arouse the communitarian impulses (*incitation à la haine religieuse*)', and so, the freedom of religion will be curtailed if a word or deed, even if religious, threatens to arouse communitarian impulses.

The communitarian impulses may be aroused in two ways. One way is to target the constituents of communitarian identity by 'incit[ing] to religious and *madhhabiyya* hatred and spread[ing] divisiveness (*fitna*) among the *ṭawā'if*'. Another consists in the 'violat[ion of] the rights of others by defaming their religious rituals (*Diffamation Religieuse*) [*sic*] with words and opinions that exhibit disdain, sarcasm, mockery, libel or slander [towards] other religions'. Either of the two kinds of actions would be 'considered a crime', for the subject would have 'transgressed his right to exercise his freedom'.

The state has reason to override its principled neutrality and intervene in religion. The concept of 'public order' is the formal principle by which the state gives itself a reason to act, 'the sensibility' its substantive support, constitutive of the context in which an act would constitute a crime. Earlier, when commenting on the Convert's comparison between Christianity and Islam, the judge concludes that it did not contain words that might defame Islam, adding the clause, 'in the conception of an ordinary citizen [who is characterized by] a normal [*tabīʿiyya* , as opposed to excessive, *al-mufraṭa*] religious sensibility'.

Now, towards the end of his argument, having found the Pastor and Convert not guilty, he adds a reminder. It must be borne in mind, he states, that 'the standard of criminalisation . . . resides in the first place in the extent to which [the actions would] hurt the feelings of the ordinary person [who is] endowed with a normal religious sensibility (*al-hasāsiyya*) (*l'indignation doit être de nature à blesser les sentiment* [*sic*] *religieux d'un* [*sic*] *personne moyenne dotée d'une sensibilité religieuse normale*)'.[10]

The first clause articulates a distinction between intelligibility and the sensibility, but it also proposes their interconnection in such a way as to make them mutually reinforcing. The appropriate or 'correct' conception – moderate, sanctioned, authorised – of religion (or one's specific religion, e.g.

[10] This last sentence is reproduced *verbatim* (without citation) in the transcript from a ruling issued by the European Court of Human Rights in 1994: CEDH, 20 September 1994, Otto Preminger Institut c/ Autriche, no. 13470/87. Cited in 'Religion et Cour européenne des droits de l'Homme', *La Revue des droits de l'homme* [En ligne] 7 (2015), http://journals.openedition.org/revdh/1384 (last accessed 9 July 2020).

Islam) is constitutive of the 'natural religious sensibility', which, in its turn, when exercised or put on display in action or practice, confirms the conception – naturalises it, so to speak. The conjunction of both is the 'average' (or ordinary) human being who embodies them, and for whom the correct conception of religion and religious sensibility are – it goes without saying – attuned. The judge's proclamations about the Christian religion – what is essential to it and what is not – and what is offensive to the Muslim and what is not are acts by which to set the threshold at which the sensibility is (in) vulnerable to stimulation (offence).

The Muslim (in this case; it could be the Christian in another) is expected to have the correct conception of their religion (a function – is it not? – of official Islamic institutions, e.g. Dar al-Fatwa in Lebanon, and the office of the Mufti of the Lebanese Republic). Moreover, the Muslim is also expected to be tolerant of – be accepting of – others and other religions, including the ones attempting to convert him by proselytising. It follows, then, according to the judge's reasoning, that the Muslim's correct understanding of Islam involves an opening to the possibility of conversion and proselytisation, which, in so far as they are a way of 'bearing witness' (again, according to the judge), are essential to Christianity and being Christian. (The question urges itself at this point: is this reciprocal and to what extent? In respect of what 'essential' features of Islam, as defined by what authority?)[11]

Two earlier judicial decisions offer some insight into this. On 9 May 2007, 'the Single Criminal Judge in Tripoli [issued a rul[ing] . . . against the activist Joseph Haddad'. The case was 'initiated by the Public Prosecution' following a complaint against the activist 'by an Islamic student group in Tripoli'. Haddad had allegedly 'writ[ten] . . . a number of articles, among which "The

[11] 'Religious sensibility' could mean two different things. In one sense, a 'religious sensibility' is religious in so far as it concerns or involves an 'opening' to the divine, the sacred, for example, 'transcendence', 'numinence', and so on. In another sense, it involves a sort of 'defensiveness' regarding what pertains to one's religion, especially in regards to how it is construed, understood, conceptualised. Georges Hélal, 'Raison et sensibilité: deux sources de la recherche de sens', in *Raisons d'être: Le sens à l'épreuve de la science et de la religion* [online] (Montréal: Presses de l'Université de Montréal, 2008). Available at: http://books.openedition.org/pum/17065 (last accessed 1 June 2023).

Abducted God (*Al-Ilah al-Makhtuf*)", which appeared to cast doubt on the existence of God. The group 'saw that the articles . . . mocked veiled women (*al-muḥajjabāt*) and the veil (*al-ḥijāb*) in a way that is offensive to the feelings of Muslims and touches on scandalous sexual topics'.[12]

The judge dismissed the complaint, arguing that the two offences of '*taḥqīr al-dīn* (defamation of religion)' and '*ithārat al-naʿarāt al-ṭāʾifiyya* (arousing the communitarian impulses)', of which the group accused the writer, must be 'subjected to the standards of tolerance (*maʿāyīr al-tasāmuḥ*)'. Otherwise, they would be abused, put to use 'for purposes exactly antithetical to the ones for which they are designed'. The two offences, which 'represent the limits of the freedom of expression', would, if not used with caution and moderation, lead to the 'extracting [of] what was written, intended, or aimed at out of the context (*siyāq*) and content (*maḍmūn*) of common sense (*al-mafhūm al-ʿām*)', and 'impos[e] on it narrow and literal interpretations that divert it from its intended meaning'. That would lead to the throwing around of random accusations, and it is that that would 'arouse communitarian impulses and exacerbate the causes of conflict, competition, and *fitna*' (rather than the other way round, as was assumed in the initial claim).

The two limiting prohibitions against the defamation of religion and the arousal of the communitarian impulses, which are supposed to reinforce the secular value of tolerance are mutually supportive (and subversive), and must be interpreted in accordance with a hermeneutics that maintains their secular character – i.e. with tolerance. The judge does not even consider if the words are offensive or non-offensive to an 'Islamic' sensibility, but calls first into question the basis of the complaint, which does not fit within his understanding of the purpose of the two prohibitions against defamation and incitement. The claim itself is the result of a 'literalism' towards which the judge displays hardly any tolerance, the reason being that the concept that operates as the organising principle of his argument and the sensibility it articulates is 'moderation' – against which 'literalism' is measured and found excessive (or extreme). The judge urges instead a 'moderate' (secular, liberal?) hermeneutics that seeks the meaning of signs in the 'context' and the overall 'sense' in which they occur.

[12] Legal Agenda, '*Al-Mufakkara Tudhakkir*'.

Sensibility: Religious, Aesthetic

Eight years earlier, on 1 December 1999, the Single Penal Judge in Beirut ceased the prosecution of the musician Marcel Khalife for 'singing a Qur'anic verse' that he 'had taken from [a] poem . . . by [Palestinian poet] Mahmoud Darwish'.[13] The complaint against him included the claim that the musician's 'chanting (*al-inshād*) of the verse violated the principles of [Islamic] jurisprudence (*al-qawāʿid al-fiqhiyya*)'. The judge dismisses the charges on the basis of two premises. The first is the anthropological claim that 'all societies have manners of conduct (*anmāṭ min al-sulūk*) that are known to touch on various aspects of life, without care to religious norms (*al-qawāʿid al-dīniyya*)'. The second is a legal principle, namely, that 'it is not possible to consider any action that violates or does not agree with religious norms a criminal act except according to the Penal Law'.

While seeking justice in the law – that is, secular justice – the plaintiff frames the complaint, nevertheless, in terms of the singer's violation not of law, but of Islamic *fiqh*, provoking the judge's affirmation of the second premise (the legal principle). The judge then points out that the musician sang the verse with 'poise and dignity (*wiqār wa razāna*) that emanate from a deep feeling of the [verse's] human content'. The singing of the verse does not constitute, therefore, 'any defamation of the sacrality of the Qur'anic text (*qudsīyyat al-naṣṣ al-qur'āni*) . . . and carries absolutely no denigration of religious rites (*taḥqīr al-shaʿā'ir al-dīniyya*) . . . explicitly or implicitly'.

The complaint is that the singing violates rules – that is, it lacks the 'objective' criteria that would identify it as 'properly' or 'appropriately Islamic' – not that it defames religion or the sanctity of the Qur'an. Thus, the complaint is that the singing of the Qur'anic verse is not done according to rules of practice – that is, rules that describe the proper ways in which the recitation of the Qur'an is to be carried out (i.e. the discipline of Qur'anic recitation). It says nothing about the style of delivery, the quality of the singer's voice, or the values which the performer puts on display, which, as the judge suggests, might constitute defamation if, for example, they were executed in a tone of mockery.[14]

[13] Ibid.

[14] During a conversation with the Mufti of the Republic in 2007, I was struck by his meticulous attention to the way I took notes, especially, but not exclusively, the citing of verses of the Qur'an and some hadith. These could not simply be quoted or just written down as any other, secular, text.

It would seem that the plaintiff and the judge are talking about two different things, or two senses of the verbal noun, '*al-inshād*': *reciting* the Qur'an according to rules elaborated in the Islamic tradition on the one hand, and the secular practice of *singing* (*al-ghinā'*) on the other. The translation from one to the other is secured by judicial prerogative, which operates a shift from specifically 'Islamic' concerns to universal secular claims, such as the anthropological assertion about human societies just mentioned, or that singing the Qur'an is just another 'conduct that touches on various aspects of life' that could be done 'without care to religious rules'.

The judge translates the complaint that the musician recited the verse without regard to rules of recitation – that is, *sang* and did not *recite* – into aesthetic propositions and formal criteria by which singing is artistically judged, such as poise and dignity. These 'emanate from a deep feeling of the human content of the verse', which, as the judge finally rules, 'denies any profanation of the sacrality of the Qur'anic text'. The judge's judgment falls on the musician as artist, on the performance as singing. The judge seems to have in mind here the idea that art (or at least some kinds of art) is a passage to aesthetic experiences that provide access to deeper, human truths – the same truths that are sought in religion (or, indeed, that religious truths are human truths).

Thus, in as much as aesthetic experiences may lead back to religion, it turns out as well that the 'religious sensibility' is itself a kind of aesthetic sensibility (of a religious, rather than secular, sort).[15] It is the basis of legal reasoning and judgment, as in the following case of an appeal against a lower court ruling to ban a book of comic strips. The appeal argued that 'the elements of the crime of defamation of religion do not exist', since the freedom of expression is 'guaranteed by the Lebanese Constitution and international treaties'. Moreover, the appellants argued, 'Satire [or parody, *al-kumīdia*, an Arabic

[15] Compare this passage by Saint John of the Cross (1542–91) as an example of what is also called 'the religious sensibility': 'God communicates so well His supernatural Being [to the soul] that it seems God Himself; it possesses what God does; the union . . . is such that all the things of the soul are none but one with the things of God, the soul is transformed; it participates in what God is, it appears to be God rather than soul; it is God through participation.' Cited in Hélal, '*Raison et sensibilité*'.

adaptation of the word 'comedy'] has a noble social purpose that requires legal protection'.

> The judge's analysis of the book and the censored depictions. 'The book' in question 'is a book of comics'. It 'contains . . . under [the title] "Lebanese Recipes for Revenge", the recipe of "*ḥarq al-dīn*"'. The Arabic phrase translates literally into 'the burning of religion', but is commonly used as a (mild) curse (or as a way to avoid saying graver ones), in a figurative sense in various grammatical modalities, in different contexts and circumstances, to mean a wide variety of different sorts of things that bear no obvious connection with the literal sense of the words (which, when taken literally, verge on nonsense). The judge singles out another strip entitled, '*Ecce Homo*' (the judge includes the names of the authors of both).
>
> The ingredients of the first recipe, namely, 'matches and a gallon of benzene', accompany a drawing of 'a human being wearing a white gown with the sign of the cross on it', 'a black belt around his waist', and 'a white skullcap on his head' – the judge adds, between parentheses, 'the [man in the] drawing resembles Christian clergymen'. The frame shows 'a hand pouring gasoline over him, lighting a matchstick, and setting him on fire'. A subsequent frame shows a 'human being in a white gown from head to toe' – the judge adds, between parentheses, 'the drawing looks like that of pious Muslims *al-muslimīn al-multazimīn*' – suffering the same fate as the first, in the same method. In a third frame, 'nothing remains except black ash and people asking, "And [what about] censorship? Jews? Druze? Buddhism? Vegetarianism?"'.
>
> The second story depicts 'a [Roman] centurion . . . killing a legionnaire' with whom he had just had 'a homosexual relationship'. Afterwards, 'the army, on an order from Caesar, pursues the new *ṭā'ifa* . . . accusing them of the aforementioned crime, and kills them'. A frame depicting the aftermath of 'the massacre . . . shows . . . two crosses with two persons on them, the one . . . in the foreground bearing resemblance to . . . Christ . . . as he has usually been depicted in paintings with a religious character (*dhāt ṭābiʿ dīni*)'. A centurion stands before him yelling, '*C'est toi qui est pd* [*sic*]' ('It is you who is a faggot').
>
> Regarding the first comic strip, the judge's argument proceeds on the basis of two distinctions, one between the (individual) mind (or subjectivity) and the law, another between comedy and defamation. 'While it might occur in the mind of some (*fi dhihn al-baʿḍ*) to give a comic (*al-fukāhi*) character to the first drawing', the judge states, 'in the view of the law . . . it is considered to

> be defamation of the "monotheistic religions (*al-diyānāt al-samāwiyya*)"'. The point of contestation, however, is not the expression 'burning religion' itself, which the judge calls 'a representation of blasphemy', but rather the kind of meaning to assign to it, and the sensations it is to provoke, in the context of the publication in question – whether it has a 'comic character' or constitutes 'defamation' (the judge does not consider the possibility that it could be both; it would seems that the religious does not accommodate comedy or 'fun', but is necessarily serious).

'Comedy, or what is comic,' it seems, does not go without saying – or, rather, it goes without saying, but only within the bounds of what is accepted as 'humour'. This aesthetic acceptance comes not on its own, or 'naturally', but is the result of the interplay among the moral, legal, religious and political considerations within which it is embedded. Regarding the second strip, the judge argues that 'the cross is the symbol of the Christian religion which is officially recognised in Lebanon, and the operation of crucifixion and the resurrection are at the core of the aforementioned religion'. The 'allusion (*al-iyhā'*) that the prosecution of the new sect in the Roman period took place as depicted . . . the trivialization of the . . . crucifixion . . . and calling the crucified "homosexual" is considered defamation of the Christian religion'.

The judge and the authors, the readers who find the strip funny, and those who find it defaming of religion, despite their differences, all agree on one thing – one thing that enables their disagreement – namely, that the words and images that compose the sequences constitute signs that stand for recognisably religious things (personages, gestures, events, symbols). They all presuppose a secular, representational 'mode of figuration' that presides over their perceptions and sensations, their response to signs in one way or another – indeed, to recognise a sign when they see it, and know what it signifies.

Conclusion

The Lebanese state is concerned about religion. It places under surveillance religious activities and representations, and the words and gestures that touch upon them in public space – that is, a space that is not formally designated as sacred or religious. It is on the watch regularly for 'signs' and the media in which signs travel within, along and across its borders. Sometimes, an action or enunciation makes an appearance, suddenly, in the shape of an event, troubling the stillness of public space, compelling the state to act to reassert the peace, typically through judicial action.

Other times, however, a word or image comes to the attention of its agencies, arouses their suspicions in silence, during the course of their routine observation of the circulation and dissemination of signs. In such a case, they take action by informing the judicial authorities, which initiate an investigation and, if need be, prosecution. In yet another kind of case, it is a citizen or group of citizens that initiates the process, out of concern for the integrity of the public space, but more often because their religious sentiments are offended or their religion is mocked. One reason why the circulation of signs is a matter of concern is the potential they have to offend the religious sentiments, to defame religion and cause unrest. They constitute a violation of the public order.

The judiciary must decide if (or demonstrate that) the word, gesture or image offends the religious sentiment or not, or defames religion. In other words, the judiciary must show that they fall within the scope of what the Penal Law defines as (this kind of) crime, or, conversely, if the categories and rules of the Penal Code, in terms of which the accusation is made, apply to them. This involves the transformation of the word, gesture or image into a sign that signifies religion, or making a connection between the image, gesture or word and the religious sentiment or religion.

The judiciary proceeds on the basis of a set of fundamental principles with the aim of ensuring that its ruling is just (legal or constitutional and, therefore, valid). Three stand out. The judiciary must abide by the principles of the neutrality of the state towards religion, the freedom of religion (of conscience and belief), and the preservation of public order. The three are interconnected, as the state's neutrality implies the individual's right to exercise any form of religion (or none) and impartiality towards any (officially recognised) religious community (or religion), within the bounds of public order, and it is a matter of public order that the state remain committed to neutrality.

For the judiciary to proceed, and for it to be able to determine if an offence to the religious sentiments or a defamation of religion has occurred (if the act or image remains within the scope of religious freedom and does not threaten the public order), the judiciary must determine two things. First, it must determine what is 'properly' religious, or what is proper to a particular religion, and then if the word or action falls within its scope, or touches on it. In other words, judicial reasoning must pronounce on religion, doing so prior to ruling that an offence or defamation has occurred. Second, it must determine the separate, but related, question of whether, and in what way, offence or defamation has occurred, considering the action or representation *and* the sensibility they affect, and with which they are taken up.

Judicial reason, then, encompasses religion and aesthetics. It assumes the charge of determining the religious *and* the threshold of sensibility, the point at which a sensibility could tilt towards the abnormal, excessive or pathological. It presupposes a sensorium, common to Muslims and Christians, constitutive of their coexistence, and shaping the ways in which they speak and act towards each other and religion, the ways in which they see, hear and feel what they say to and about each other, and about religion.[16]

[16] See Charles Hirschkind, *The Ethical Soundscape: Cassette Sermons and Islamic Counterpublics* (New York: Columbia University Press, 2006) for the ethics (and aesthetics) of listening among Muslims in Egypt, and his interrogation of 'the secular body' in 'Is there a Secular Body?', *Cultural Anthropology* 26, 4 (2011): 633–47. See Talal Asad in the same issue, but also, for the idea of 'sensible body', Asad, *Secular Translations*.

EPILOGUE

What does Lebanese law tell us about secularism and the secular (in Lebanon)? A few years after the French High Commissioner gathered the 'spiritual representatives' of the Muslims (the Sunni mufti) and Christians (the Maronite Patriarch) on the steps to the Palais des Pins in Beirut to proclaim the founding of the State of Greater Lebanon in 1920, an agent of the French Mandate in Syria and Lebanon, a Captain Philippe Gennardi, conceded that 'the experience of *sécularisation* has failed in the states under our mandate'.[1] The captain's task was to carry out a series of measures that would extend the *Droit Civil* over marriage, its consequences, and the family ('*statuts personnels*'). The French had made three different attempts in the 1920s and 30s, all of which failed to bring about the desired result, the last failure putting paid to any such efforts in what was then the near future.[2] The Mandate admitted that 'th[e] method [of *sécularisation*] is applicable in independent states where the national sentiment may be easily developed', but 'is impracticable in the state under mandate or protectorate'. The French seemed to have been hopeful that the Civil Law's annexation of that vital swathe of life that is marriage and the family would '[have] permit[ted] a unified national life based on the essential quality of personal right'.[3]

[1] Cited in Nadine Méouchy, 'Réforme des juridiction religieuses en Syrie et au Liban (1921–1939): raisons de la puissance mandataire et raisons des communautés', in Pierre-Jean Luizard (ed.), *Le choc colonial et l'islam: les politiques religieuses des puissances coloniales en terres d'islam* (Paris: La Découverte, 2006), p. 365.

[2] Thompson, *Colonial Citizens*, p. 153.

[3] High Commissioner Gabriel Puaux, in Thompson, *Colonial Citizens*, p. 152.

A century later, the idea of a 'failed secularisation' in Lebanon is still common currency. It moves scholars, self-proclaimed secularist activists and anti-secularists alike, some in the pursuit of a definitive success, others as a confirmation of the triumph of piety. This conclusion is still taken as a directive for political action ('legal reform'), and not just by those oblivious to colonial or imperial pasts. The idea that the Lebanese legal arrangement is the point at which secularisation fails in Lebanon motivates the secularising critics of 'religious personal status laws' as much as it informs the attitudes of those who insist on keeping marriage and the family outside the purview of the Lebanese state's judicial power. The latter consider that the Lebanese legal arrangement is a bulwark against secularism and the liberal, European or 'Western' values to which the former aspire. The 'failure of secularisation' is the 'success of religion', and vice versa.

What goes without saying between the religious and their secularising critics about the mutual exclusivity of the religious and secular is reinforced by the fact that, in so far as they are in agreement about the 'failure of secularism', they both consider the secular to be a legal matter or a matter of and for law, and conversely, that it is in the law that the secular resides – that the law is a matter of and for the secular. Is it possible to disconnect the two, to think about the secular (in Lebanon, in this case) on its own terms – or, rather, to find an articulation of the legal and secular without reducing them to, or identifying them with, each other? Is there a way, that is, to relinquish the thesis of a 'failure of secularisation' in the legal sense, and still take seriously the possibility of a distinctively 'Lebanese secular(ism)'?[4]

I should like to think that I did so in this book, by taking a path through Lebanese law and, beyond it, towards a concept of 'the secular' that is embedded in it. I did so by asking what does Lebanese law, in its current arrangement, do to and for the religious? The answer I propose is that Lebanese law in its current arrangement 'does' three things: (1) it secures a place for Christians and Muslims (for the religious), securing them in it; (2) it enables

[4] 'Can Secularism Be Other-wise?', in *Varieties of Secularism in a Secular Age*, edited by Michael Warner, Jonathan VanAntwerpen, and Craig J. Calhoun (Harvard University Press, 2010) pp. 282–99.

and constrains Muslims and Christians (the religious) to articulate their religious difference and distinctiveness; (3) it contains the religious passions of Christians and Muslims (the religious). In this resides a possibility to disaggregate the law and the secular. While it is the case that Lebanese law secures the placement of the religious, enables and constrains religious articulations of difference and distinctiveness, and ensures the containment of the religious passions, the three – the placement, articulations and containment of the religious – could conceivably still be completed differently, non- or extra-legally. While they are embedded in Lebanese law and the Lebanese legal arrangement, they nevertheless constitute separately a secular domain of concepts, practices and attitudes – they articulate a distinctively secular sensibility or form of life.

The law enters into the constitution of this sensibility (the coexistence of Muslims and Christians in Lebanon) in so far as it is the privileged (but non-exclusive) medium of its articulation. How is what I am calling 'sensibility' to be characterised? I would suggest that it is structured by and gives expression to a single, secular principle, that of coexistence. This principle, I suggest, shapes what it is to say 'Muslims' and 'Christians' *in* Lebanon, and it does so differently in each case, as each case is a specific articulation of religious difference and of the religious and legal (the law). Put differently, 'Muslims' and 'Christians' are in Lebanon two articulations of the religious *and* the legal, religion and 'law'.

There is perhaps no more obvious a site in which the relationship between the religious and 'legal' is played out than the substantive 'the religious'. Lebanese law offers no formal or official definition of a concept of 'religion', but it is possible to derive from it several senses of 'the religious' as: (1) individuals and groups (communities); (2) marriage and its consequences (the family); (3) passions, affects, beliefs, doctrines, and so on; (4) the monotheisms, the 'Abrahamic faiths', or the 'Religions of the Book'.[5]

These observations carry consequences for the 'secular(ising) critique' of the Lebanese legal arrangement – that which targets, specifically, the religious jurisdictions. For, any general proposition to 'secularise Lebanon' by way

[5] Reduced, historically, to Muslims and Christians.

of legal reforms to abolish the religious jurisdictions of personal status – a proposition to carry out the task to which the French Mandate had set itself and 'failed' – would be met (and has been met) with different Christian and Muslim responses. It would reinforce, thereby, claims of right (and the sense of threat) to 'religious difference', since that difference consists in the different relationship which Muslims and Christians (the religious) have with Lebanese positive law (and, more generally, secular power).

If there is a keenness to call into question the Lebanese legal arrangement, the terms of the critique cannot be 'civil marriage', 'sectarianism' or secularism, for there is no consensus over these terms in Lebanon. On the contrary, they are the purview of particular 'parties' in the debates, put forward polemically against each other, to block each other's attempts to take change in a direction appropriate to them. Words like 'sectarianism' and secularism are not explanatory or analytical concepts, but belong to the discursive formations through which the coexistence of Muslims and Christians is articulated – by means of which Christians and Muslims 'perform' or 'practice' their coexistence.

'Liberal secularists' are participants in the debate, and what they provide is only one alternative among several and is as contested as they are. alternative that is already contested. What is required, perhaps, is an acknowledgment of what secularism and the secular consist in in the Lebanese context, or that what there is there is already 'secular(ism).' What is required, perhaps, is a laying to rest the 'failure' or 'incompleteness' thesis, and of the sense of 'secularism' as a state doctrine or ideology, whether in opposition to or as emancipation from religion. A way out might be to concede that a concept of the secular is already operative in Lebanon, is at the basis of the Lebanese state, embedded in its legal arrangement (though not identical to it). This concept, I propose, is common to Muslims and Christians: it is constitutive of their mode of belonging to their respective religions, which it (re)presents as two equally valid, interchangeable, and comparable forms of life, and which presupposes (and depends on) their singular and singularly dispassionate bodies.

Any effective critique will have to take as its target or call into question, one would think, the principle of 'religious difference': the coexistence of *Muslims and Christians* in Lebanon and, indeed, of the religious. Doing so means that religion itself – as well as 'Christianity' and 'Islam' – are also called into question, invited into the discussion. This, however, is what secularism or secular reason cannot tolerate, or cannot risk. It is not a coincidence that Lebanese law – Penal Law – circumscribes freedom of speech precisely at the point when it begins to touch on this.

REFERENCES

Bibliography

Abillama, Raja. 'Contesting Secularism: Civil Marriage and Those Who Do Not Belong to a Religious Community in Lebanon', *PoLAR: Political and Legal Anthropology Review* 41, S1 (2018): 148–62.

Abillama, Raja. '"The Love That Muslims Have for Mary": Secularism and Christian-Muslim Coexistence in Lebanon', *Comparative Studies of South Asia, Africa and the Middle East* 42 1 (2022): 51–62.

Agrama, Hussein Ali. *Questioning Secularism: Islam, Sovereignty, and the Rule of Law in Modern Egypt* (Chicago: University of Chicago Press, 2012).

Akarlı, Engin Deniz. *The Long Peace: Ottoman Lebanon, 1861–1920* (Berkeley: University of California Press, 1993).

Asad, Talal. *Formations of the Secular: Christianity, Islam, Modernity* (Stanford: Stanford University Press, 2003).

Asad, Talal. *Secular Translations: Nation State, Modern Self, and Calculative Reason* (New York: Columbia University Press, 2018).

Asad, Talal. 'Trying to Understand French Secularism', in Hent de Vries and Lawrence Eugene Sullivan (eds), *Political Theologies: Public Religions in a Post-Secular World* (New York: Fordham University Press, 2006), p. 500.

Atallah, Elias. *Le Synode libanais de 1736. Tome I: Son influence sur la restructuration de l'Église maronite. Tome II: Traduction du texte original arabe* (Paris: Letouzey et Ané, 2001).

Aubin-Boltanski, Emma. 'Fondation d'un centre de pèlerinage au Liban', *Archives de sciences sociales des religions* 151 (2010): 149–68, http://journals.openedition.org/assr/22386.

Aubin-Boltanski, Emma. 'La Vierge, les chrétiens, les musulmans et la nation', *Terrain* 51 (2008): 10–29, http://journals.openedition.org/terrain/10943 (last accessed 1 June 2023).

Cammett, Melani Claire. *Compassionate Communalism: Welfare and Sectarianism in Lebanon*. Ithaca: Cornell University Press, 2014.

Chamussy, Henri. 'Le dialogue islamo-chrétien au Moyen-Orient', *Confluences Méditerranée* 66, 3 (2008): 179–90.

Chelala, Nazih. *Al-Talaq wa Butlan al-Zawaj Lada al-Tawa'if al-Masihiyya: Ijtihadat al-Mahakim al-Ruhiyya wa Dirasat Fiqhiyya Kanasiyya* (Beirut: Manshurat al-Halabi al-Huquqiyya, 2005).

Clarke, Morgan. *Islam and Law in Lebanon: Sharia within and without the State* (Cambridge: Cambridge University Press, 2018).

Deeb, Lara. 'Beyond Sectarianism: Intermarriage and Social Difference in Lebanon', *International Journal of Middle East Studies* 42, 2 (2020): 215–28, https://doi.org/10.1017/S0020743819000898 (last accessed 1 June 2023).

Deringil, Selim. '"There is No Compulsion in Religion": On Conversion and Apostasy in the Late Ottoman Empire: 1839–1856', *Comparative Studies in Society and History* (2000): 547–75.

Donahue, Charles. 'Comparative Reflections on the "New Matrimonial Jurisprudence" of the Roman Catholic Church', *Michigan Law Review* 75, 5/6 (1977): 994–1020.

Doumanis, Nicholas. *Before the Nation: Muslim-Christian Coexistence and Its Destruction in Late Ottoman Anatolia* (Oxford: Oxford University Press, 2013).

Dumont, Louis. *Essais sur l'individualisme: une perspective anthropologique sur l'idéologie moderne* (Paris: Éditions du Seuil, 1985 [1983]).

Dumont, Louis. *Homo Hierarchicus: le système des castes et ses implications* (Paris: Gallimard (Collections Tel), 1978 [1966]).

Elgawhary, Tarek. *Rewriting Islamic Law the Opinions of the 'Ulamā' towards Codification of Personal Status Law in Egypt* (Piscataway: Gorgias Press, 2019).

Fabre-Magnan, Muriel. 'Les sujets de droit', in M. Fabre-Magnon, *Que sais-je?* (Paris: Presses Universitaires de France, 2014), pp. 97–107.

Farha, Mark. 'Secularism in a Sectarian Society? The Divisive Drafting of the 1926 Lebanese Constitution', in Asli U. Bali and Hanna Lerner (eds), *Constitution Writing, Religion and Democracy* (Cambridge: Cambridge University Press, 2017), pp. 101–30.

Farha, Mark. 'Stumbling Blocks to the Secularization of Personal Status Laws in the Lebanese Republic (1926–2013)', *Arab Law Quarterly* 29, 1 (2015): 31–55.

Gerber, Haim. *Islamic Law and Culture, 1600–1840* (Leiden: Brill, 1999).

Goyard-Fabre, Simone. 'Sujet de droit et objet de droit: défense de l'humanisme', *ARSP: Archiv für Rechts- und Sozialphilosophie/Archives for Philosophy of Law and Social Philosophy* 81, 5 (1995): 517–31.

Grifith, Sidney. 'Sharing the Faith of Abraham: The "Credo" of Louis Massignon', *Islam and Christian–Muslim Relations* 8, 2 (1997): 193–210, https://doi.org/10.1080/09596419708721120 (last accessed 1 June 2023).

Hallaq, Wael B. 'A Prelude to Ottoman Reform: Ibn Abidin on Custom and Legal Change', in Israel Gershoni, Hakan Erdem and Ursula Woköck (eds), *Histories of the Modern Middle East: New Directions* (Boulder: Lynne Reiner, 2002), pp. 37–61.

Hallaq, Wael B. *Shari'a between Past and Present: Theory Practice and Modern Transformations* (Cambridge: Cambridge University Press, 2009).

Hanf, Theodor. *Coexistence in Wartime Lebanon: Decline of a State and Rise of a Nation* (London: Centre for Lebanese Studies in association with I. B. Tauris, 1993).

Hélal, Georges. 'Raison et sensibilité: deux sources de la recherche de sens', in Solange Lefebvre, *Raisons d'être: Le sens à l'épreuve de la science et de la religion* [online] (Montréal: Presses de l'Université de Montréal, 2008). Available at: http://books.openedition.org/pum/17065 (last accessed 1 June 2023).

Hillenbrand, Carole (ed.). *Syria in Crusader Times: Conflict and Coexistence* (Edinburgh: Edinburgh University Press, 2020).

Hirschkind, Charles. *The Ethical Soundscape: Cassette Sermons and Islamic Counterpublics* (New York: Columbia University Press, 2006).

Hirschkind, Charles. 'Is there a Secular Body?', *Cultural Anthropology* 26, 4 (2011): 633–47.

Hughes, Aaron W. *Abrahamic Religions: On the Uses and Abuses of History* (Oxford: Oxford University Press, 2012).

Hussaini, Talal. *Al-Zawaj al-Madani: Al-Haqq wa-l-ʿAqd ʿAla al-Aradi al-Lubnaniyya* (Beirut: Dar al-Saqi, 2013).

Imam, Muhammad Kamaleddine, and Jaber ʿAbd el-Hadi Salem Al-Shafiʿi, *Masa'il al-Ahwal al-Shakhsiyya al-Khassa bi-l-Zawaj wa-l-Furqa wa Huquq al-Awlad fi-l-Fiqh wa-l-Qanun wa-l-Qada* (Beirut: Manshurat al-Halabi al-Huquqiyya, 2003).

Jacques, Francis. 'Qu'est-ce qu'un texte religieux?' *Raisons politiques* 4, 4 (2001): 40–56.

Jeuland, Emmanuel. 'Le droit au juge naturel et l'organisation judiciaire', *Revue française d'administration publique* 125, 1 (2008): 33–42.

Khadduri M., and H. J. Liebesny (eds), *Law in the Middle East* (Washington, DC: The Middle East Institute, 1955).

Krynen Jacques. *Le Théâtre Juridique : Une Histoire De La Construction Du Droit.* (Paris: Gallimard, 2018).

LaDue, William. 'Conjugal Love and the Judicial Structure of Christian Marriage', *Jurist* 34 (1974): 36–67.

Lochon, Christian. 'Les chrétiens dans l'Orient: l'apport de l'histoire des religions à la coexistence religieuse en Méditerranée', *Cahiers D'Histoire* 145 (2020): 81–99.

Mahmood, Saba. 'Can Secularism Be Other-wise,' in Varieties of Secularism in a Secular Age, edited by Michael Warner, Jonathan VanAntwerpen, and Craig J. Calhoun (Cambridge, MA: Harvard University Press, 2010) pp. 282–99.

Mahmood, Saba. *Religious Difference in a Secular Age: A Minority Report* (Princeton, NJ: Princeton University Press, 2016).

Makdisi, Ussama. *Age of Coexistence: The Ecumenical Frame and the Making of the Modern Arab World* (Berkeley: University of California Press, 2019).

Makdisi, Ussama Samir. *The Culture of Sectarianism: Community, History, and Violence in Nineteenth-Century Ottoman Lebanon* (Berkeley: University of California Press, 2000).

Mauss, Marcel. 'Une Catégorie de L'Esprit Humain: La Notion de Personne Celle de "Moi"', *Journal of the Royal Anthropological Institute of Great Britain and Ireland* 68 (1928): 263.

Méouchy, Nadine. 'Réforme des juridiction religieuses en Syrie et au Liban (1921–1939): raisons de la puissance mandataire et raisons des communautés' ['Reforming the Religious Jurisdictions in Syria and Lebanon'], in Pierre-Jean Luizard (ed.), *Le choc colonial et l'islam: les politiques religieuses des puissances coloniales en terres d'islam [The Colonial Shock and Islam: the religious politics of colonial powers in the land of Islam]* (Paris: La Découverte, 2006), pp. 359–82.

Méouchy, Nadine, Peter Sluglett, Gérard D. Khoury and Geoffrey Schad (eds), *The British and French Mandates in Comparative Perspectives/Les mandats français et anglais dans une perspective comparative* (Leiden: Brill, 2004).

Meziane, Mohamad Amer, *Des empires sous la terre: Histoire écologique et raciale de la sécularisation* (Paris: La Découverte, 2021).

Mikdashi, Maya. 'Religious Conversion and Daʿwa Secularism: Two Practices of Citizenship in Lebanon', *Journal of Middle East Women's Studies* 11, 2 (2015): 254.

Mikdashi, Maya. 'Sex and Sectarianism: The Legal Architecture of Lebanese Citizenship', *Comparative Studies of South Asia, Africa and the Middle East* 34, 2 (2014): 279–93.

Mikdashi, Maya, *Sextarianism: Sovereignty, Secularism, and the State in Lebanon* (Stanford: Stanford University Press, 2022).

Moumtaz, Nada. 'From Forgiveness to Foreclosure: *Waqf*, Debt, and the Remaking of the *Ḥanafī* Legal Subject in Late Ottoman Mount Lebanon', *The Muslim World* 108, 4 (2018): 593–612, https://doi.org/10.1111/muwo.12265 (last accessed 1 June 2023).

Moumtaz, Nada. *God's Property: Islam, Charity, and the Modern State* (Berkeley: University of California Press, 2021).

Mouton, Stéphane. 'Personnalité juridique et sujets de droits', in Xavier Bioy (ed.), *La Personnalité Juridique* (Toulouse: Presses de l'Université Toulouse 1 Capitole, 2013), pp. 47–56.

Neirinck, Claire. 'La personnalité juridique et le corps', in Xavier Bioy (ed.), *La Personnalité Juridique* (Toulouse: Presses de l'Université Toulouse 1 Capitole, 2013), pp. 57–67.

Noonan, John T. Jr. *Power to Dissolve: Lawyers and Marriages in the Courts of the Roman Curia* (Cambridge, MA: The Belknap Press of Harvard University Press, 1972).

Nucho, Joanne. *Everyday Sectarianism in Urban Lebanon: Infrastructures, Public Services, and Power* (Princeton, N.J.: Princeton University Press, 2017).

Opwis, Felicitas. Maṣlaḥa *and the Purpose of the Law: Islamic Discourse on Legal Change From the 4th/10th to 8th/14th Century* (Leiden: Brill, 2010).

Opwis, Felicitas. '*Maṣlaḥa* in Contemporary Islamic Legal Theory', *Islamic Law and Society* 12, 2 (2005): 182–223.

Al-Qadi, Ahmad bin Abd al-Rahman bin 'Uthman. *Daʿwa al-Taqrib Bayn al-Adyan: Dirasa Naqdiyya fi Dawʾ al-ʿAqida al-Islamiyya* (Riaydh: Dar Ibn al-Jawzi, n.d.).

Quinn, Gary J. 'A New Look at Christian Marriage', *Journal of Religion and Health* 10, 4 (1971): 387–98.

'Qur'an'. *The Islamic World: Past and Present*. Esposito, John L. (ed.). Oxford Reference. Oxford University Press. https://www-oxfordreference-com.avoserv2.library.fordham.edu/view/10.1093/acref/9780195165203.001.0001/acref-9780195165203-e-275 (last accessed 1 June 2023).

Rabbath, Edmond. *La formation historique du Liban politique et constitutionnel: essai de synthèse*, 2nd edn. Publications de l'Université Libanaise, 1 (Beyrouth: Libraire Orientale, 1986).

Rahhal, Wadiʾ. *Al-Qawaʿid al-ʿAmma li-l-Ahwal al-Shakhsiyya, al-Jizʾ al-Thani: Ahkam al-Zawaj al-Dini wa-l-Madani* (Publisher not specified, 1997).

'La répression du blasphème, LC 262, Janvier 2016', *Revue internationale de droit comparé* 68, 1 (1997): 233–38, https://doi.org/10.3406/ridc.2016.20609.

Robinson, Neal. 'Massignon, Vatican II and Islam as an Abrahamic Religion', *Islam and Christian–Muslim Relations* 2, 2 (1991): 182–205, https://doi.org/10.1080/09596419108720957.

Shaery-Yazdi, Roschanack. 'Rethinking Sectarianism: Violence and Coexistence in Lebanon', *Islam and Christian-Muslim Relations* 31, 3 (2020): 325–40.

Stuart, Eileen F. *Dissolution and Annulment of Marriage by the Catholic Church* (Sydney: Federation Press, 1994).

Sullivan, Winnifred Fallers. *The Impossibility of Religious Freedom* (Princeton, NJ: Princeton University Press, 2005).

Taylor, Charles. *A Secular Age* (Cambridge, MA: The Belknap Press of Harvard University Press, 2007).

Thompson, Elizabeth. *Colonial Citizens: Republican Rights, Paternal Privilege, and Gender in French Syria and Lebanon* (New York: Columbia University Press, 2000).

Weiss, Max. *In the Shadow of Sectarianism: Law, Shiʿism, and the Making of Modern Lebanon* (Cambridge, MA: Harvard University Press, 2010).

Yanagihashi, Hiroyuki. 'The Doctrinal Development of "*Marad al-Mawt*" in the Formative Period of Islamic Law', *Islamic Law and Society* 5, 3 (1998): 326–58.

Zarka, Yves Charles. 'L'invention du sujet de droit', *Archives de Philosophie* 60, 4 (1997): 531–50.

Judicial Cases

Abou Eid, Elias (ed.). *Al-Qararat al-Kubra fi-l-Ijtihad al-Lubnani wa-l-Muqaran /Les grands arrêts de la jurisprudence libanaise et comparée*. Beirut.

Badawi, Hanna (ed.). *Al-Huquq al-Lubnaniyya wa-l-ʿArabiyya*. Beirut.

Beirut Lawyers' Association. *Al-ʿAdl: Majallat Naqabat al-Muhamin.* Beirut.

European Court of Human Rights. 'E.S. vs. Austria' (Application no. 38450/12), https://hudoc.echr.coe.int/eng#{"itemid":["001-187188"]} (last accessed 1 June 2023).

Lebanese Ministry of Justice. *Al-Nashra al-Qadaʾiyya*. Beirut.

Lebanese Ministry of Justice. *Majmuʿat Ijtihadat Haiʾat al-Tashriʿ wa-l-Istasharat fi Wazarat al-ʿAdl.* Beirut: Manshurat Sader al-Huquqiyya.

Lebanese University. http://www.legallaw.ul.edu.lb/Default.aspx (last accessed 1 June 2023).

Legal Agenda. '*Al-Mufakkara Tudhakkir bi Thalthath Ahkam Raʾidat Hawla al-Tasamuh al-Dini fi Lubnan: al-din, al-hasasiyya al-mufrata, wa hurriyat al-taʿbir w al-ibdaʿ*', 30 July 2019, https://www.legal-agenda.com/article.php?id=5764 (last accessed 1 June 2023).

Al-Mustashar. https://almustachar.com/home (last accessed 1 June 2023).

Université Saint Joseph. Faculty of Law and Political Science. *Al-Sharq al-Adna: Dirasat fi-l-Qanun*. Beirut.

Codes of Law

Al-Zein, Aref Zaid. *Qawanin wa Nusus wa Ahkam al-Ahwal al-Shakhsiyya wa Tanzim al-Tawaʾif al-Masihiyya fi Lubnan* (Beirut: Manshurat al-Halabi al-Huquqiyya, 2003).

Al-Zein, Aref Zaid. *Qawanin wa Nusus wa Ahkam al-Ahwal al-Shakhsiyya wa Tanzim al-Tawaʾif al-Islamiyya fi Lubnan* (Beirut: Manshurat al-Halabi al-Huquqiyya, 2003).

Al-Zein, Aref Zaid. *Qawanin wa Nusus al-ʿUqubat fi Lubnan* (Beirut: Manshurat al-Halabi al-Huquqiyya, 2009).

Bakkar, A. 1987. *Qadaya al-Ahwal al-Shakhsiyya wa-l-Jinsiyya*, 2nd edition. Beirut.

Codes of Canon Law.. https://www.vatican.va/archive/cdc/index.htm (last accessed 1 June 2023).

Young, George. *Corps de Droit Ottoman, Vol. II* (Oxford: Clarendon Press, 1905).

INDEX

'Abducted God, The' (Haddad, Joseph), 186–7
Abu Hanifa, *madhhab* of, 133, 135
Abu Zahra, Mohammad, 136
accusation, act of, 177
administrative reality, 53, 56
alimony, 127–8, 137–9
annulments, 38, 58, 60, 64–5, 66–7, 69, 94–6, 100–4; *see also* Maronite annulments
Antiochian Catholic Apostolic Primary Orthodox Church, 48–9
art, 189
asylum, 63n

baptism, permanent mark of, 88
belief, freedom of, 54, 77, 79, 87–8, 171–3, 180–2, 192
  CLC (Commission of Legislation and Consultations), 46–7
  Convert and Pastor case 178–85
  Lebanese Constitution, 46, 54, 61–2, 179
  limitation, 82
belonging *see* place
binary oppositions, 3
blasphemy, 162, 191
body, the, 3–4
  dispassionate, 24, 197
  legal, 23, 62
  securing in place, 16–18, 35, 36, 55
  see also medical discourse
bureaucracy, 33–5, 38

Cassation Court, 58, 59–60, 66, 67, 71–3, 82, 84, 86
Catholicism, 66–7, 88, 154
  marriage, 93–100
  see also Maronite Church
censorship, 172n, 189–90
Christian–Muslim coexistence, 151–2, 167, 168–70, 172
  dialogue, 152–6, 162
  religious offences, 160–3
  Virgin Mary apparition, 156–60
Christianity, 67–8, 186, 191
  Catholicism, 66–7, 88, 93–100, 154
  Christian–Muslim coexistence, 151–63, 167, 168–70, 172
  conversion, 87–9
  Convert and Pastor case, 174–84

Christianity (*cont.*)
Evangelical Church, 174–6
Islam, relationship with, 14–15, 143
Islam, tolerance of, 149–50
Islamic–Christian National Dialogue Committee, 155–6
marriage, 98
personhood, 97
place, securing in, 17–18, 21, 35–45
state, relationship with, 14–15
see also Maronite Church
citizenship, 9–10, 11
CLC (Commission of Legislation and Consultations), 45–8, 50–1
codification, 21–3
coexistence, 12, 23–7, 172
law and, 20–3, 196
limits (limitations), 50–6
principles of, 3, 16–20
as secular arrangement, 13–16
tabdīl al-dīn, 62–3
see also Muslim–Christian coexistence
comedy, 189–91
Commission of Legislation and Consultations (CLC), 45–8, 50–1
communitarian impulses, 162–3, 177–8, 184, 185, 187
conjugal love, 97, 98, 101, 104–6, 109, 114–16, 129–30
conjunctive relationships, 14–15
conscience 62, 78–9, 80; *see also* belief, freedom of
consent, 96–100, 103–4, 113–14, 119
conspiracy, 176
constitution *see* Lebanese Constitution
conversion, 59, 60, 72–3, 74–5
belief, 87–8
conspiracy to convert, 178
Convert and Pastor case, 174–84
displacement, 72
divorce after, 57–8, 59, 64–5, 66–7, 71, 87, 88–9
fraudulent, 63n, 73, 74, 75–6, 77–8
freedom to, 61
human rights after, 59
inheritance after, 57, 60, 67–9, 79, 81, 82
intentions, 75–9
jurisdiction, 58–9, 64, 66, 67, 68, 69, 71–3, 81–2, 89
legal context of, 63
legal displacement, 89–90
legally effective, 67, 68, 70–1, 79–81, 86
narratives of, 63–5
personal rights, 70
proselytism, 181, 183, 186
right of, 46–7, 79, 180, 181
shariʿa courts, 83
sincerity, 70–4
subject of law, 77
to Islam, 67–8, 81, 83–7
United States, 63n
in writing, 80
see also *tabdīl al-dīn*
Convert and Pastor case, 174–84
courts
Cassation Court, 58, 59–60, 66, 67, 71, 72–3, 82, 84, 86
civil, 58–9, 67, 68, 77, 79, 85, 86, 88, 89–90
Maronite, 73, 82–4, 90–1
religious, 58, 73, 87–9, 94, 95–6
see also shariʿa courts
custody, 127–8, 130, 131–2, 137–9, 140–1

Day of Annunciation, 152–3, 159
death-sickness, 135
defamation, 177–8, 183–4, 185, 187–93
DGPS (Directorate General of Personal Status), 31–2

Directorate General of Personal Status (DGPS), 31–2
distinctiveness, 3
divorce
after conversion, 57–8, 59, 64–5, 66–7, 71, 87, 88–9
shari'a courts, 128–30, 134–5, 137, 139, 140
see also annulments

equality 13, 14, 15
Evangelical Church, 174–6

family, 3, 16, 19
alimony, 127–8, 137–9
codification, 21–2
conduct 137–42
custody, 127–8, 130, 131–2, 137–9, 140–1
ḥaḍāna, 132
maṣlaḥa, 132–3
shari'a courts, 127–8, 130, 131–41
see also inheritance; marriage
forgiveness, 149–50, 165
France, 164n, 194
freedom of expression/speech, 172, 181, 198

Gennardi, Philippe, 194
government, 45
Gregorian Armenian Orthodox *ṭā'ifa*, 46–7
Gregorian Orthodox Independent Catholicossate, 46–7
group/individual binary opposition, 51–2

HAC (Higher Advisory Committee), 51–2
ḥaḍāna, 132
Haddad, Joseph, 186–7
'Abducted God, The', 186–7
hierarchical relationships, 14, 15, 43
Higher Advisory Committee (HAC), 51–2
holidays, 152
human rights, 51–2, 55, 180
after conversion, 59
humour, 189–91
Hussaini, Talal, 52n

Ibn Abidin, Muhammad Amin, 133–4
'idda, 135n
identity, 31–2, 86, 113
documents, 53–4
see also personhood
individual/group binary opposition, 51–2
inheritance
after conversion, 57, 60, 67–9, 79, 81, 82
shari'a courts, 128–9, 132, 134, 135, 137, 139
interfaith relations, 153n
Islam, 36, 84–6, 186
Christianity, relationship with, 14–15, 143
Christianity, tolerance of, 149–50, 165–6
conversion, 67–8, 81, 83–7
Convert and Pastor case, 174–84
family, 127–8, 130, 131–3
general interest, 142–4
inheritance, 68
Islamic–Christian National Dialogue Committee, 155–6
marriage, 121–4, 125–6, 135–6
Muslim–Christian coexistence, 151–63, 167, 168–70, 172
Muslims as legal subjects, 126–31
offending, 166
place, securing in, 17–18, 21, 35–45
Qur'an, the, 166, 188–9
sensibility, 125, 126
state, relationship with, 14
Sunni, 36, 83–4, 85, 80
see also shari'a courts

John Paul II (pope)
'New Hope for Lebanon, A', 156–7
judge of examination, 164–5
judgement 71
judicial events, 4–8
jurisconsults, 45
jurisdiction, 4–8, 21, 35
Cassation Court, 71–3
co-existence, 21, 23
conversion, 58–9, 64, 66, 67, 68, 69, 71–3, 81–2, 89
Maronite courts, 73, 87–9
transfer, 64
see also shariʿa courts
Khalife, Marcel, 188–9

law, the, 3–4, 167
codification, 21–3
coexistence and, 20–3, 196
divisions of, 6–7
evasion, 70–4, 75–6, 77, 78
judicial events, 4–8
Lebanese Constitution, 9, 10, 13–14, 15, 46, 54, 61–2, 151, 179
Lebanese Penal Code, 151, 160–5, 170
marriage, 6
neutrality, 179
reformist, 167, 168
religion and, 76
religious offence, 172–4
sanction, 21, 23
secular positive, 26
secularism, 8–12, 195–6
see also conversion; courts; jurisdiction
Law of 1951, 'The Recording of Personal Status Documents', 37–8, 79–80
Law of Personal Status and of Judicial Procedures for the Catholic *Ṭawāʾif* [Communities], 39
Law of *Sharʿi* Judiciary, 133
Lebanese Constitution, 9, 10, 13–14, 15, 151
belief, freedom of, 46, 54, 61–2, 179
Lebanese Penal Code, 151, 160–5, 170
Lebanon, 156, 194
'Lectures on Islam and Christianity in Lebanon' lecture series, 153
'Lectures on Justice in Christianity and Islam' lecture series, 153
legal norms, 179
legal principles, 179
legal subject, the, 3–4
legal texts, 133–7, 142–5, 166, 188–9
Legislative Decree No. 60 L./R., 41–3, 44, 45, 52
Article 23, 72, 87–8
recognition, 48–9
ṭāʾifa, not belonging to, 53
love, 98; *see also* conjugal love

madhhab, 31–6, 38, 40, 59, 60, 62
registering, 53–5
managerial (regulatory) secularism, 8, 10, 11, 12
Maronite annulments, 57, 60, 64–5, 66–7, 70, 87, 88–9, 95–6
character, 101–3, 104, 106–7, 108, 110, 111–14, 117, 118
consent, 96–100
medical discourse, 95, 96, 99n, 100–1, 102–3, 104–6, 107–8, 111–20
medico-legal reports, 106–14
simulation, 103–4, 107–8, 112, 113
witness accounts, 108–11
Maronite Church, 87–9; *see also* Maronite courts; Maronite marriage
Maronite courts 73, 82–4, 87–9, 90–1

Maronite marriage, 95–6
conjugal love/sexual relationships, 97, 98, 101, 104–6, 109, 114–16
consent, 96–100, 103–4, 113–14, 119
personhood, 97
see also Maronite annulments
marriage, 3, 6, 16, 19, 24, 82, 194
Catholic, 93–100
Christian, 98
civil, 121, 194, 197
codification, 21–2
community, 111
crisis, 100–11
definition of, 135–6
Islam, 121–4, 125–6, 135–6
law, 21–2
personal status, 38, 39
registration, 21–2
religion, 82
shariʿa courts, 121, 131–41, 140
virtues of, 144–5
see also divorce; Maronite marriage
maṣlaḥa, 132–3
Massignon, Louis, 154
masturbation, 116
Matta, Jocelyn, 165–8
medical discourse
Maronite annulments, 95, 96, 99n, 100–1, 102–3, 104–6, 107–8, 111–20
shariʿa courts, 129–30, 140
Meziane, Mohamad Amer, 1n
Moubarac, Youakim, 154
mukhtār, the, 31–3
Muslim–Christian coexistence, 151–2, 167, 168–70, 172
dialogue, 152–6, 162
religious offences, 160–3
Virgin Mary apparition, 156–60
Muslims, 26, 166; *see also* Islam

National Day for Christian-Muslim Dialogue/Day of Annunciation, 152–3, 159
negative neutrality, 179
neutrality, 179
'New Hope for Lebanon, A' (Pope John Paul II), 156–7
Nokkari, Mohammad, 152–3

objective public order, 181–2
official holidays, 152

partial (incomplete) secularism, 8–10, 11–12
Pastor and Convert case, 174–84
Paul VI (pope)
'Relation of the Church to Non-Christian religions, The', 154
penal code *see* Lebanese Penal Code
personal status, 8–9, 24–5, 31–2, 36–41
documents, 53–4, 67, 75–6
individual/group binary opposition, 51–2
religious laws of, 143
respect for, 61
ṭā'ifa, not belonging to, 50–2, 53–5
personhood, 97
place, 3, 16–17
jurisdiction, 21, 23
law, 195
personal status 36–40
recognition, 41–5
securing, 17–18, 21, 23–4, 35–45, 55
political secularism, 8
politics, 6n, 45–50
Muslim–Christian coexistence, 153, 154, 155
positive neutrality, 179
private, the, 10
proselytism, 181, 183, 186

public, the, 20, 162
public order, 49–50, 179, 181–2, 192
  disruption of, 72–3, 75–6, 77, 78, 179, 184–5
punishment, 149–50, 151, 161, 162, 164

qādi al-taḥqīq, 164–5
Qur'an, the, 166, 188–9

reality, 53, 56
recognition, 41–5
  CLC, 46–8, 50–1
rehabilitation, 164, 167
'Relation of the Church to Non-Christian religions, The' (Pope Paul VI), 154
religion, 35
  Antiochian Catholic Apostolic Primary Orthodox, 48–9
  codes, 42–3
  courts, 58, 73, 87–9, 94, 95–6
  crimes against, 165, 184–91, 192, 198
  declaring, 31–5, 40
  defamation of, 177–8, 183–4, 185, 187–93
  difference/distinctiveness, 3, 15, 16, 19, 21–2, 23, 25, 143, 172, 196–7
  Evangelical Church, 174–6
  Gregorian Armenian Orthodox, 46–7
  interfaith relations, 153n
  knowledge, 167, 168
  law and, 76
  madhhab, 31–6, 38, 40, 53–5
  marriage, 82
  Muslim–Christian coexistence, 151–63, 167, 168–70, 172
  offences against, 149–51, 160–6, 172–3
  offending different religions, 179
  passion, 3, 16, 19–23, 24, 26, 160–3, 196
  proselytism, 181, 183, 186
  respect for, 165–6
  system of, 41–4
  ṭā'ifa, 32–6, 41–55
  tolerance, 149–50, 165–6, 171–2, 186, 187
  tourism, 158
  see also belief, freedom of; Christianity; Islam; Maronite Church; religious sensibility
religious, the, 2, 3, 12, 18, 19–20, 35, 76, 194–7
  courts, 58
  law divisions, 5–7
  as private, 10
  secularism, 197–8
  state, relationship with, 8–10
religious offences, 160–3, 166, 172–3
  forgiveness, 149–50, 165
  punishment, 149–50, 151, 161, 162, 164
  rehabilitation, 164, 167
religious passions, 3, 16, 19–23, 24, 26, 160–3
  codification, 21
  law, 196
  sanction, 21, 23
  tolerance, 22–3
religious sentiment, 159, 160–3
religious sensibility, 19–20, 21, 151–2, 185–7, 189, 193, 196
  shari'a courts, 124, 125, 126
religious tolerance, 149–50, 165–6, 171–2, 186, 187
religious tourism, 158
Rmeileh, 150

sanction, 21, 23
satire, 189–91
sectarianism, 2n, 7, 155n, 161, 162–3, 169, 170, 197

secular sensibility, 196; *see also* religious sensibility
secularism, 1–3, 18, 154–5, 158, 167–70, 194–8
  courts, 58
  failed, 194–5, 197
  Gennardi, Philippe, 194
  law, 8–12, 195–8
  law divisions, 4–8
sensibility (form of life), 27, 196; *see also* religious sensibility
sexual, the 10
sexual relationships, 97, 98, 101, 104–6, 109, 114–16, 129–30
shariʿa courts, 15n, 83–4, 86, 121–2, 124–31
  conduct, judging, 137–42
  conversion, 83
  divorce, 128–30, 134–5, 137, 139, 140
  family, 127–8, 130, 131–41
  inheritance, 128–9, 132, 134, 135, 137, 139
  Islamic general interest, 142–4
  judicial conduct, 141–2
  legal texts, 133–7, 142–5
  marriage, 121, 131–41, 140
  Muslims as legal subjects, 121–6
  religious sensibility, 124, 125, 126
Shariʿa Courts Law, 39
signs, 191, 192
simulation, 103–4, 107–8, 112, 113, 140
singular, positional relationships, 14–15
sovereignty, 51–2
state, the, 10–11, 158
  coexistence, 13–14
  crimes against, 161–2
  founding, 194
  hierarchical relationships, 14–15
  individual, the, relationship with, 40
  neutrality of, 177–9, 182, 185, 192
  recognition, 44, 45–9
  religion, 185, 191–2
  religious, the, relationship with, 8–10
  singular, positional relationships, 14–15
State Advisory Council, 48–9
status *see* personal status
subject/body, 22, 62
subjective public order, 181–2
Sunni Islam, 36, 83–4, 85, 80
suspicion, 18n

tabdīl al-dīn, 25, 63–70, 76, 89–90
  problem of, 59–63
  will, the, 79–83
  see also conversion
tabdīl al-madhhab, 65–6
ṭāʾifa, 32–6, 41–55
  civil, 50–1
  not belonging to, 50–1, 53–5
  privilege, 52–3
  public order, 49–50
  recognition, 45–51
  status, 50–2
tolerance, 22–3
  religious, 149–50, 165–6, 171–2, 186, 187
Tripoli, 150

United States, 63n

vaginismus, 105, 115–16
Virgin Mary, 163, 166
  apparition, 156–60

EU representative:
Easy Access System Europe
Mustamäe tee 50, 10621 Tallinn, Estonia
Gpsr.requests@easproject.com

www.ingramcontent.com/pod-product-compliance
Lightning Source LLC
Chambersburg PA
CBHW051123160426
43195CB00014B/2324
9781399507554